Let 'er Rip

*The Colts in Indianapolis:
A Look Back, A Look Ahead*

By Terry Hutchens

*A Division of Howard W. Sams & Company
A Bell Atlantic Company*

Published by Masters Press
(A Division of Howard W. Sams & Co., A Bell Atlantic Company)
2647 Waterfront Pkwy. E. Dr., Suite 300
Indianapolis, IN 46214

© Terry Hutchens

All rights reserved.

Published 1996

Printed in the United States of America

96 97 98 99 00 01 02   10 9 8 7 6 5 4 3 2 1

No part of this publication may be reproduced, stored in a retrieval system or transmitted, in any form or by any means, electronic, mechanical, photocopying, recording or otherwise, without the prior permission of Masters Press.

Library of Congress Cataloging-in-Publication

Hutchens, Terry, 1958-
  Let 'er rip / by Terry Hutchens.
     p. cm.
  ISBN: 1-57028-096-7 (alk. paper)
  1. Indianapolis Colts (Football team)--History. I. Title.

GV956.I53H88 1996
796.332'64'0977252--dc20   96-26112
                                                                                                 CIP

Acknowledgments

A project this size could never be successfully completed without the support and assistance of a great number of people.

My sincere gratitude goes out to Colts director of public relations Craig Kelley, assistant Todd Stewart and the entire public relations staff in providing me with complete access to past newspaper clippings as well as helping to arrange interviews with several players. I had several requests over a five-month period and not once did Craig say no. Again, without his cooperation this book would have been 10 times more difficult.

Thanks also to the Colts players and members of the coaching staff, past and present, for their openness and willingness to participate in the book. A special thanks goes out to Jim Harbaugh, who not only wrote every word of the foreword by himself but spent extra time with me in the fine-tuning process of the book.

The majority of the photos in the book, as well as the cover, were shot by Paul Sancya of the *Indianapolis Star* and *News*. Paul is an excellent photographer who did a superb job of chronicling the ups and downs of the 1995 Colts on film. The cover photo in particular perfectly captured the mood of *Let 'Er Rip*. Don Larson, the official team photographer for the Colts, provided eight pictures including all of the photos for the history chapter. Guy Reynolds, an *Indianapolis Star* and *News* photographer, was in the right place for the final play of the 1995 season and provided a photo of Aaron Bailey just missing the ball in the end zone.

The four caricatures of Ted Marchibroda, Bill Tobin, Vince Tobin and Lindy Infante were done by Michael Wellin of Indianapolis, an excellent artist with a keen eye for detail. If you'd like to use Michael professionally, he can be reached by writing to: P.O. Box 55642, Indianapolis, Ind., 46205 or by calling (317) 251-8839.

Special thanks are also extended to Duke Tumatoe for his wonderful *Lord Help Our Colts* lyrics that help the book come alive. Tumatoe went back through his personal archives searching for little ditties that could somehow add some extra personality to the book. Booking of Duke Tumatoe and the Power Trio is handled by Live Entertainment and can be made by calling (317) 475-9975 or (317) 630-0180.

Thanks also goes out to the *Indianapolis Star* and *News* under the direction of managing editor Frank Caperton. Had I not covered the Colts for the *Indianapolis News* for five seasons I would never have had the opportunity to get close enough to the principals to be able to write such a book and become an expert in my field.

The most important thank you goes out to my family for their support while daddy pursued a dream. Thank you Susan for always challenging me to be the best that I can be. There were several evenings when I was cubbyholed somewhere trying to pound this book out. And thank you Bryan and Kevin for serving as a daily reminder of what life is all about and what is truly important in this world in which we live.

And finally, my prayers go out to the family of Colts owner Robert Irsay and to the owner himself as he wages a daily fight to recover from a November 1995 stroke that left him hospitalized. Though often misunderstood, Irsay is still the man that brought professional football to Indianapolis and the one single person most responsible for the success of the 1995 Indianapolis Colts. Mr. Irsay, Let 'er Rip.

Credits

Cover Photos © Paul Sancya
Inside Photographs © Paul Sancya, Don Larson and Guy Reynolds
Illustrations © Michael Wellin
Edited by Kim Heusel
Cover Design by Phil Velikan
Text Layout by Kim Heusel

Table of Contents

Acknowledgments iii
Foreword vii
1 — Good to the Last Drop 1
2 — Lord Help Our Colts 11
3 — Rebuilding the Colts 39
    Step 1: Ted Marchibroda
4 — Rebuilding the Colts 49
    Step 2: Bill Tobin
5 — Rebuilding the Colts 61
    Step 3: Vince Tobin
6 — Rebuilding the Colts 71
    Step 4: Lindy Infante
7 — Erickson, Flipper and the Marshall Plan 81
8 — Same Old Colts? 95
9 — Jim Harbaugh: Captain Comeback 105
10 — Giant Killers 121
11 — Up and Down 133
12 — Expansion Foes 143
13 — Controlling Their Own Destiny 151
14 — The Playoffs: California Here We Come 161
15 — The Playoffs: We're Going to Kansas City 173
16 — The Playoffs: One Step From the Super Bowl 183
17 — Unfinished Business 197
Let 'er Rip 205
About the Author 207

Foreword

By Jim Harbaugh

Once upon a time in 1995, fifty men on 56th Street shocked the National Football League. Sound like a fairy tale? Let me go on.

We began our march in mid-February 1995. Long before the pads went on, long before the first preseason game, long before the draft, about 50 men had a mission in mind. March rolled in and about every pollster had the Colts at the bottom — or fighting for the bottom — of the AFC Eastern Division. All of the "experts" said we would finish right where we belonged — in last place. Everyone believed the pollsters except for those 50 guys on 56th Street. We had a goal and that goal in our minds could not be altered by "expert" predictions, but rather only by our actions.

Through the drudgery of off-season training, the team grew closer than any that I have been involved with. Every time another doubter picked us last, it seemed to make the grind easier to bear. With the season approaching, trades, the draft and changes occurred as they always do in the NFL, but nothing seemed to shake the 50 guys on 56th Street. We believed in each other, in ourselves and in our ability to reach our goal.

The season began in our house with Cincinnati where the Bengals gave us a good, old-fashioned butt-kicking. We did everything we could to prove the "experts" right. The media started echoing the same reports as years past — phrases like "Same Old Colts!" and "Here We Go Again!" National and local experts alike felt the polls were right. Everyone doubted our chances of finishing the season intact, everyone that is except for about 50 guys on 56th Street. We pulled ourselves together and began a journey that had fight, bite and scratch written all over it. Every week was a new war, and for us to win everyone had to be ready to play.

As a player, you never know when you will be asked to step up; when it happened we didn't miss a step. We had our peaks and valleys in September but looming in our future was the dreaded month of October. The doubters came out of the woodwork. National and local alike, the "experts" didn't give us a chance of coming out of October alive. We had to face the undefeated Rams, the Dolphins, the World Champion 49ers and, finally, the silver and black of the Raiders. Doubt, negativity and fear were the operative emotions of the "experts" when they spoke of our upcoming October. No one believed, no one that is except 50 guys on 56th Street.

The Rams' winning streak ended in Indy. We went to Miami and had to tie a Colts' team record in order to come back and win. The 49ers rolled into Indy and limped out with a loss. We went to the West Coast to finish October with a loss to the Raiders. Not bad for a team that was sentenced to death before Halloween.

The season continued with ups and downs, but one factor always remained the same — all the outsiders continued to doubt while 50 guys on 56th Street continued to believe. There was a magic to our team that everyone who wore a Colt uniform could feel. We all worked toward a common goal with total focus. In wins and losses one thing was sure, there was no quit in the 50 guys from 56th Street. We ended the season 9-7, or should I say we began there.

Everyone outside thought we had a great year at 9-7 and that we should be proud of our accomplishments. Everyone was satisfied with our season, everyone except for 50 guys on 56th Street. We knew that the race was just about to start and that anything could happen.

We took our underdog show on the road to San Diego and shocked the NFL Wild Card week with a win. No one had given us a chance to win that game. We were double-digit underdogs with some of our big guns injured. Fifty guys on 56th Street didn't read the papers, listen to the reports or feel sorry for themselves. We knew we could control 70,000 plus in San Diego if we stuck together and fought, and fight we did.

Our next double-digit underdog trip was to Kansas City where the Chiefs had amassed the best record in the NFL. We were a dome team venturing into the cold, hostile sea of red. The "experts" called this one a no-brainer. "The Chiefs would have to not show up at Arrowhead to lose this one," one report in a Kansas City newspaper read. Again the 50 men from 56th Street, a dome team on the road, did what many considered to be impossible, and we were on our way to the AFC championship game against Pittsburgh. Fifty men from 56th Street working together had calmed the sea of red.

Pittsburgh — steel town, tough town, terrible towels.

Steelers — Hungry from last year, not going to let it happen again.

Colts — Dome team, injured, lucky, no chance.

That's the way it read as we prepared for the biggest game of most of our lives. It was the same story from the experts and the same story from the 50 Colts on 56th Street. We ended up one play away, you pick it, from going to the Super Bowl.

I will always remember the magic of the 1995 Indianapolis Colts season. But more importantly, it will be those 50 guys on 56th Street that will forever live in my memory when I think about that magical season.

I will never forget them.

Let 'er Rip

*The Colts in Indianapolis:
A Look Back, A Look Ahead*

1

Good to the Last Drop

Aaron Bailey can still see the ball in the air.

He can see himself maneuvering for position in the end zone, timing his jump just right and keeping his eye on the ball as it bounces through a maze of fingertips in pinball-like succession.

At just the right moment, he leaves the ground with the spiraling football in his sights. He reaches out but comes up short and begins descending downward among a sea of black and gold Pittsburgh Steeler jerseys. A split second later he's in the right place at the right time when the ball trickles through several defenders and comes to rest firmly in his hands.

He rolls over, cradling the pigskin just as he gets his hand between the turf and the football. When he stands up with the ball in his possession, the official does a quick mental inventory before raising his arms upward to signal touchdown. The 5-foot-10 wide receiver spikes the ball with authority, is mobbed by his teammates and eventually jogs back to the middle of the field where the grandfatherly Ted Marchibroda is waiting with an ear-to-ear grin, a slap on the back with his rolled-up game plan and the customary "Attaway" greeting in a way that's vintage Marchibroda.

It's a storybook finish. Another Goliath has fallen, and the Cinderella Indianapolis Colts live to play another week. Next up — Dallas in the Super Bowl.

But for one week anyway, Bailey is the toast of the town. ESPN shows the highlight what seems like a million times a night, Bailey does Letterman and Leno on Tuesday and Wednesday of the following week, and the play is forever remembered right alongside Franco Harris' Immaculate Reception for the touchdown that lifted Pittsburgh over Oakland in a 1972 playoff game.

Interview requests pour into the Colts' public relations office in landslide proportions, causing P.R. director Craig Kelley and assistant Todd Stewart to work a series of 18-hour days. Bailey agrees to do every one, and a player whose previous career high point was a regular season touchdown catch in a comeback win over Miami is elevated to hero status.

Then he wakes up.

The same way, mind you, that he has been jarred awake hundreds of times since that game-ending moment on January 14, 1996, in the AFC Championship game at Three Rivers Stadium. Palms sweaty, a pillow on the floor by his bedside and a bad taste in his mouth of what might have been. He knows he may never have a chance like that again and he wishes he could somehow change the outcome.

"I wish I could just stop time, go back into that end zone and make sure that ball didn't slip away," Bailey said. "I would do anything for that to happen. I really thought I had it, but it somehow got away."

And with it came the end of the most successful season in the 12-year history of the Indianapolis Colts. Not since the days of Johnny Unitas, Tom Matte and Norm Bulaich, of Bubba Smith, Mike Curtis and Ted Hendricks, when the team was still in Baltimore, had the Colts reached the AFC championship game.

In fact, between that AFC championship appearance following the 1971 season and the 1995 three-game run against San Diego, Kansas City and Pittsburgh, the Colts had only played in a total of four playoff games in 23 years.

Had Bailey found a way to hang on to what would have been a truly remarkable catch, the Colts' next appearance would have been in Tempe, Ariz., in Super Bowl XXX, their fourth postseason game of the '95 season.

But it wasn't in the cards.

If only Quentin Coryatt had intercepted a Neil O'Donnell pass around the Colts' 40-yard line, or if Lamont Warren had picked up a crucial first down when he appeared to have running room as the Colts were trying to run out the clock in the final four minutes.

Or had the back judge been looking down to see Kordell Stewart step out of the end zone and then come back in to catch a touchdown pass late in the first half that kept the Steelers close at intermission.

Woulda, coulda, shoulda.

But as Bailey is well aware, the way this game will forever be remembered — fair or unfair — is how close the second-year wide receiver came to making one of the greatest and most timely catches in the franchise's 43-year history, if not in the history of the National Football League.

The play in the huddle was called "Rocket." To the football fan, it was the Hail Mary, a prayer seldom answered yet often used in desperate situations at the end of a game. And this was truly a desperate situation. The Colts had no timeouts, the ball at the Pittsburgh 29-yard line, five seconds on the clock and the Steelers clinging to a precarious 20-16 advantage.

On the drawing board, Bailey was supposed to get to the end zone first, while Brian Stablein, the team's best vertical jumper, was to attempt to tip the ball up in the air where either Bailey or Floyd Turner would be able to catch it.

It wasn't much of a chance, but it was the only chance the Colts had. Playoff victories over San Diego and Kansas City on the road had set the stage for the AFC title game in Pittsburgh, and the entire season rested on the outcome of one final play.

As Jim Harbaugh peered into the huddle, confidence was still high. Captain Comeback had led this team back before and it appeared destiny was on the Colts' side.

"I know there wasn't anyone in that huddle that didn't believe 100 percent that we could still pull it out," said guard Joe Staysniak. "We had worked the magic before and there was no reason to think we couldn't do it again. We had gotten that far by making big plays in big situations and we just expected to do it one more time."

Despite the fact that the odds are incredibly against you when you have to go to the Hail Mary as a last resort, Stablein said he and his teammates just felt the Colts were a team of destiny.

"The attitude and the way we were rolling in the playoffs, we felt something was going to happen and we were going to win the football game," Stablein said. "It wasn't a real panic mode when we went into the two-minute offense. We all knew what we had to do, we had been in this situation a whole bunch of times before and people had always made the plays. We just felt somebody was going to make the big play one more time."

Pro Bowl left tackle Will Wolford, who had several moments like this one before in playoff runs with Buffalo, tried not to think about all the implications riding on the play.

"I just wanted to focus on what I needed to do on that final play," he said. "I think we all felt that way. None of it was going to matter if Jim got sacked behind the line. We had to do our job just to give Jim and the receivers a chance to do their jobs."

As he called the play, Harbaugh looked like an old-fashioned gladiator, a bruised and battered quarterback with just one final throw in him. With blood oozing from a split right index finger, Harbaugh sent Turner, Stablein and Bailey flanked to his right and Sean Dawkins to the left and then broke the huddle as a sense of anticipation sent a wave of electricity through the crowd of 61,062 in attendance at Three Rivers Stadium.

"I believed the entire game we were going to find a way to win," Harbaugh said looking back on the AFC title game. "I believed it before the game. I believed it during the game. I believed it with all my heart.

"We had always played like a team, and that's what had set us apart," he added. "I really believed that we somehow would find a way to win that game."

As they reached the line of scrimmage, the Steelers not surprisingly had elected to stay with their deep prevent scheme, with six defensive backs on the field. Five of them would wind up in Bailey's vicinity just to the right of the center of the end zone when the ball eventually made its downward descent.

The initial moments of the play worked perfectly. Harbaugh dropped back several steps, rolled to his left, and did his best to buy his receivers some time. Steeler defenders began to make a push and the veteran quarterback rolled out a little more. Then, like he had done so many times during the season, Harbaugh tried to use his running ability as his ally as he approached the line of scrimmage.

But this time no one was buying the notion that Harbaugh might try to run the final 29 yards on the game's final play. Somehow, someway, the quarterback was

Let 'er Rip

Floyd Turner (88) and teammate Brian Stablein watch with two Pittsburgh defenders as Jim Harbaugh's pass drifts toward the end zone on the final play of the 1995 AFC Championship Game. Aaron Bailey, the Colt who nearly caught the ball hasn't entered the picture yet. (Photo by Guy Reynolds)

going to get the ball in the air for one final jump ball in the Three Rivers Stadium end zone.

And he did. A few steps before the line of scrimmage, Harbaugh stopped, launched the ball in the air and watched along with millions of others coast-to-coast as the rest of the play would unfold. In terms of what he had hoped to accomplish from his end, Harbaugh had just about worked his part to perfection.

"I wanted to make sure we at least had a chance, that was the thought that kept going through my mind," Harbaugh said. "When I let it go it looked like it was heading for the right place. After that I became a spectator like everyone else."

On the other end Bailey was surrounded by a host of Pittsburgh defenders, a scene that looked a lot like a group of chunky single women waiting for the bride to toss the bouquet over her shoulder, each one willing to do just about anything to get that prize in his hands.

"As I was running down the field all I kept thinking was 'Please Jim, don't throw the ball out of the end zone'," Bailey said. "All I wanted was a chance. I knew if I had a chance I was going to catch the ball. I just knew it. It was a gut feeling.

"When I got to my spot in the end zone, before I turned around to look back for the ball, I saw the eyes of one of the Pittsburgh defenders and to me that told the whole story," he said. "His eyes were just getting big, and I knew the ball must be on its way down. That's when I turned and looked up, and I knew we had a chance."

Steeler defender Darren Perry never took his eye off the ball after it left Harbaugh's right hand.

"The ball was up there so long, it looked three times its normal size," Perry said. "And everything just seemed to be going in slow motion."

In the end zone, Bailey quickly got tied up with a Steeler defender or two. At one point, someone was holding his right arm, and there was constant shoving and jockeying for position among the receivers and defenders. The officials weren't going to decide this one with an interference call in the end zone, and everyone on the field knew it. Unless a Colt was tackled trying to catch the ball, the yellow flags were going to remain firmly tucked in the officials' pockets.

"It all only lasted a split second of real time, but a lot was going on out there in the end zone," Bailey remembers. "For a moment I couldn't get my arm free but as the ball started coming down I was able push myself free and try to get into position."

As Bailey went up, Steeler defender Randy Fuller — not Colt teammate Stablein — tipped the ball, but as it changed direction it appeared to be headed right for Bailey, who got a hand on it just as he was falling to the turf. He appeared to have it in his grasp for a second but the replay clearly showed the ball come out and hit the end zone turf.

"Originally I was supposed to be the jump guy but the ball was thrown a little bit inside to Aaron," Stablein said. "So I was just trying to work my way inside and be in the vicinity if the ball was deflected. But I really thought Aaron had caught it when I was there. You couldn't really tell because everything happened so quickly. The ball was about five inches from me. If anybody had hit it I might have had a chance to catch it."

"For a moment I thought he had it," said defensive tackle Tony McCoy, watching with his teammates from the sideline. "The crowd got quiet and I think they thought we had it for a second, too."

Harbaugh was another one who thought at first the Colts' season of destiny had been extended with one more miracle.

"On the field, I thought he caught it," Harbaugh said. "When I saw the replay, I thought he caught it. When I saw the replay about the third time, I finally saw the ball hit the ground.

"You hate to lose it that way but it really summed up the season for us," he said. "We had fought, scratched and clawed the whole year long. Heck, we were down at halftime against New England in the final game of the regular season and we had to win just to make it into the playoffs.

"You don't think we had experienced these feelings before?" he said. "That final play was symbolic of our team. We fought until the end but just came up a little short."

Bailey hoped for a moment that no one had seen the ball hit the turf.

"I don't know how the referee saw it come out," Bailey would say in the locker room moments after the defeat. "I grabbed the ball, put it underneath me and tried to put on my act, as if I caught it.

Let 'er Rip

Indianapolis receiver Aaron Bailey battles a host of Pittsburgh defenders for the ball on the last play of the 1995 AFC Championship Game. (Photo by Don Larson)

"I guess I'm a lousy actor."

Fuller said later he was afraid Bailey was too good of an actor.

"I knew it was incomplete, but I was worried the referee might not have seen it that way. Luckily for us he did."

High atop Three Rivers Stadium in the visitors' radio booth, WIBC play-by-play announcer Bob Lamey had his own roller coaster of emotions on the final play.

"When the play started and everyone knew it was the Hail Mary, I think I figured our chances were pretty much zilch," Lamey said. "So I was kind of half way laid back and anticipating the worst. Then Jim threw it up in the air and everybody goes for it and there's this mass of humanity.

"The first two things I saw were Floyd Turner coming out of the mass with his hands up in the air, and one of the Steelers, and I don't remember which one, with his hands on his helmet as if to say, 'What happened?'," Lamey added. "I thought Aaron caught it. And then immediately after I said he caught it I realized he didn't. And so you run the gamut of emotions from absolute exhilaration to disappointment.

"It was just one of those things," he said. "It happened, it was an impossible play, and it came within a whisker of maybe being the greatest play in NFL history."

Mike Chappell, Colts beat writer for the *Indianapolis Star*, was on the field for the final play, but more than 50 yards away from the action. He too said at first he thought Bailey had made the catch. In fact, given the way the season had unfolded, he pretty much expected Bailey to come down with it.

"I thought he caught it," Chappell said. "We were on the field and your first reaction was to look at the scoreboard and the replay screen. I remember standing next to (Quentin) Coryatt and he's looking because he doesn't know, either. And you think, God he really caught the ball because of the way he reacted. Then you see it on the board that he didn't and you kind of just walk away.

"But for that split second everybody pretty much held their breath," he added. "And until you see that he didn't catch the ball, you're thinking 'These guys are going to the Super Bowl'."

In the rowdy confines of several drinking establishments in downtown Indianapolis, where the noise levels were too high to hear the audio on the game's final play, many Colts fans were certain Bailey had made the catch. Upstairs in the plaza area of Union Station, a large throng began celebrating as Bailey came up holding the ball in his hands.

"We're going to the Super Bowl!" several fans screamed as they began running the length of the Union Station Food Court, jumping in the air, and celebrating what they believed was a most improbable victory. "This is unbelievable. We're going to the Super Bowl!"

"Bring on Dallas," said another. "We can beat anybody."

But as many in the crowd continued to celebrate, suddenly the NBC cameras panned a shot of Pittsburgh coach Bill Cowher, with a huge smile on his face, running across the field to shake Marchibroda's hand. A quick shot of a luxury box high atop Three Rivers Stadium showed a jubilant Kaye Cowher, the coach's wife.

Within 30 seconds, reality began to set in for Colts fans and quickly the sound of the television could once again be heard. After a commercial and a couple of interviews, they showed the replay once again and this time the official in the corner could be seen waving his arms to signal an incomplete pass.

Still, there were those who refused to believe it. Many fans, who felt the Colts had been screwed by the officials on at least one other occasion earlier, felt their team had been a two-time victim of bad officiating.

One fan who called the postgame show on WIBC, the flagship station of the Colts, was still insisting three hours later that Bailey had made the catch. It was only when he was told by one of the hosts that Bailey had admitted in an interview that the ball had come loose, that the fan finally gave up his dream.

Let 'er Rip

Despite the acting of Bailey (80), Stablein (86) and Turner (88), the officials correctly ruled that Jim Harbaugh's pass on the last play of the 1995 AFC Championship Game was incomplete. (Photo by Guy Reynolds)

"Oh, I didn't hear him say that," the fan from Brownsburg, Ind., replied. "Well, if Bailey says it I believe him but I still think it was awful close."

Four months later, Bailey said people still were coming up to him in shopping malls and telling him that they knew the truth, that he had indeed caught the ball.

"It's one of those things that people just don't want to accept," Bailey said. "I guess I can't blame them. I don't really want to accept it, either."

Even on an official state document, a proclamation from the Indiana General Assembly congratulating the Colts on their successful season, there's a hint of disbelief concerning the season's final play.

In House Concurrent Resolution No. 82, it reads in part that "Whereas, the Steelers game came down to the last play, a 'Hail Mary' pass from Jim Harbaugh to Aaron Bailey." and "Whereas, whether or not Aaron Bailey caught the pass will be the topic of discussion and debate among Colts fans for years to come; the officials, however, ruled that he did not."

◆   ◆   ◆

Four months later, Bailey admitted he had stopped thinking about the play every day. But that doesn't mean he's getting over it.

"I don't think about it every day, but it's still every other day or two out of every three days, something like that," Bailey said. "I'm sure that will be the case for a long time to come. I know I'll think about it for the rest of my life. In some ways it will haunt me, but at the same time I realize that it may have put Aaron Bailey on the map.

"I'm hoping people won't remember me as the one who dropped the ball, but rather as the guy that almost came up with the miracle catch."

Bailey has come to hate instant replay, especially what he calls the "super slow motion replays." People will walk up to him and say, "Man, you had it right there on your stomach, how come you couldn't just hang on?" Bailey just shrugs his shoulders and shakes his head. If only he could go back in time and change the outcome, his life would be totally different.

"I'm a very religious person and I believe that God has a plan for my life," he said. "Maybe he didn't think I was ready for all that would have happened had I made that catch. And maybe I wouldn't have been.

"The tough thing for me when I look back on that play is that when you slow things down, it just looks so easy," he said. "It was like 'Why couldn't I just have reached out there and grabbed it?' It was right there. I can still see it like it was happening this minute. The ball was there for the taking, and I just couldn't quite come up with it."

Ironically, Bailey says the play for him anyway was as if it were run in super-slow motion.

"It was like a dream sequence," he said. "When I first looked up and saw the ball, it looked big and very catchable. I thought it was coming right for me. I just wanted to jump up and somehow snag it out of the air.

"When it did come down, I felt like I had it for a second, but just before I got my hand underneath it it hit the ground," he said. "The funny thing was I was pretty sure it had hit the ground but at first I really didn't know for sure. Then I was laying on my side and I knew it had touched the turf, but I wanted to try and make the official think I caught it anyway.

"You have to give the official a lot of credit," he said. "He was in the perfect position to make that call, and he got it right."

They say it's a game of inches, and Bailey is a believer. One lesson the final play of the AFC championship game taught him was just how thin a line there is between good players and great players in the NFL.

"I believe I'm a great player, and I really think I have a great future ahead of me in the NFL, but at the same time it's frustrating to think about how close our team came to going to the Super Bowl," he said. "I spend a lot of time talking about me in the context of what I could have done to win that game for us, but all season long it was a team effort, and I've always been a 100 percent team player.

"What that game comes down to for the Colts is that it just wasn't meant to be," he said. "People are going to say forever that the best team won, and that the best team then went to the Super Bowl and got pounded, but I don't believe the best team won.

"I don't believe the Pittsburgh Steelers were the best team," he said. "Not that day. Not ever. So many plays in that game could have turned things out a lot differently, but you can't worry about that now."

Bailey says he's heard a phrase going around about the Colts that is painful, yet very true.

"People say we were good to the last drop," he said. "I guess that's true, but what I wouldn't give to go back and find a way to catch that ball."

2

Lord Help Our Colts

For the die-hard Indianapolis Colts fan, laughter has always been the best medicine. Which makes a lot of sense when considering how the boys in blue have fared throughout their 12 seasons in Indianapolis. Never has the team won more than 10 games in a regular season and only four times have the Colts finished better than .500. As of 1996, they had yet to play a home playoff game and had only made it to postseason play twice — in the strike-shortened 1987 season and during their incredible three-game playoff run of 1995.

And even in '95 it wasn't as if the Colts whisked through their schedule with an air of dominance. Rather, the '95 regular season was very, well, Colts-like. First they lost the season opener to hapless Cincinnati, then six weeks later knocked off San Francisco. They beat Miami twice, but dropped games in the second half of the season to New Orleans and expansion Carolina.

Needing a win against New England just to make the playoffs in the season finale, the Colts trailed 7-0 at halftime before Tony Siragusa threw a table or two in the locker room at the half, which seemed to light a fire under his teammates, and they rallied for a 10-7 playoff-clinching victory.

As harried a pace as it was, the season was vintage Indianapolis Colts. The formula never changes. Win a few games you should lose, drop a couple you should win, go into the final few weeks with a remote chance to make the playoffs, and finish somewhere around the .500 mark.

For the real Colts fan, mediocrity has been an accepted way of life. Seven times since 1987, the Colts have won either seven, eight or nine games. Good enough to be in the hunt, but usually just a game away from the big time.

And so Colts fans have learned to laugh — because it's a lot more fun than crying. Not to mention the fact it comes in handy when your favorite team becomes the brunt of jokes everywhere you go. Admit to being a Colts fan while in any other NFL city and the jokes are usually quick to follow.

Why are they considering replacing the artificial surface in the RCA Dome with cardboard? Because the Colts always look better on paper. Or, The Colts always have a lot on the ball — unfortunately it's rarely their hands.

Think of the Colts and comic relief, and musician Duke Tumatoe comes to mind. With the Colts off to an 0-13 start in 1986, he was asked by popular Indianapolis morning radio host Tom Griswold of *The Bob and Tom Show* on WFBQ to write a song about the Colts' woes. He wrote a blues tune with changeable lyrics called *Lord Help Our Colts* and it became an immediate staple for Colts fans throughout the city. Ten years later, Tumatoe's weekly diatribe during the Colts season is one of WFBQ's most popular Wednesday morning features.

The verse changes from week to week, but the refrain usually goes:

> *Lord help our Colts. Lord help our Colts.*
>
> *Ple-e-e-e-a-a-a-s-s-s-e-e-e. Lord help our Colts.*
>
> *Oh I sing the blues for the men who wear Horseshoes,*
>
> *Lord help our Colts.*

From Eric Dickerson to Jeff George, Craig Erickson to Jim Harbaugh, Tumatoe has never had a shortage of material when it comes to writing about the Colts.

George was one of his favorite targets, but as controversial of a figure as he grew to become in his hometown this wasn't a startling fact. As *Indianapolis Star* columnist Robin Miller once said about the bearded wonder, picking on George was almost too easy. "It's like clubbing baby seals," Miller would say.

Hearing that line, Tumatoe broke into an ear-to-ear grin. But it was obvious he didn't disagree. George did everything in his power to earn his cocky, prima donna reputation, and those in the media did their best to make it come alive. A few weeks before George's first NFL game in September 1990, Tumatoe pondered the following thought in verse:

> *Will Jeff George be the answer?*
>
> *Will he be our pride and joy?*
>
> *Or will we all someday wish*
>
> *he'd stayed at Illinois.*
>
> *Lord help our Colts.*

A few weeks later, after Bruce Smith, Cornelius Bennett and the Buffalo Bills gave George a rude baptism to the NFL, Tumatoe's verse went like this:

> *Jeff George will be a great one.*
>
> *That's what everyone has said.*
>
> *But right now he's 0 and 1*
>
> *and he's got an aching head.*
>
> *Lord help our Colts. Lord help our Colts.*
>
> *As Cornelius Bennett did tell*
>
> *Jeff, welcome to the NFL.*
>
> *Lord help our Colts.*

But the jabs have never been reserved for just one player. Tumatoe has rarely played favorites during his 10 seasons singing about the Colts. In fairness, the lyrics are not designed to be negative but rather clever in either a winning or losing forum.

Lord Help Our Colts

Because of his arrogant attitude, Indianapolis Colts quarterback Jeff George became a favorite target for the media as well as songwriter Duke Tumatoe, who often made George the subject of Lord Help Our Colts, *his weekly musical comment about the Colts' latest performance. (Photo by Don Larson)*

Unfortunately, the Colts have lost a whole lot more than they've won since moving to Indianapolis in 1984. In their first 12 seasons in Indy, including the four playoff games, the combined record was 78-117.

When things have gone well, Tumatoe's blues tune has been known to take on a more upbeat approach. When winning in 1995, the refrain often changed to:

Go Colts. Go Colts. Kick the crap out of the NFL.

Early that season, after the Colts went to the Meadowlands and rallied to beat the Jets in week 2, the weekly song went like this:

> *Rocking and rolling the Meadowlands.*
> *The Colts had the Jets in the palm of their hands.*
> *Oh sure they were down by three touchdowns.*
> *But they knew they could beat Rich Kotite's clowns.*
> *Go Colts. Go Colts. Beat the crap out of the NFL.*
> *Harbaugh came in and saved the day.*
> *How come when he starts he doesn't play that way?*
> *Golly Mike Cofer can give you a scare.*
> *Just kicking that ball everywhere.*
> *Wide right. Go Colts. Kick the crap out of the NFL.*

Tumatoe calls himself a football fan, but not necessarily a Colts fan. He grew up in Chicago as a fan of the Bears and moved to Indianapolis in 1982. The song has caused him to become a fan in some ways, but he admits he really doesn't have any NFL allegiances anymore.

"The song has forced me to pay attention to (the Colts), and I am a football fan, so it has been interesting," Tumatoe said. "I've gotten to know some of the players and I wish the Colts well. They're much easier to like now than they were a few years ago. It was hard to like the teams with George and Dickerson and those guys. It was hard to feel much warmth for them.

"It's a lot easier to watch this bunch of guys and hope that they win," he said. "So I guess I am becoming more of a Colts fan the last couple of years."

Tumatoe says he watches the games on Sunday, or watches the highlights on television, and then sits down for an hour or so and pounds out the lyrics. In past seasons, the writing has been easy at first but harder as the season wears on.

"Usually the first 12 or 13 weeks of the season it's not hard at all and then if they're having a really bad year the last few weeks are tough," he said. "It gets tough because you can only beat a horse so much. When it's laying there dead, you can't really do a whole lot more to it."

September has not been a good month for the Colts since moving to Indianapolis in 1984. In their first 12 seasons in Indy, the Colts had only had one winning September. Their overall record in the month was 11-33. Needless to say, it has often made for the same kind of early season *Lord Help Our Colts* lyrics.

> *September blues again*
> *Once more it's a mess.*
> *September for the Colts*
> *is like an audit from the IRS.*
> *Lord Help Our Colts.*

Since joining the WFBQ team in the mid-1980s, Tumatoe has only had his lyrics censored once. It was in 1987, the week after a plane had crashed into the side of the Ramada Inn near the Indianapolis airport. In what he admits were inappropriate lyrics, Tumatoe had written about something to do with the Colts game against the Jets that weekend and tying in the plane references to the Ramada tragedy.

"It was obviously a line I had written in very poor taste and luckily I had a discussion with (Tom) Griswold before I went on the air," Tumatoe said. "In every other situation they've never asked me what the lyrics were and I've never played them for anybody before I went on the air. But we were having this discussion, and Tom said, 'I hope you're not saying anything in the song this week about the Jets and the hotel and that thing.' And I said as a matter of fact I am. And he said please take it out. So I did."

At first the station's management asked him to be as positive as possible with his weekly Colts lyrics. But after a few attempts at writing something positive about a less than positive product, station management came to Duke with a new message. "Just let it flow," they said, and Duke has done just that over the years.

Duke Tumatoe and his band, the Power Trio, have a life all their own outside of Indianapolis. To many Colts fans, Tumatoe is "that big guy that sings that song about the Colts." The truth, however, is that *Lord Help Our Colts* is a very small part of Tumatoe's success as a musician. He has eight albums on the market as of 1996 and plays approximately 200 dates a year in several Midwestern states.

"I actually have two quite distinctly different careers going," Tumatoe said. "I travel all over the country to perform, my albums have been on Warner Brothers and some major blues labels, and I play festivals and shows all over the place. And *Lord Help Our Colts* is an aside to my career. But I never play those songs outside of the city of Indianapolis. It's just like a jingle that I do. And it's fine and it's fun and we've made a lot of money with it. But it's just a portion of what I do.

"But people in Chicago, Detroit, Kansas City, Minneapolis, Pittsburgh, Louisville and St. Louis to name a few, they don't know anything about this aspect of my career," he said. "But a lot of people in Indianapolis think that's what my career is when in fact it has very little to do with it."

Tumatoe's jabs often take in the officials and don't stop with the players or coaches, either. Tumatoe has been known to go all the way to the top of the Colts' chain of command. One version in the summer of 1995, started out with several seconds of laughter and then went straight to:

> *It's the Colts. Just the Colts.*
> *How do they do it? How do they screw it — up?*
> *Lord help our Colts. Lord help our Colts.*
> *Not to bust anybody's dreams.*
> *But the same guys still own the team.*
> *Lord help our Colts.*
> *Got themselves a new quarterback.*
> *Lots of guys they say can play.*
> *But I'm still ticked off*
> *That Steve Emtman got away.*

> *Lord help our Colts. Lord help our Colts.*
> *But this year if the chance came*
> *The Colts could probably beat Notre Dame.*
> *Lord help our Colts.*

Duke Tumatoe has taken the shell of his *Lord Help Our Colts* song and changed it at times to fit close to a dozen other NFL teams and a few major-league baseball franchises such as the Cleveland Indians and Detroit Tigers. When radio stations across the country call, Tumatoe will change the tune to fit whatever team is singing the blues.

But the one constant through the years remains the original version of *Lord Help Our Colts*. And in that version, the ending has remained the same since Day 1 in 1986 and will continue on in the hearts of Colts fans for years to come. Every Wednesday morning during the football season, the song concludes with a tongue-in-cheek prayerful suggestion:

> *Everybody please, get down on your knees.*
> *And Lord help our Colts.*
> *Do it.*

◆ ◆ ◆

Robert Irsay refers to April 2, 1984, as his most memorable day in football, the day he walked into the Hoosier Dome with Indianapolis mayor Bill Hudnut to the cheers of 20,000 new Colts fans gathered for the owner's arrival to their city.

Interestingly, just five days earlier — March 28, 1984 — is remembered in Baltimore as one of the worst days of all time. That night, under the cover of darkness, Irsay ordered 15 Mayflower moving vans to the Colts' 14-acre complex in the Baltimore suburb of Owings Mills.

The Colts packed up the green and yellow 18-wheelers with business records, official books and equipment of the club. The secretaries desks were loaded up without even emptying their contents. The weight room downstairs was hurriedly packed up. At 11:15 p.m., the first van was on its way. Seven hours later, the last van left the parking lot bound for Indianapolis.

On a chilly, rain-mixed-with-snow evening, the Baltimore Colts were headed for the Hoosier capital.

The move almost never took place. Despite the fact that owner Robert Irsay had threatened to move his club for some time, most insiders believed it was all a bluff to attempt to bring sagging attendance figures back up. The main problem in his mind was a deteriorating Memorial Stadium, and the city simply refused to refurbish it.

In an article in the *Indianapolis Star* in 1989, Jim Irsay said just how difficult the decision had turned out to be.

"There was a lot of hesitancy on dad's part to move," the younger Irsay said. "That's why it took so long for him to make the decision. A lot of people don't realize it, but he was trying hard to work it out with the Baltimore people. It was very difficult for him to pull the trigger.

"I remember talking with him right after one of the last meetings he had with the Baltimore officials," Irsay added. "He didn't want to move, but he felt he had to for financial survival."

The straw that broke the camel's back was when the Maryland legislature was in the process of passing legislation for the use of eminent domain laws to force the franchise to remain in Maryland. It turned out to be the final shove the elder Irsay needed, and within hours the Mayflower vans were at the Colts' practice facility.

"I think my dad was just waiting until there was only one single option, and that as it turned out was to move to Indianapolis," Jim Irsay said. "I remember the final day in Baltimore as clear as a bell. I was sitting in my office and I was on the line with Dick Syzmanski, our ex-general manager. And he was saying, 'You guys will never move. Your dad will never move. It's all bark and no bite'. And I said, 'Well Syzy, I don't know. I think this is more than that.' Then all of a sudden someone peaked their head in my office and told me my dad was on the other line. When I picked it up, he said 'We're moving, get ready, we're leaving tonight'."

On the other end, the city of Indianapolis was waiting with a sweetheart deal. The Colts signed a 20-year lease, renewable up to 10 years, to play in the Hoosier Dome (later renamed the RCA Dome). The Colts had to pay the Capital Improvement Board $250,000 annually plus $25,000 per playoff game. The CIB also received five percent of gross ticket sales through an admissions tax, which amounted to about $465,000 per year.

The Colts were also to pay for ticket takers, security guards and personnel on game days, which amounted to about $200,000 per season.

In return, the CIB guaranteed the Colts annual revenue of $7 million from ticket sales and broadcast revenues of more than $800,000 for the first 12 years. If not met, the CIB agreed to pay the difference.

The Colts also received the first $500,000 annually from suite rentals in the Dome, as well as a $12.5 million loan from Merchants National Bank for 10 years at eight percent interest. The CIB would pay the difference between the prime rate and the eight percent level.

But the kicker was the practice facility. The CIB agreed to build a permanent practice facility near Eagle Creek on West 56th Street and the land cost the Colts $1.

"I feel we were very blessed to have landed in Indianapolis," said Jim Irsay. "There were a lot of good things happening in this city and we were lucky to get in on the ground floor on a lot of them. I really don't think it could have worked out any better for our organization."

Robert Irsay quickly immersed himself in the local community upon his arrival in Indianapolis in 1984. Through a series of fund-raising events at his party pavilion on his estate in Carmel, Ind., the Colts owner estimates he gives or raises close to $750,000 per year for local charities.

"I've lived a good life, and I've been able to do a lot of things," Irsay said in a 1992 interview. "And now it gives me great pleasure to see what my money is going for. We've done a lot of work for charities here, and we're looking at the kids, the people, the recipients and we really get a kick out of it. It's money well spent."

Irsay began building his fortune in 1952 when he formed the Robert Irsay Company of Skokie, Ill. After building the business into one of the largest heating, ventilating and air conditioning companies in the world, Irsay sold his company in 1971 to a firm listed on the New York Stock Exchange.

Irsay also has been involved in real estate, including development of several million square feet of business and office space for Walgreen drug stores in three states.

Upon arriving in Indianapolis, he turned the general manager reins of his organization over to his son, Jimmy. The younger Irsay had grown up with the Colts and learned all aspects of the day-to-day operations of an NFL team in a hands-on environment.

"Baltimore was a tremendous learning experience for me," Jim Irsay said. "Basically I just lived with the Colts and learned from the Colts. I remember watching film with Ted Marchibroda when I was just in high school. He'd let me come up at night and watch film and talk football with him. And then being around the players was another big plus.

"A normal kid just doesn't get that opportunity to come in at 11 o'clock at night and eat a pizza with Bert Jones or Lydell Mitchell," he added. "They really treated me as one of their own, and would say things to me that made me feel that they really trusted me. As I grew up in the organization I pretty much worked in every single area at some point by the time I got out of college."

Jim Irsay was general manager for 10 seasons before Bill Tobin came in prior to the 1994 season and assumed the responsibilities of director of football operations. When Robert Irsay suffered a stroke in November 1995 and was hospitalized for an indefinite amount of time, the younger Irsay's role with the club expanded greatly.

"Right now I'm basically overseeing the whole organization and trying to restructure with an idea of where we are and where we're headed," Jim Irsay said. "My responsibilities are of even a larger global nature than they were a year ago. Right now I think the global picture warrants a detailed analysis. To quote Bob Dylan, 'I want to know my song before I start singing.'

"I need to look at everything before I start deciding what courses of action we need to take to get us out of the 1990s and into the next decade," he said. "I've been in this thing since I was 12 years old and I know this business well. It's like if as a kid you grow up with the traveling circus, when you get up on the high wire it's just not that big of a deal. It has become second nature. That's kind of where I'm at and it's a very exciting time."

The cast of characters that came through Indianapolis in the Colts' first 12 seasons in the city brought with them enough interesting baggage to fill the pages of several books.

The head coaches alone were as diverse a group as could be imagined. From the military-like Frank Kush to the green-behind-the-ears Rod Dowhower. From the smooth-talking Ron Meyer to the soft-spoken, difficult to rile Ted Marchibroda. To Lindy Infante, who may be the most even-keeled of the five.

Kush came with the club from Baltimore after a successful 1983 campaign that saw him lead the Colts to a 7-9 record. Not a great mark until you consider it was seven victories more than the 0-8-1 strike-shortened 1982 squad had been able to produce the year before.

Kush was a disciplinarian and there was no mistaking his coaching style.

"My coaching philosophy is a disciplined approach which emphasizes conditioning and the fundamentals of the game in addition to mental preparation," Kush was quoted as saying in his bio in the 1984 Colts media guide. "But above all, everyone must be motivated toward the same objective — success."

Kush didn't last long in Indianapolis, 15 games to be exact. After the Colts started 4-11, the veteran coach quit and was replaced by Hal Hunter. Hunter coached the Colts for the final game of the 1984 season, a 16-10 loss to the Patriots at New England.

General manager Jim Irsay said Kush was never happy in Indianapolis. Having spent a considerable amount of time in Arizona, Kush had hoped the Colts would relocate in the warm confines of Phoenix rather than Indianapolis.

"I think Frank was really disappointed when we ended up here instead of Arizona," Irsay said. "Once that fate was sealed I think he was gone. I had the utmost admiration for him. With the exception of Ted Marchibroda, I think he had the biggest impact on me of any of the coaches that came through here."

Irsay admired Kush's leadership qualities.

"He's a very good leader, a military type of guy who I always believed was an excellent coach," Irsay said. "Like any coach, you really had to help him in terms of coordinators and assistants, but left alone he was a great football man."

Mark Herrmann, who prepped locally at Carmel and played his college ball at Purdue, was a member of that inaugural Colts team in 1984, after playing his first NFL season in Baltimore. He left after the '84 season but came back in a backup role to Jeff George during the 1990-92 seasons.

Mention Kush to the former NFL quarterback and Herrmann has to smile.

"Frank was a real hard-nosed guy, a real football guy," Herrmann said. "He didn't put up with any shenanigans. Camp was unbelievable. Three hours in the morning, three hours in the afternoon and very intense. I just remember a lot of fights breaking out in training camp.

"It just seems like we left it all in training camp and once we got to the season we were pretty much shot," he said. "Frank is just one of those old-school football guys. I got along with him fine. He was hard on the linemen but he was just an old football guy who would battle you to the end."

The next chapter of Colts football began in 1985 with the hiring of Rod Dowhower. Irsay still wonders aloud if Dowhower was ready for his first — and perhaps last — NFL head coaching position.

"Rod was a real talented guy," Irsay said. "I feel sorry for Rod in a way because on paper he was ready but unfortunately there is no school for head coaches in this league. He came in a bright guy, but he didn't really know what he was getting himself into."

Dowhower didn't get fired until the Colts started the 1986 season 0-13, but it was not difficult to see it coming following his rookie campaign. The Colts went 5-11, had a six-game losing streak and did not win a game in November.

The big story in 1985 was that of quarterback Art Schlichter, a former first-round pick out of Ohio State, in whom Dowhower put all of his confidence. When he originally named him as the starting quarterback in the preseason, Dowhower had gone out on a limb saying Schlichter's starting was "not a short-term decision."

Five weeks later, Schlichter was released and Dowhower had egg on his face.

Things did not go well in '86 either. In the second game of the regular season, quarterback Gary Hogeboom, who had been acquired from the Dallas Cowboys in the off-season, suffered a shoulder separation that was believed to be enough to keep him out the remainder of the season. On came Jack Trudeau, but the former Illinois quarterback proceeded to drop all 11 games he started. When Dowhower was then fired on Dec. 1, new coach Ron Meyer brought Hogeboom back as the starter as the Colts won their final three games.

Unfortunately for Dowhower, the one scene for which he will always be remembered in Indianapolis came in the closing minutes of a 17-13 loss to Miami in the Hoosier Dome on Oct. 26.

Standing on the sidelines, Dowhower hyperventilated and fell to the Hoosier Dome turf, splitting his pants. He was quickly surrounded by several coaches and players though, and no one knew if he had suffered a heart attack or what had happened. The truth is he was just very embarrassed by the whole situation.

"God, when he fell over on the sidelines in that game, I'm telling you I never saw anything like it," said Jim Irsay. "I thought we had just lost a head coach to the stress syndrome.

"He went Humpty Dumpty right down," Irsay added. "I couldn't believe it. That's what this league does to you. You end up on the carpet with your pants split and your butt showing. That's how tough this league can be."

Ron Meyer followed up his three-game win streak in 1986 by leading the Colts to their first playoff appearance since moving to Indianapolis in the strike-shortened 1987 season.

In '87, the Colts went 9-6 and a big reason why the team won the AFC East and made the playoffs was the three-team trade which brought running back Eric Dickerson to Indianapolis on Halloween night.

Dickerson played in the final nine games and the Colts were 6-3 in that span, winning four of their final five games. Dickerson's season totals were solid — 1,011 yards on 223 carries for a 4.5-yard average and five touchdowns. He also caught 13 passes for 133 yards.

The Colts first playoff game since moving to Indy was a 38-21 loss to the Cleveland Browns. Some termed Meyer a miracle worker and the slick coach, who many believe resembles a used-car salesman, soaked it up.

Jim Irsay said he has fond memories of the years Meyer was with the Colts.

"Ron was fun," Irsay said. "He was way different than anyone we had before. During the Dickerson deal, it was like 'Hey Jim, let's order in some beer and pizza

Lord Help Our Colts

Ron Meyer became the Colts coach in December 1986 and in 1987 led the team to its first playoff appearance since moving to Indianapolis. Although Meyer seemed to provide a spark for the Colts, it was quickly doused by Eric Dickerson's holdout in 1988 and the Jeff George debacle. Meyer was fired after the first five games of the 1991 season. (Photo by Don Larson)

and rock and roll this thing'. He was flamboyant and really had a lot of good qualities. I feel like he did a lot of good things here."

As Irsay put it, Meyer was a winner.

"He won at Nevada, won at SMU, won at New England and he won here," Irsay said. "Sometimes though, success can be your worst enemy because of the expectations that come with that success. But he has nothing to hang his head about. I think he had a good run at it."

In '88, Meyer was an unwilling participant in a season that was referred to as Team Turmoil. There were quarterback changes, holdouts, walkouts and a constant ongoing bickering among the players.

Hogeboom was benched early, Ron Solt reluctantly signed a big contract and then blasted owner Robert Irsay. A few days later, he was traded to Philadelphia. But the big trade that season was the one in which the Colts sent a pair of first-round draft picks to Seattle for linebacker Fredd Young. The trade never worked out for the Colts as Young developed a degenerative hip problem and retired three seasons later.

The season turned out to be so wacky, that in a desperation move against Tampa Bay midway through the season, Meyer installed the wishbone offense. Looking for a way to control the ball, the offense worked and the Colts won eight of their final 10 games but still missed a repeat trip to the playoffs by one game.

In '89, the Colts were 8-7 going into the final game of the season and controlled their own playoff destiny with a road game against New Orleans on Christmas Eve. The slogan during the week was "Win and we're in." The Colts trailed 10-6 at halftime, but the Saints blew them out in the second half and rolled to a 41-6 victory.

In 1990 Meyer suffered through growing pains with rookie Jeff George, and in '91 made it five games before he was fired after the Colts got off to an 0-5 start. A 31-3 loss to Seattle in the Kingdome sealed his fate.

Jim Irsay said he knew as that game unfolded that the next day he would be firing his coach and replacing him with Rick Venturi on an interim basis.

"After the Seattle game, I just walked out of the stadium and I said 'That's it'," Irsay said. "Things had just reached a point and we needed a new direction. It was tough because I really didn't believe Ron was totally to blame but sometimes you just have to shake things up to get the desired effect that you're looking for."

Rick Venturi was left with the unenviable task of trying to keep the ship from going below the water line.

A longtime defensive assistant that had moved with the club from Baltimore, Venturi's goal was simply to get the Colts believing in themselves. But it turned out to be a bigger task than even Venturi expected.

One by one, key players made their way to the injury list, and with them went the serious chances for victories.

Eleven games later, the Colts had won just one game and Venturi's brief head coaching stint had come to an end. In two head coaching positions — four years at Northwestern and 11 games with the Colts — Venturi won a total of two games. The answer to the trivia question as to who the two victims were will go down in history as the University of Wyoming and the New York Jets.

As for Meyer, his loss of employment was not a financial setback. Just a few months earlier he had been granted a contract extension that guaranteed $900,000 more in salary over the next two seasons.

Think of Meyer and you think of the funny things he would say. He always had a one-liner that would cause reporters to constantly have a tape recorder running when he was around.

He was always butchering the English language, too. One day he was referring to Moses, and he talked about how "Moses had come down off the mountain with the tabloids." Did he mean the *New York Post* or was it the *National Enquirer* that Moses was clutching that day?

Lord Help Our Colts

When Ron Meyer was fired five games into the 1991 season, the task of leading the Colts fell on the shoulders of longtime defensive coordinator Rick Venturi. As key players fell to injuries, the Colts managed just one victory in the final 11 games, sealing Venturi's fate and opening the door for Ted Marchibroda. (Photo by Don Larson)

And then there were his daily references to a host of Colts players.

After the Colts drafted defensive end Mel Agee out of Illinois, Meyer said, "He looks like Tarzan, plays like Jane." When wide receiver James Bradley took a long time in training camp to bounce back from an ankle injury, Meyer said, "I've had guys come back quicker from Vietnam." On offensive lineman Pat Tomberlin, Meyer said, "He's like a golf ball in tall weeds — he's lost."

When the offensive line was having personnel problems one year, and different players were being shuffled around to fill different positions, Meyer said, "It's like shoveling shit. You can put it here or you can put it there, but in the end you have the same result."

When Ted Marchibroda came on to start the 1992 season, he also immortalized himself at the first press conference after he had been introduced to the media by general manager Jim Irsay.

Said Marchibroda: "I'm very excited to be named the head football coach of the Baltimore ... I mean Indianapolis Colts."

Old habits are tough to break.

Marchibroda was brought in with the task of rebuilding a team that had finished 1-15 the year before and in four seasons built them to respectability to the point where they finished 9-7 in '95, won a pair of playoff games and came within one miracle near-reception by Aaron Bailey of making it to the Super Bowl.

In a crazy turn of events following the '95 season, though, Marchibroda was relieved of his command and soon thereafter did return to Baltimore after all, as the new coach of the Baltimore Ravens (formerly Cleveland Browns).

Marchibroda's release came the day after Vince Tobin had accepted the head coaching job at Arizona. The Colts' choice was basically to lose Marchibroda or Lindy Infante, and they decided they preferred to put the future of the franchise in Infante's somewhat younger hands.

Still, it was a difficult decision for Jim Irsay, who went way back to the days in Baltimore with Marchibroda and respected him as one of his closest friends.

"Ted is a very special person to me," Irsay said later. "He was my last coaching selection as a general manager and I'll stand by that decision. I always said that if I wanted to sink or swim with someone, Ted would be the guy and I'm proud of that choice. He's criticized and some people wonder how he does it but he just seems to get it done."

Irsay said Marchibroda taught him several of life's lessons.

"He taught me a lot about respecting and loving the game," Irsay said. "He's a guy who puts the game before himself. In some ways he's a dinosaur in this game but you need people like that. You can't find a lot of guys that beat out (Johnny) Unitas and (Jim) Finks at the quarterback position back in the '50s in Pittsburgh.

"He was always a sentimental favorite of mine," Irsay said. "I think he's a great, great man and a very dear friend."

With Infante, the Colts have one of the most innovative offensive minds in the game. A coach who enjoys the bright lights of television cameras and the feeding frenzy that often goes with them, he remained very even keeled in his first few months on the job in Indianapolis following the '95 season.

"This is a great opportunity for me," Infante said. "I never thought when I came here that this would happen, but now that it has I just want to do the best job I can do. The Colts have had some excellent coaches before me, and I just want to fall in line with them, and I hope to continue the momentum that Ted helped to build last year."

From Kush to Dowhower to Meyer to Marchibroda and to Infante, the Colts had a most interesting fivesome of coaches to lay the franchise's foundation in Indianapolis.

But the cast of characters in Indy wouldn't be complete without a look at two of the bigger ringleaders, so to speak, in Indianapolis Colts history.

The first was Eric Dickerson, and not far behind came Jeff George. *Sports Illustrated* cover boys, always in the middle of the controversy, and a pair of players that made as much of a name for their off-the-field problems as for their successes on it.

Lord Help Our Colts

Eric Dickerson's trade to the Colts in 1987 generated lots of excitement and produced success that season, but it was downhill after that. After another good season in 1988, Dickerson began bad-mouthing his teammates and was finally traded to the Los Angeles Raiders in 1992. (Photo by Don Larson)

The cover of *Indianapolis Monthly* magazine in January 1988 displayed a picture of Eric Dickerson in a suit and tie, clutching a Super Bowl ticket in his right hand.

The headline next to Dickerson proclaimed, "WE'RE GOING TO THE SUPER BOWL!". In smaller type below it read, "Just kidding. But will this guy be our ticket there?"

The article, entitled "See Eric Run," by Sam Stall traced Dickerson's roots from his hometown of Sealy, Texas, to his days playing football for Ron Meyer at Southern Methodist University, to his five seasons with the Rams and eventually to his Halloween 1987 trade to Indianapolis.

In that article, Dickerson talked about how he was looking forward to playing in front of the people of Indianapolis, a collective group he believed were "real" fans. The laid-back style of the fans in Los Angeles just got old after a while.

"These fans are more into it," Dickerson said in the *Indianapolis Monthly* article. "In L.A. you could run an 80-yard touchdown run and they would only clap a little bit. Here, they go crazy....(The fans of Indianapolis) haven't seen me at my best yet. A 100-yard day is OK, but for me, 150 on up means I'm having a great day."

From the minute the three-way trade between Indianapolis, Los Angeles and Buffalo was announced, everyone who could get a column in print had an opinion about who got the best of the deal. The Colts had picked up Dickerson from the Rams and quickly signed him to a four-year, $5.6 million contract, a hefty raise from the $650,000 Dickerson was earning with the Rams. The Bills received Cornelius Bennett from the Colts, a player whom the Irsays had started to believe they may never have been able to sign. Los Angeles obtained a bushel basket full of draft picks. Buffalo parted with running back Greg Bell, as well as an '88 first-round pick, and its first- and second-round picks in 1989. The Colts dealt running back Owen Gill, along with their first- and second-round picks in '88 and their second-round selection in 1989.

Peter King, pro football editor for *Sports Illustrated*, immediately crowned the Colts the big winner in the trade, with the Rams close behind. It was his belief that the Bills definitely overpaid for Bennett.

Colts coach Ron Meyer, who many believe was the chief orchestrator behind the deal to bring Dickerson to Indianapolis, said he didn't think there were any losers.

"I don't look at it as anyone lost," Meyer said. "I look at is as win, win, win."

Associated Press sportswriter Dave Goldberg seemed to show a prophetic nature in a column about 10 months after the trade in August 1988. He said conventional wisdom would say the Rams benefited in the long term and the Colts in the short term. "It also holds," Goldberg wrote, "that five years from now, the Colts may regret what they did."

Goldberg explained: "For example, while Dickerson is a franchise player and got the Colts to the playoffs (in 1987), will he ever get them to the Super Bowl? He didn't with a Rams team that was as talented as the present Indianapolis group, but as the Colts did last year, seemed to lose in the first round of the playoffs every year.

"Moreover, Dickerson, at 28, may not have more than two or three solid years left. Few running backs who carry 30 times a game can survive the pounding and few — Walter Payton and Tony Dorsett are exceptions — play effectively after they're 30.

"And finally, in giving up Bennett, the Colts surrendered a player who will have an impact for at least a decade at a position that may be more important than running back."

Goldberg turned out to be wise beyond his years.

Dickerson, in an on-again, off-again relationship with management, lasted through the 1991 season before being dealt to the Los Angeles Raiders for fourth- and eighth-round draft picks. (Note: The fourth-rounder turned out to be Tony McCoy and the eighth was Ronald Humphrey). He never again would lead them to the playoffs, would take a physical pounding his final two seasons in particular and would only last one more full season before announcing his retirement from football.

Bennett turned out to be a key player in Buffalo's drive to four consecutive Super Bowls in the early 1990s, and was a dominant force in each of his NFL seasons.

The Rams squandered most of their draft picks and continued to struggle well into the mid-1990s. Among their draft selections as a result of trading Dickerson, the Rams took wide receiver Aaron Cox, linebacker Fred Strickland, linebacker Frank Stams, running backs Gaston Green and Cleveland Gary, and cornerback Darryl Henley.

But there was no denying the fact that Dickerson's appearance midway through the 1987 season paid immediate dividends for the Colts. He led them to their first playoff appearance in Indianapolis, rushing for more than 1,000 yards and scored five touchdowns. In the short term, he gave the club instant credibility.

In '88 Dickerson put up big numbers again, rushing for 1,659 yards and 14 touchdowns, and catching 36 passes for 377 yards and a score. The Colts won eight of their final 10 games and just missed the playoffs.

It was in training camp in '89 that trouble between Dickerson and management began to brew. Dickerson began by downgrading his offensive line at every opportunity. He would use words such as "awful", "terrible", "pathetic" or "pitiful" to describe some of his linemen, most specifically the guys on the right side — Ben Utt and Kevin Call.

As things didn't improve, Dickerson began to hint that he might take an early retirement. He later refused to speak to the Indianapolis media after coach Ron Meyer basically told him to "shut up" after some comments Meyer had read in the newspaper that had been attributed to his star running back. Dickerson's interesting way at getting back at Meyer was simply not to talk to the media anymore that season.

At one point early in the season when Dickerson began to hint that he wasn't being paid enough money to run behind the current Colts offensive line, WRTV Channel 6 sports anchor Ed Sorensen mentioned on the air that Dickerson was feeling low despite his high bankroll. Sorensen suggested that people who felt sorry for Eric should send him a "Pick-me-up-bouquet" as a show of compassion for the misunderstood running back.

The next day, 23 "Pick-me-up-bouquets" were delivered at various times to Dickerson at the Colts' West 56th Street practice facility. For the record, he didn't think it was nearly as funny as Sorensen did.

Prior to the 1990 season, Dickerson's verbal barrage against his teammates and management continued. In an effort to force the Colts to trade him, Dickerson did an interview on the West Coast in which among other things he said Jim Irsay deserved to be a general manager "about as much as Daffy Duck." He was also quoted that off-season as saying that running behind the Colts line "was like playing Russian roulette," and that the Colts didn't have the talent to be a representable team in the Canadian Football League.

During the summer, he staged an 11-day boycott of training camp, then when he did report he failed a physical because of a hamstring injury. Dickerson refused to take subsequent physicals, was placed on the non-football injury list for six weeks and then suspended for conduct detrimental to the team for four weeks. He was also fined one week's pay and eventually would forfeit $750,000 in lost wages and fines.

Many of Dickerson's problems likely were due to the off-season trade of offensive lineman Chris Hinton and wide receiver Andre Rison to obtain the rights to select Jeff George with the No. 1 pick overall in the draft. Dickerson was outspoken from the beginning that the deal was a mistake. In many ways, as he came to realize, the selection of George showed a significant shift in philosophy from a run-dominated offense to that of a passing game.

"To trade your best offensive lineman and one of your best wide receivers was a definite mistake in my opinion," Dickerson said in a hastily called off-season press conference shortly after the trade for George had been completed. "They had told me they were committed to making the offensive line stronger, but I think if anything, it has gotten much weaker."

In addition he basically said he was afraid he was going to get hurt playing behind a rookie quarterback.

"I don't want to be a sacrificial lamb for anyone," Dickerson said. "I don't want to be the guy that because we have a young quarterback, they'll try and take the pressure off of him and put it all on me. The load has been on me since I started playing professional football.

"My shoulders are getting tired."

When the summer came, as did the holdout and eventually Dickerson's suspension, few people were feeling sorry for the running back with tired shoulders.

Ten minutes after the suspension was announced, the first call came into the switchboard at the Colts West 56th Street complex. The caller's message was simple.

"Tell Mr. Irsay congratulations for me," the caller told the switchboard operator. "It's about time something was done."

Dickerson would last another 21 months in Indianapolis, and even somehow manage to negotiate a four-year contract extension worth nearly $10.75 million.

In 1991, though, his final season with a horseshoe on his helmet, he would again get into trouble. After failing to complete a workout, Dickerson was fined one week's pay and later suspended for four weeks. In a meeting with an off-the-field neutral arbitrator, Dickerson settled his dispute with the club, agreeing to pay the team $225,000 over a two-year span.

And he finally took his dislike for the Indianapolis media to a new, pathetic level. Early in the season, *Indianapolis News* reporter Tom Rietmann was questioning Dickerson for a spot in the upcoming *Sporting News* magazine about the running back's feelings on returning to Los Angeles on Sept. 15 for a game against the Raiders.

Dickerson just shook his head and walked over toward his locker. When Rietmann followed him and asked the question again, the running back got upset and began shouting at the reporter. As he shouted he grabbed Rietmann by the shirt and gave him a solid shove. At that point, defensive back Michael Ball and a few other players separated the two parties and the volatile moment was over.

Dickerson later apologized for the incident. Ironically, two weeks later, Rietmann left the beat but it had nothing to do with the incident. The move had been planned for some time, but the timing turned out to be bad for the reporter following "The Shove."

When it was eventually all said and done, Dickerson got his wish. In an off-season move prior to 1992, the Colts dealt him to the Los Angeles Raiders for a pair of draft picks. Finally, a troublesome chapter in Colts history had come to an end.

"It was a bad situation that we tried every way possible to make good out of," said Jim Irsay a few years later. "Still, if I had to do it all over again, I would still make the trade. From a potential standpoint and from one of instant credibility, that deal put the Indianapolis Colts on the map. No one could have anticipated the problems that would arise. I will always stand by that decision."

◆ ◆ ◆

April 20, 1990.

It should have forever gone down in Indianapolis Colts annals as the day the franchise turned the corner.

Two or three seasons later, when the Colts had made it to the Super Bowl, they should have been able to look back at that late-April date as a major reason they had come so far.

Instead, two seasons later they were coming off a 1-15 debacle and the Super Bowl was the farthest thing from their minds.

And as for April 20, 1990, the day they obtained quarterback Jeff George was little more than a black smudge on the franchise's white linen.

In the beginning it looked like a marriage made in heaven.

George, who had led Warren Central High School on the east side of Indianapolis to back-to-back state football championships in 1984 and 1985, had returned home to lead the town's professional team, the Indianapolis Colts, in pursuit of a Super Bowl.

It seemed so right, and yet almost from the minute the Colts inked George to a six-year, $15 million deal that included a $3.5 million signing bonus, public sentiment was against the Colts and their prize quarterback.

The big problem, which really had nothing to do with George, was the perception that the Colts gave up way too much to acquire his services. For the privilege to select George as the No. 1 player overall in the 1990 draft, the Irsays had to give Atlanta offensive lineman Chris Hinton, wide receiver Andre Rison and their No. 1 pick in 1991.

But the other problem in many people's minds was a feeling that the Colts had become a little too mesmerized by a pair of workouts that George gave prior to the NFL draft. On March 29 and April 5, throwing under a bubble installed over Memorial Stadium at the University of Illinois campus, George put on a show. About halfway through the April 5 workout, George stopped the scouts in their tracks. Asked by Atlanta scout Ken Herock to throw a deep ball, George dropped back and unleashed an 81-yard bomb to Illinois teammate Mike Bellamy.

Colts receivers coach Milt Jackson said that was the telling tale.

"When we saw that throw, we'd seen enough," Jackson said.

And a workout legend was born.

But beyond that, there were several dissenting opinions as to just how valuable George would be. ESPN draft analyst Mel Kiper Jr., a longtime Colts basher, was one of the most outspoken, claiming George was the eighth-best quarterback in the 1990 draft, a far cry from the player who should be selected No. 1 overall in the NFL.

"He's an average quarterback at best," Kiper said.

Dave Thomas, editor of the *Poor Man's Guide to the NFL Draft*, was even more to the point in an interview with a Seattle newspaper just weeks after the Colts selected George in the draft. In fact, Thomas was almost prophet-like in his assessment of what would transpire with the boy with the golden arm.

"George emerged because he was like the new girl on the block," Thomas said. "Everybody fell in love, but they didn't check with the old neighbors to see what a bad girl she was. The Colts better make sure they have a big stock of Excedrin, because they're going to need it."

George had an immediate response to his critics.

"I don't think I have to prove anything to the Mel Kipers or anyone else that says Jeff George isn't for real, because they haven't seen me play," George said at the time. "They're going by what went on when I was younger at Purdue or things like that. I think I got the last laugh by being drafted No. 1, and I'll just let my performance on the field speak for itself."

But the instant criticism wasn't only levied by the national and local media. The fans, as well as future Colts teammates, were quick to speak up against the deal.

From the moment the details of the trade for George began to circulate in Indianapolis, the switchboard at the Colts West 56th Street practice facility began to light up. Even though Indianapolis officials claimed the response was 50-50, insiders said that more than 90 percent of the calls were not positive.

George may have been a hometown boy, but he was returning home with a lot of excess baggage. Many fans in central Indiana still hadn't forgiven him for his decision to leave Purdue after one year and go to the University of Illinois. Those that knew him best said he was a spoiled brat who was coddled by his parents to an extreme and was very accustomed to getting his own way.

The consensus was the Colts were getting a million-dollar talent, but unfortunately they had to accept the rest of the package as well. Not short on confidence, George made it clear from the outset that he was the player who would take the Colts to the next level.

"I honestly believe that I'm the guy to take this team to the Super Bowl," George said shortly after arriving on the scene. "Every team needs a leader and I'm ready to accept that responsibility."

And then there was the players' reaction, many of whom felt the club mortgaged the future for the right to bring George on board. Eric Dickerson said a questionable offensive line had just been made weaker with the loss of Hinton. Incumbent quarterbacks Chris Chandler and Jack Trudeau both took it personally, with Chandler eventually having his wish to be traded granted, and Trudeau left to only dream that he could go, too. "I want to go where I can play," Trudeau said at the time. "You know they didn't give him $15 million to sit on the bench."

Said Chandler prior to his own trade out of Indianapolis: "The trade really tore us down and hurt a lot of guys. And it's going to be hard for them to look at this guy (George) as their leader."

Through it all, George remained cocky and confident, qualities that while it's true helped him through some rocky times would eventually pave the way for his exit from a hostile hometown environment.

Jim Irsay defended the selection early, saying that chances had to be taken to achieve success.

"The only question that matters is whether Jeff George is going to be a legitimate big-time NFL quarterback in the upper echelon," Irsay said. "If he is, then you don't look back and you robbed the bank. If he isn't, obviously you made a mistake.

"You can win without a quarterback and patch it together, but the Montanas, the Kosars, the Kellys stay consistent. They give you a chance to win every time. When you don't have them, you're always kidding yourself thinking this second-rounder or third-rounder can do it."

Nearly four years later, when the Colts orchestrated a March 1994 trade — ironically with Atlanta — to send George packing for a conditional first-round pick, the organization was left to pick up the pieces and figure out exactly what went wrong.

Many of George's problems he brought upon himself. When criticism arose, he always believed in fanning the flames rather than admitting a mistake and trying to learn from it.

Once when he was asked late in the 1992 season why he always got booed in the Hoosier Dome, George said it had to do with two reasons. "I'm good and I'm good looking," he said. Later that day, George approached the reporter who had asked the question originally and made his point even more clear. "You know what I said about being good and good looking?" George quipped. "I just want you to know I was serious. I want to see that in the newspaper."

On several occasions throughout his nearly four years with the Colts, George let his confidence in his own abilities spew forth in almost uncontrollable terms. Asked if he was the person to lead the Colts to the Super Bowl, George once said, "Everyone knows you need a quarterback like myself to get where you want to go."

When George once said that he was the guy, Duke Tumatoe had a question for him in song.

> *Jeff says he's the guy*
>
> *I say, the guy for what?*
>
> *I bet if Jeff could find a way*
>
> *He'd kiss his own darn butt*
>
> *Lord help our Colts. Lord help our Colts.*

One of the criticisms early in his career from his own teammates had to do with the quarterback's work ethic — or lack thereof. Teammates said George would be the last one to arrive in the morning and the first one to be out the door when practice had ended. His reaction was not to deny the reports. "I have more God-given ability than the next guy," George said. "I don't have to work as hard."

Let 'er Rip

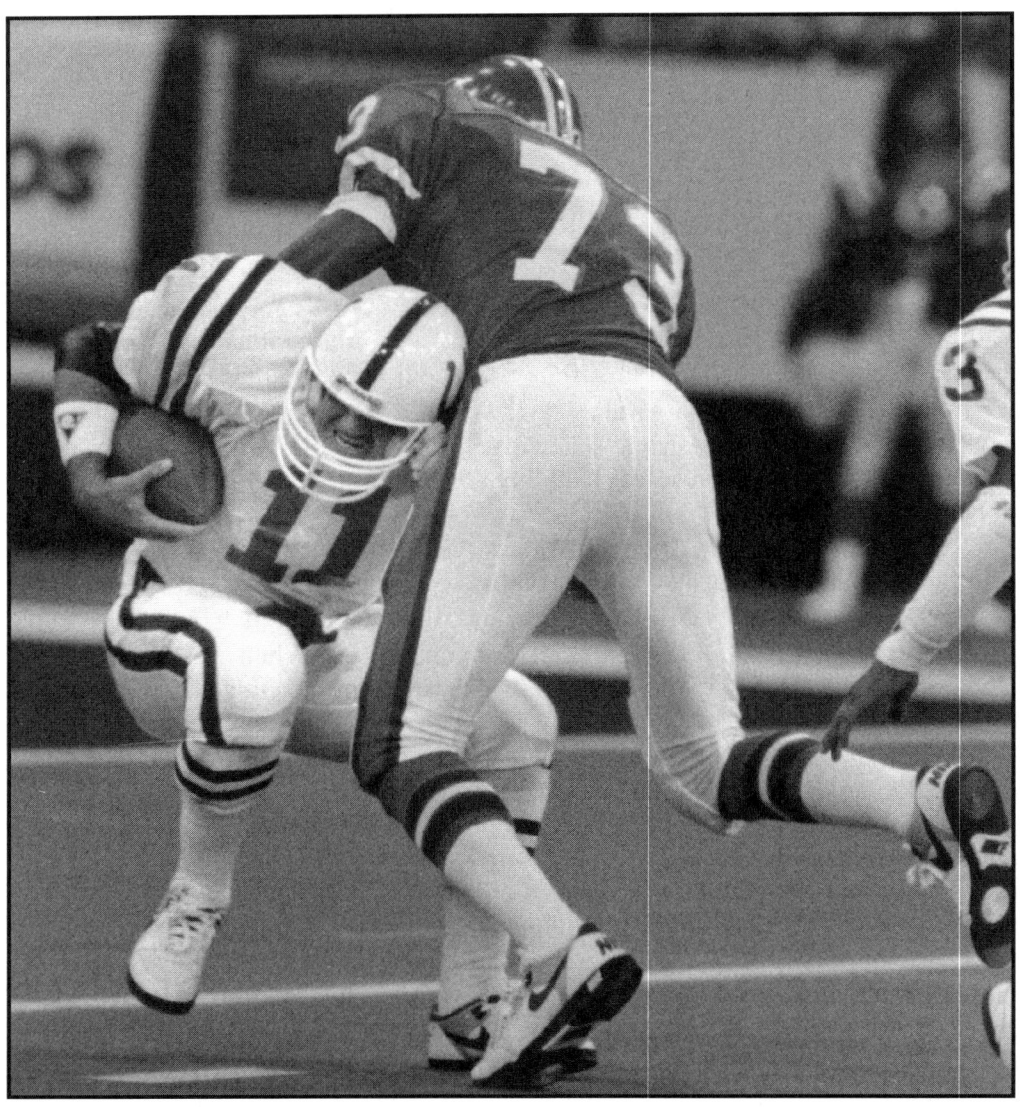

Although he posted impressive statistics, Jeff George could not escape his cocky attitude nor the results of a Colts team that allowed the young quarterback to be sacked 56 times during the 1991 season. (Photo by Don Larson)

As a rookie, George posted better-than-average numbers. He completed 54 percent of his passes for 2,152 yards and had a record of 5-7 as a starter. Most importantly he threw more touchdown passes (16) than interceptions (13), becoming only the eighth of 34 rookie starting quarterbacks in the NFL since 1961 to accomplish the feat.

His second year, the Colts' miserable 1-15 season of 1991, George started all 16 games. At the time, his two-year statistics were the best of any quarterback that had been selected No. 1 overall since the NFL and AFL merged in 1967. And he was in pretty good company. The others included Terry Bradshaw (1970), Jim Plunkett (1971), Steve Bartkowski (1975), John Elway (1983), Vinny Testaverde (1987) and Troy Aikman (1989). Of that group, he had more attempts (819), completions (473), yards (5,062), a better completion percentage (.578) and was the only one to throw for more touchdowns (26) than interceptions (25).

On the negative side, however, he was becoming a bruised and battered quarterback as well. In 1991, he was sacked 56 times for 481 yards which established club records in both categories. In his first 29 games, he was sacked at least once in all but one of those contests.

Following a 17-6 loss to the Jets that year, George decided it was time to unload his frustrations on his line play. In a story in the *Indianapolis Star*, George said, "It's tough out there when you make mental errors like we've been making. Either you know the pass protection or you don't. It's been a problem all year. We know what's coming, we're just picking up the wrong guy. ... To get beat by not knowing what's going on is wrong. If you don't know what's going on, ask questions. I haven't been in the league that long and I'm not a real expert, but I know what's going on. I know when this guy needs to block that guy. Some of it is common sense. You learn that in high school."

The physical beating led to several injuries in his Colts career. He missed three games with an abdominal strain in his rookie season, six games with separate injuries to his right hand and right thumb in 1992, and three games in '93 after he held out the entire training camp, a decision which cost him $144,000 in daily fines.

George's frustrations came to a head late in the 1992 season after he was pulled by Ted Marchibroda in favor of Jack Trudeau in the fourth quarter of a December game in the Meadowlands with the Colts trailing the Jets 6-3 at the time. Even though Trudeau rallied the Colts to a victory, George sat by himself on his helmet, sulking at the far end of the sidelines for the rest of the game. He threw his helmet and didn't offer his teammates congratulations following what would be the game-winning touchdown.

Duke Tumatoe saw it this way:

> *Jeff got mad and threw his helmet*
> *And said Ted must take the blame*
> *But Jeff, you were the one*
> *who was screwing up the game.*
> *Lord help our Colts. Lord help our Colts.*
> *Jeff, the picture might get clearer*
> *If you look straight in the mirror*
> *(Don't ask your mom for her thoughts either)*
> *Lord help our Colts.*

The following week the boos grew louder in the Hoosier Dome and criticism became more intense in the local media. *Indianapolis Star* columnist Robin Miller hit a nerve with the bearded wonder in a column a few days after George threw his tantrum in the Jets game.

Wrote Miller: "George, who didn't make things any better by refusing to talk to the press afterward, is young, but needs some maturation. He's not a bad kid, but I think he's gotten some bad advice and too much in-house brain washing during his career."

Those criticisms were mild compared to what Miller wrote in an '87 column, shortly after George decided to leave Purdue. There, he took to task George's parents, Dave and Judy (calling them Rave and Judicious in the story) for coddling their son throughout his early years.

One week after the Jets game, following a victory over Phoenix where George started and was repeatedly booed by the paying customers in the Hoosier Dome, the quarterback and the columnist had a verbal altercation in the Colts locker room.

As Miller interviewed defensive lineman Tony Siragusa, George stepped in to confront the columnist about a recent story. He poked a finger in Miller's chest before being pulled away by defensive end Sam Clancy.

"You can say or write anything about me that you want but keep my family out of it or I'm going to get you," George screamed.

Miller replied that such action would likely cost the quarterback a lot of money to which George replied, "Yeah, but it would be worth every penny."

As he walked away, George let loose a verbal barrage on Miller calling him a prick and a skinny mother f-----. George also told Miller to watch his backside when he was out in public because George's brothers and friends would be looking for him and "they're going to kick your ass."

"OK, I'll be careful Jeff," Miller replied, fanning the flames in a mocking tone. "I'll make sure I stay off the streets."

"You better you skinny little mother f-----."

The following summer George was a no-show at training camp and for 36 days no one knew where he was for sure. There were sightings everywhere from Florida to Mexico to Broad Ripple, a yuppie section of town just north of the heart of Indianapolis.

Apparently attempting to force a trade, George finally caved in and returned when the daily fine total had reached $144,000 and the time was about to arrive when the Colts could suspend him without pay for the remainder of the season. Needless to say, the holdout didn't sit well with the majority of his teammates, who believed George's selfish act was going to cost them down the road in the 1993 season.

Veteran right tackle Kevin Call was one of the most outspoken.

"I don't see how he can mend any fences," Call said. "He's pretty much torn them all down. You don't forgive these things. He wants the fans to leave him alone. I mean, grow up and learn a little bit. If you don't want to get into the limelight, then get out. Go be a trash man, or whatever it was he studied in school."

Duke Tumatoe summed it up this way:

> *Jeff, Jeff, Jeff, Jeff, Jeff, Jeff*
> *you ego-maniacal jerk*
> *Writing these songs with you around*
> *is just a lot less work.*
> *Lord help our Colts. Lord help our Colts.*

From now on when I boo I will always think of you.
Lord help our Colts.
We'll call you the guy, the bearded wonder, whatever you want
just as long as you come back quick.
I'll even make Bob and Tom promise
not to call you a dick.
Lord help our Colts. Lord help our Colts.
If you come back and play
we'll all chip in and buy you your own bidet.
Lord help our Colts.

George eventually returned, played out the season, and in the next off-season got his wish when new director of football operations Bill Tobin dealt him to Atlanta for the Falcons' 1996 first-round selection. The Colts would eventually use the pick to select Syracuse wide receiver Marvin Harrison.

Tobin summed up the chapter in Colts' history thusly on the day George was traded away: "I don't think anybody will ever know why it didn't work the way they thought it would in 1990. He was the first pick in the draft, he was going home to play in his hometown. Everybody thought that was the ideal situation. Everybody expected the Colts to have him as their quarterback for years and years to come. For whatever reason, it didn't work out the way it was planned.

"It was time to cut the cord and move in another direction for him and for us," Tobin said. "It gives us a lot of options. It's a great trade in that it's a win-win-win situation for the Colts, for George and for the Falcons."

The Colts' first seven seasons in Indianapolis were nothing to write home about, with just one playoff appearance in a 1987 strike-shortened season that would contain an asterisk as two of those victories were by a replacement team.

Still, the Colts didn't actually hit rock bottom until Dec. 22, 1991.

On a warm, sunny day in Tampa, Florida, the hapless Colts put the finishing touches on a 1-15 season with a 17-3 loss to the equally inept Buccaneers at Tampa Stadium.

The game had been billed as the Repus Bowl (that's Super spelled backward) as the 2-13 Bucs faced the 1-14 Colts. The 28,043 fans in attendance that day found out something they didn't think was possible — there was a team in the NFL that was worse than their beloved Buccaneers.

The Colts were pitiful to the very end. Jeff George threw for 203 yards but was sacked five times, the Colts lost four fumbles and as a team lost for the 10th time in 11 tries under interim head coach Rick Venturi.

As the team came off the field, a television reporter caught up with Eric Dickerson, who had just rushed for 19 yards on 11 carries in the game. Asked what he was feeling at the moment, Dickerson said, "Relief." A moment later, he added, "Get a good look because this is the last time you'll ever see me in a Colts uniform."

It turned out to be a prophetic remark as in the off-season new head coach Ted Marchibroda would have a major role in trading Dickerson to the Raiders. One of the two draft picks in particular that the Colts received for Dickerson, a fourth-rounder in the 1992 draft, was spent on Florida defensive tackle Tony McCoy.

Murphy's Law played a big role in the 1991 Colts season. If something bad had a chance to happen to the Colts, it would.

The team suffered through injuries, injuries and more injuries. When the season ended, a total of 12 players were listed on injured reserve, including nine on the offensive side of the ball.

The offensive line in particular was beset with an incredible number of injuries. When the season opened the Colts had Zefross Moss at left tackle, Bill Schultz at left guard, Ray Donaldson at center, Brian Baldinger at right guard and Kevin Call at right tackle. By the time it was said and done, the only constant in the chaos would be Call, who started all 16 games.

Everyone else missed at least one game, and several missed the majority of the season. Two in particular were victims of the Los Angeles Coliseum Colts Massacre (also known as the Wrath of Bubba) on September 15. Former San Francisco 49er offensive lineman Bubba Paris, brought in just after the beginning of the regular season to shore up the line, took out Donaldson and Irv Pankey within five plays of each other. Both injuries turned out to be for the season. Donaldson broke his leg when Paris stepped on him in a pile up. Four plays later, Paris pulled on a play and stepped on Pankey's ankle, fracturing it as well.

Two games later, in a 31-3 loss at Seattle, Moss would leave the game on crutches with an ankle injury and Dixon had a severely strained calf. At the end of the game the only two offensive line reserves were Mark Cannon and Pat Snyder, a pair of long snappers with zero NFL offensive line experience between them.

"In the Seattle game, we were on our goal line, about to get stuffed and (George) called a 20 draw," said running back Eric Dickerson. "One of the linemen said, 'Is that a run or pass?' That's not the first time that has happened. I mean it's like 'C'mon guys, you've got to get a clue'."

Said quarterback Jeff George: "I have faces in the huddle and I don't even know all their names."

But it wasn't just the linemen. Albert Bentley tore knee ligaments in week 2 and was out for the season. Anthony Johnson missed the final nine games of the season after being poked in the eye and suffering blurred vision. Jack Trudeau missed the second half of the season with a broken thumb. Donnell Thompson and Matt Vanderbeek missed the final month of the season on injured reserve.

"It was crazy, like nothing I had ever seen before," said linebacker Jeff Herrod. "Guys were just dropping like flies. Every time someone would go down you'd be afraid to look to see who it was. It just seemed like there was a curse on.

"It was like somewhere, someone had a voodoo doll and they were using us as a pin cushion."

After they slipped to 0-8, Dickerson could hold his tongue no more.

"This is just embarrassing," he said. "I don't know if a lot of these guys realize it but we're 0-8 and if things don't get better a lot of these guys are going to be out of here, including me and probably some of the other players. I don't think they know what's at stake.

"I think a lot of them look at this as a fun game, and just come and get a paycheck, but there's more to it than that," he said. "If we go 0-16 — and I pray to God we don't — and it comes time for other teams to look at this team for players ... nobody's going to want any of them. I mean I wouldn't want any of them. I just wouldn't, that's a fact.

"I think a lot of these guys just don't give a damn and that's the problem," he added. "And honestly I think I care too much. I think that's one of my problems."

Dickerson had reached the boiling point, and even though his statistics couldn't really back up his words, he continued to fire away with both barrels.

"There's nothing I can do," he said. "It's like sending you to Vietnam with a BB gun. You know what happens when you get out there with a BB gun or a sling shot? It would be no help at all."

Asked if he thought the Colts could turn things around, Dickerson said, "We are not, more than likely, going to go 8-8." Asked to elaborate he put it in even simpler terms. "It's always darkest before it goes totally black."

The Colts would lose their first nine games of the season before something good would happen. They had not scored a touchdown in their last 21 quarters when they headed to the Meadowlands on Sunday, Nov. 10, to take on the Jets. The game would turn out to be their only highlight, in a season filled with despair.

The touchdown streak came to an end against the Jets — and how. In the first 568 minutes and 53 seconds of the season to that point, the Colts had scored a total of four touchdowns. Then against the Jets, in a 13-minute, 5-second stretch, the Colts scored four more.

George, who had three touchdown passes in the first nine games, tied a career best with three in the 13-minute span against New York. Two went to Jessie Hester and the other to Billy Brooks.

The final score: Indianapolis 28, New York 27.

"It feels like we just won the Super Bowl," George said. "Maybe this will be the spark that we need to get this thing turned around."

That wasn't the case. The Colts went on to lose their final six games, and set a franchise record for most losses in a season. The Colts managed just 143 points in 16 games including just 24 in the first quarter all season.

The Colts ranked last in total offense (234.3), last in rushing offense (73.1) and 27th (out of 28 teams) in pass offense (161.2). Defensively, the Colts were last against the run allowing 145.4 yards per game.

The Colts had hit the bottom of the barrel. There was no place to go but up and it appeared as if there would be a new coach in town by the time the 1992 season rolled around.

Whoever the new guy would be it would take some big-time rebuilding to turn around the likes of the 1991 Colts.

3

Rebuilding the Colts

Step 1: Ted Marchibroda

Jessie Hester looked around the visitors' locker room at Tampa Stadium in late December 1991 and could only shake his head.

A few moments earlier, the Colts had put the finishing touches on a gut-wrenching 1-15 season, and the wide receiver openly questioned what the future for the club would hold.

"We all have a bad taste in our mouths right now and I hope we never forget the way we feel at this moment," Hester said. "We're embarrassed. We're the worst team in the NFL and that doesn't feel too good. It just makes you wonder what is going to happen between now and next year's training camp.

"I'm sure a lot of changes are planned but you just wonder where they're going to start."

Let 'er Rip

At the top of course. Ron Meyer had only lasted the first five games of the '91 campaign before being fired and replaced on an interim basis by Rick Venturi. With too many injuries to too many key players to count, Venturi had done his best to keep the ship afloat but only a 28-27 victory over the Jets stood between the Colts and an imperfect 0-16 season.

Vice president and general manager Jim Irsay knew he had to find the perfect person to turn the tide and get the Colts back on their feet again. Venturi applied for the job, but the Colts needed a blood transfusion from the outside. Michigan State's George Perles was interviewed, as was San Francisco assistant Mike Holmgren. Buddy Ryan expressed interest, but never got a formal interview.

On top of Irsay's short list was Ted Marchibroda, a former head coach of the Baltimore Colts from 1975-79, and currently the offensive coordinator for the AFC champion Buffalo Bills.

The dilemma for Irsay was he could not talk with Marchibroda until after the Super Bowl, and by waiting that long he would likely lose a chance to hire his other top choice, Holmgren. Irsay opted to gamble and wait to speak with Marchibroda. Holmgren in the meantime accepted the head coaching position at Green Bay and Irsay was left with his fingers crossed.

They didn't stay crossed for long. Within hours of the Bills' 37-24 loss to Washington in Super Bowl XXVI in Minneapolis, the Colts and Marchibroda had enjoyed a lengthy discussion. Quickly a decision was reached, and even more quickly Marchibroda was on his way to a press conference in Indianapolis to announce his hiring as the Colts coach.

"In the back of my mind I've always been excited about (Ted) coming back here and finishing the job that he started," said Jim Irsay at that initial press conference. "Really the last time we had a dominant type of team where we consistently won over a period of time was when he was the head coach.

"I was hoping it would work out with Ted because I don't think there's another individual out there who can do the job that needs to be done as well as he can," he added. "I wanted to take the opportunity to talk to a few people before we made the big decision but really sentiment doesn't play into it, only winning.

"You can bring in whoever, but if the wins don't follow with that choice, the popular coach will become unpopular and the choice will become unpopular, too."

When Marchibroda came on board in late January 1992, the Colts' four key returning offensive weapons were quarterback Jeff George, running backs Eric Dickerson and Albert Bentley, and wide receiver Bill Brooks.

George, about to begin his third season in the league, was considered an NFL star of the future, who just needed a quarterback's coach such as Marchibroda to mold him into one of the game's elite players. Dickerson was unhappy — as was the case during the majority of his five seasons with the Colts — but the thinking was a new coach could be just the spark the veteran needed to resurrect his career. Bentley was bouncing back from a knee injury that had cost him the 1991 season but all

Rebuilding the Colts: Ted Marchibroda

Colts coach Ted Marchibroda found the going tougher than expected when he took over in 1992. Inheriting a team thought to have a bright future led by a quarterback expected to be an NFL star, Marchibroda's expectations had to be rearranged after holdouts, injuries and disappointing performances by key personnel. (Photo by Paul Sancya)

indications were that he was close to 100 percent for '92. And Brooks had caught a career-high 72 balls for nearly 900 yards the year before and had moved into second place all time in Colts history for receptions.

As he sat in that first press conference after accepting the Colts coaching job for the second time in his career, Marchibroda had to have figured all of those players would play a significant role in his master plan to rebuild the Colts from the ground up. Every rebuilding plan needs its share of cornerstones, and offensively anyway those seemed to be the likeliest candidates.

Marchibroda, always known as a quarterback guru, spent his first few days talking about why he believed Jeff George was an indication that the future for the franchise was bright.

"I always felt that Jeff was the key because he had all the tools to be a great quarterback," Marchibroda would say later. "I said at the time that Jeff may be as fine a passer as there is in the NFL and I still believe that today. He has all the intangibles that you just can't coach. He's got a strong arm, a quick release and pinpoint accuracy. That's not a bad starting point for any coach coming in."

Still, 10 months later when he would look back on his first season as the Colts coach, Marchibroda had to shake his head at what had become of his cornerstone players.

George was upset after being pulled in a Dec. 13 game against the Jets at the Meadowlands and was still steaming. "Ted made his decision and that's something he's going to have to live with," was George's mature response the week after he was pulled in favor of backup Jack Trudeau midway through the fourth quarter with the Colts trailing 6-3. Trudeau wound up leading the Colts to a fourth-quarter TD and a 10-6 victory, but all of that was lost on the 26-year-old man-child. He preferred to sit by himself at the end of the bench and pout. Even when Trudeau came off the field following the eventual game-winning score, George didn't offer as much as a hand in congratulations.

The following summer he would be a no-show for training camp and miss the first few games of the regular season, among other things still unhappy about his treatment by the head coach.

Dickerson never carried the ball one down for Marchibroda; instead, he was traded on draft day in April to the Los Angeles Raiders for fourth- and eighth-round draft picks. The malcontent running back had said walking off the field in Tampa in December that it was the last time anyone would see him in a Colts uniform. He got his wish.

Bentley, in one of the best kept secrets of the '92 training camp, did not make the final cut to 47 players the first week of September. Marchibroda worried that Bentley's knee was not up to 100 percent and felt it was in the best interests of the organization to let Bentley go. Bentley eventually was picked up by Pittsburgh but never carried the ball for the Steelers and had just one kickoff return for 17 yards before being released. He later would retire from football.

Brooks was the fourth-leading receiver on the '92 team with 44 catches but it was obvious his role had diminished decidedly under Marchibroda, offensive coordinator Nic Nicolau and receivers coach Dwain Painter. The following season, when his contract was up, Brooks narrowed his choices to the Colts and Bills before opting to sign with Buffalo.

Despite all the changes in personnel, however, there was a constant in the chaos for the '92 Colts. The bottom line was the team finished 9-7, and Marchibroda had tied an NFL record for the greatest single-season turnaround by improving the Colts by a total of eight victories. Interestingly, the record he tied was his own. In 1975, his first year with the Baltimore Colts, Marchibroda took a team that had finished 2-12 the year before and guided it to a 10-4 record, the first time in league history that a team had moved from last to first.

The leading rusher in '92 was Rodney Culver with 321 yards and Reggie Langhorne, the former Brown who had resurrected his career with a 65-catch season. The tight end had once again become part of the offense with Kerry Cash and Charles Arbuckle playing key roles for the Colts down the stretch as Indianapolis won its final five games.

One of the finest draft classes in the club's 40-year history had infused the veterans with new excitement and enthusiasm. Players such as Steve Emtman and Quentin Coryatt, despite injuries that hindered their progress, had given the veterans new reason for hope. Other draftees such as Ashley Ambrose, Jason Belser, Stephen Grant, Culver and McCoy would eventually play key roles in the rebuilding process.

More than anything else though, it was as if there had been a weeding out of the bad and a reseeding of the good as optimism was again high in Indianapolis.

Trudeau, who had seen his share of the bad since being drafted by the Colts in the second round in 1986, said a big reason for the change was a new attitude among his teammates.

"We brought in a new staff and some new players and the attitude just was a whole lot better," Trudeau said. "Ted's a different type of coach. With him, you'd better be prepared to work a lot preparing for a game, which was a definite change from the past. Ron Meyer's attitude was that we were pros, and to go out and get it done. With Ted, we studied more. He's a real positive individual and his attitude rubbed off on some people."

Coming out of '92, optimism with the Colts was once again high, but Marchibroda cautioned that optimism by dishing out a dose of reality. He made it clear that much of the club's success was a direct benefit of a fifth-place schedule and that the five-game win streak to end the season, although enjoyable, had to be kept in context. Although the Colts did beat Buffalo in that run, the other four opponents were New England, the Jets, Phoenix and Cincinnati. And in the run the Colts only scored 17 points or more one time.

His point was that the Colts had a long way to go and were certainly not going to approach the next off-season as if the club had a pat hand. A busy off-season bolstered the offensive line, adding Will Wolford and Kirk Lowdermilk up front. Though both were big improvements from a skill standpoint, they also brought with them other intangibles, most notably that of players who could be counted on for leadership in the clubhouse.

The weeding out of bad eggs also continued. Marchibroda believed veteran center Ray Donaldson was replaceable, and the Colts did not re-sign him. Chip Banks had overstayed his welcome and did not return. Jon Hand had concluded another unproductive season, and though he would return to play in '93 and '94, the patience of the coaching staff was wearing thin.

The '93 draft was also key because it produced offensive starters Sean Dawkins and Roosevelt Potts. Slowly the pieces were falling into place. However, the unknown, a 36-day holdout in July, August and September by Jeff George would send Marchibroda and his staff scrambling to compensate on offense.

When he would look back on the 4-12 nightmare of 1993, Marchibroda would point to several areas of concern. The offense had sputtered, the defense couldn't stop the run, and overall, the Colts had several long days at the office. He rarely made much mention, in public anyway, of just how much George's holdout had affected the club's ability to perform.

But like it or not, George was the straw that stirred the drink, and the glass was empty so long the Colts never did seem to click until it was far too late.

George, the player Marchibroda had hoped would be like a flower that would blossom and be part of a beautiful bouquet, turned out to be a thorn in his side.

Through the holdout, Marchibroda remained as interested as the next guy as to what was going on in George's head, but he claimed throughout the months of waiting that he had no contact with his quarterback.

Had they had more of a charmed relationship, one would have expected George to have at least confided in his head coach the reasons why he was not in camp. Instead, Marchibroda remained in the dark. That had to be particularly difficult for Jim Irsay, who had dreamed the veteran coach and the young player would develop a relationship that would enable George to live up to the expectations that had come with being the first player selected in the 1990 draft.

In Marchibroda, Irsay had a coach who was a veteran of 30 previous seasons in the NFL. More importantly, he had a man who gave instant credibility to his belief that George could develop into a big-time quarterback. Many insiders felt a big reason for George's slow maturation process at the NFL level was the fact he had not had a true quarterback coach working with him on a daily basis.

Which was why the addition of Marchibroda to the picture seemed like a perfect fit. Marchibroda's single biggest claim to fame was his work with quarterbacks. He had been credited with much of the success of players such as Jim Kelly, Randall Cunningham and Bert Jones in recent years, and had worked with Roman Gabriel, Sonny Jurgensen and Billy Kilmer in past seasons.

At that first press conference in January of '92, Marchibroda made it clear that he believed he had struck gold by coming to a franchise that had a quarterback such as George in place.

"One of the reasons I'm excited is wherever I've been with an outstanding quarterback, we've won," Marchibroda said. "Jeff may be as fine a passer as there in the NFL. I think No. 1, we're not going to try to make Jeff George another Jim Kelly. We want Jeff George to be Jeff George.

"Right here in Indianapolis we have a rare quality in Jeff George," he added. "He's the kind of gentleman you certainly hope to work with."

It didn't take long for Marchibroda to realize that the word "gentleman" didn't fit his prize quarterback, a player who was long on self-confidence but short in the self-discipline department. Though Marchibroda publicly defended George until long after he left in the spring of '94 for the greener pastures of Atlanta, so much of George's ways were everything Marchibroda disliked about the modern day player and against the grain of his own philosophies for team success.

Rather than throw into the end zone from 50 yards away on the final play of a half and risk an interception, George always preferred the dump-off 16-yard completion that would improve his stats. Instead of talking about what the team was doing, George wanted to talk about how he was going to lead the Colts to the Super Bowl. Rather than privately air his dirty laundry when it came to shortcomings on the part of his teammates, George on more than one occasion was caught on the big screen berating a teammate, either to his face or from 30 yards down the field.

In the end, it was clear that George was a player who had been used to getting his own way and didn't take kindly to anyone stepping on his toes. And because playing for a coach whom he didn't completely respect was too much to ask of the bearded wonder, the Atlanta trade was consummated in the spring of '94.

When it was all said and done, both parties did their best to paint a rosy picture of the situation.

"I still believe Jeff is a tremendous talent and he can have a great future in the NFL," Marchibroda said. "But a time comes when you have to move on and that's what happened here. I wish him nothing but the best."

Though George rarely agreed to talk about his days in Indianapolis after landing in Atlanta, the company line he adopted was to say nothing but good things about his former employer.

"I have good memories of the time I spent in Indianapolis but I just needed a change," he said. "I have a lot of good friends there but now I need to concentrate on taking this team to the Super Bowl."

◆   ◆   ◆

The off-season prior to the 1994 season laid the groundwork for what was to eventually come in 1995 — a playoff contender in Indianapolis.

Owner Robert Irsay, saying he was tired of not getting enough bang for his buck in player expenditures and wanting a football man to come in and turn his organization around, hired Bill Tobin as vice president and director of football operations.

Jeff George and Jack Trudeau hit the road, as did receivers Reggie Langhorne and Jessie Hester who had combined for 149 catches and 1,873 yards the year before. Jim Harbaugh and Don Majkowski were given the reins to the offense, and some high picks in the draft produced running back phenom Marshall Faulk, linebacker Trev Alberts, as well as offensive linemen Eric Mahlum and Jason Mathews, and running back Lamont Warren.

Heading into the '94 season, Marchibroda was back to his optimistic self.

"Without a doubt this is the best team I've had in my three years here," he said. "Talent-wise it's the best, and there has been a dramatic change in the ballclub in terms of attitude and leadership.

"We've had excellent drafts the last three years and when you put all the components together the outlook has to be better," he added. "The players came into camp in shape with a real concern for this football team."

The season was a strange one. The Colts appeared several times on the verge of making a run at the playoffs, but they couldn't put together back-to-back victories. After an emotional 17-15 victory over Seattle early in the season, they bounced back to give a game away in a 16-6 loss to the lowly Jets at the Meadowlands. The following week, Harbaugh was brilliant in a rare road victory against Buffalo, but the next week the Colts dropped a 41-27 debacle to a Washington Redskins team that had only won one of its first eight decisions.

Two late-season losses to New England proved to be the Colts' undoing, and an 8-8 finish kept them out of the playoffs for the 10th time in 11 seasons.

This time the off-season brought a change at quarterback when the Colts acquired Craig Erickson from Tampa Bay on draft day, a move that Bill Tobin was rumored to not completely endorse. A strong supporter of Harbaugh since he drafted

Ted Marchibroda, left, and quarterback Jim Harbaugh celebrate after the Colts defeated New England 10-7 in the final regular-season game of 1995, clinching a spot in the playoffs. (Photo by Don Larson)

him with the Chicago Bears, Tobin felt Erickson was a good player but it's believed he felt there should have been an open competition for the starting job in training camp.

Instead, Marchibroda wasted little time in naming Erickson as the No. 1 QB heading into camp, and quickly the pressure grew on the head coach. If Erickson was a success, Marchibroda's decision would have been hailed. If he were to fail, there would be no place to hide.

When Erickson did falter, and Harbaugh came on to lead the Colts deep into the playoffs in '95, many insiders believed Marchibroda's job for '96 was definitely in doubt. When the Colts reached the AFC title game, the general feeling was that Marchibroda had saved his job, but the general feeling turned out to be incorrect.

Twenty-six days after leading the Colts to within one catch of Super Bowl XXX, the Colts announced a decision to sever ties with Marchibroda, claiming a financial agreement and length of contract had made further negotiations not worthwhile. The

Colts wanted Marchibroda back for one-year at the same salary of the year before — $500,000. Marchibroda wanted a two-year deal and believed he deserved to be rewarded financially for the club's success in '95.

"I think this is something that had been planned for a while," Marchibroda said the day after the Colts announced that their coach of the last four years would not be back for '96. "Bill (Tobin) and I are not total buddies. We're working partners. This is the direction he decided to go and I have to live with it."

Interestingly, those were the same words spoken by Jeff George two years before in reference to Marchibroda. It was just another golden example of how what goes around, comes around.

◆   ◆   ◆

One of Marchibroda's favorite ways of describing a good player in his days as head coach in Indianapolis would be to say, "He's a Colt."

To Marchibroda's way of thinking, a Colt was someone who was willing to go the extra mile to get the job done. Someone who believed in the team concept and was always working toward the same goal. A player who took pride in the horseshoe and was proud to wear the symbol on his helmet.

In that vein, Marchibroda was a Colt.

Even when the wheels came off less than a month after he took the Colts to the threshold of the Super Bowl, the veteran of nearly 35 NFL seasons refused to badmouth his employer. He had nothing but good things to say about Bob and Jim Irsay, he was very fond of the city and very proud of his players.

"The Irsays gave me two opportunities and I feel like I repaid them this year," Marchibroda said in his final press conference, held on a Friday night at the downtown Westin Hotel. "I feel I did the job I was brought in to do and that was to coach the Colts back to respectability.

"It was a great ride."

Indeed it was. Marchibroda's only big regret was that he wouldn't be there to see the fruits of his labors in the future. Instead, a week later he was hired by Art Modell to coach the Baltimore Ravens (formerly the Cleveland Browns), proving once again that good people always find a way to land on their feet.

"I had hoped to be a part of next season and I expected the Colts to be in the Super Bowl," Marchibroda said. "But I guess it just wasn't meant to be."

In all honesty, Bill Tobin and the Colts were caught between a rock and a hard place when the '95 season finally came to an end with the 20-16 loss to Pittsburgh in the AFC title game. Because of Indianapolis' success, a raid was on to hire away members of the Colts coaching staff — namely defensive coordinator Vince Tobin and offensive coordinator Lindy Infante.

It was very similar to how Marchibroda became a Colt in the first place, four years before following Buffalo's ascent to the Super Bowl.

The Colts' decision to take their one-year, $500,000 offer to Marchibroda off the table came the same day that Vince Tobin accepted the head coaching job with the

Let 'er Rip

Arizona Cardinals. Had Marchibroda been retained, the Colts would have also likely lost Infante, a possibility they didn't want to risk.

In the end, it came down to a decision between keeping Infante, who had been a major player in the Colts' success in '95, and Marchibroda, who for the majority of the '95 season they didn't believe they were going to bring back for another season.

Looked at in that light, it's not that surprising that Marchibroda was let go and Infante eventually named head coach.

The bottom line, however, was that the Colts rebuilding process from the ashes of a 1-15 season in 1991 began with the hiring of Ted Marchibroda. It was Marchibroda who weeded out a lot of the bad eggs and filled the roster with "Colts". It was Marchibroda who had a big hand in four drafts that produced a total of 22 players who were still on the roster for the '95 run. Eleven of those players were starters in '95.

It was Marchibroda who deserves a big chunk of the credit for an about face from NFL joke to respectability.

"I was just happy to be a part of it," Marchibroda said as he saddled up and headed into the sunset. "I have coached a lot of different places, but I will always hold a special place in my heart for what it means to be a Colt."

4

Rebuilding the Colts

Step 2: Bill Tobin

The winds of change blew into Indianapolis on January 7, 1994, and it didn't take the organization long to realize the new kid on the block meant business.

There would be no more acceptance of status quo, no shortcuts to success and no room for anyone who wasn't 100 percent committed to the team.

When Bill Tobin took over the reins of all football operations of the Indianapolis Colts just after the new year dawned in 1994, he was commissioned with the task of returning the organization to one of consistent respectability.

In many ways, the move to bring in Tobin was owner Robert Irsay's way of saying it was time to change dealers. Son Jim Irsay had served as the club's general manager since the move to Indianapolis in 1984, and the bottom line figure was just one trip to the playoffs, that coming in the strike-shortened 1987 season.

The elder Irsay believed the Colts needed more of a football man running the show. In a March 1994 column in the *Indianapolis Star*, Irsay said his decision to bring in Tobin should not be perceived as a lack of confidence in his son's abilities.

"I'm not dissatisfied with Jimmy at all," Irsay said at the league meetings that spring in Orlando, Fla. "He came in at 24 years old as a general manager and he had a lot to learn. We made a mistake by not surrounding him with the type of talent that a Bill Tobin brings. Tobin has a complete knowledge of the football business. He knows the people, he knows talent and he knows football. That's what we've been looking for."

With those things in mind, the elder Irsay began pursuing Tobin toward the end of the '93 season, but kept his interest a secret from his son. A few phone discussions led to a lunch in Carmel, Ind., on Jan. 4. Two days later an offer was extended. A phone tip, however, to ABC affiliate WRTV Channel 6 in Indianapolis leaked the fact that Irsay and Tobin had met for lunch.

Jim Irsay was attending league meetings at Dallas at the time. When contacted by reporters from both the *Indianapolis Star* and the *Indianapolis News* in his Dallas hotel that night, Irsay said he was aware that a meeting had taken place but wouldn't elaborate. The truth, however, was that he had no idea of what the reporters were talking about.

"I said I knew about the meeting and that I didn't want to say much about it but that was B.S.," Irsay said. "The truth is I had a zinger thrown at me and my instincts just took over. I was always taught to never act like you don't know. But I didn't know. I didn't know anything was going on. I was as surprised as the next guy."

It wasn't until later that evening that he first heard from his father that Tobin was close to becoming a member of the Colts' front office.

"I sat down and talked with Jimmy about it ... afterwards," Robert Irsay said. "I kept it a very big secret. Bill wanted it that way and I wanted it that way.

"Some reporters and people say I have cut Jimmy's wheels off," he added. "I haven't cut his wheels off, I'm just putting more wheels on to get us on a fast track. Jimmy is the general manager. I just created another position between Jimmy and Ted, and there are several teams doing things like that.

"Jimmy had all those years, now I want a crack at it," Irsay concluded. "That's why I made the decision to bring in Tobin."

Two days after the initial lunch, Robert Irsay made Tobin an offer he couldn't refuse. Not only would he be the primary voice in all football decisions, but he had the "C" word on his side as well. He was given "Control".

But before he would accept the offer, Tobin told the owner that he wanted Jim Irsay involved in future discussions.

"I told Bob I wouldn't go any farther unless Jimmy was at the next meeting and I had his blessing," Tobin said. "I didn't want to get between blood and blood. I may be country, but I'm not dumb."

After it was agreed that Tobin would be brought on board, Jim Irsay said the initial transition was difficult but eventually he began to appreciate his new role. In fact, a few years later, when Robert Irsay suffered a stroke and would spend an indefinite amount of time in an Indianapolis hospital, Jim Irsay began taking over the day-to-day operations of the team.

"It was difficult at first," Jim Irsay said. "It was a little bit like being a prizefighter and having your trainer throw in the towel. Any good fighter, guys like Frazier and Ali, or Hagler and Leonard, they never want to throw the towel in and that's kind of the way I felt, too. You just don't want to stop."

As he looks back at it now, however, Irsay believes it was the best move for all parties.

"It gave me a chance to step back and start learning the big picture," Irsay said. "It allowed me to assess what had happened over the first 10 years and realize just how young I was and how much I had ahead of me. I think overall it was really healthy and very good for me. I think bringing Bill Tobin on board was a blessing for everyone concerned."

Soon thereafter, a new era of Colts football was born. Though the elder Irsay had to rubber-stamp Tobin's recommendations, the new Colts front-office boss was given complete authority to turn things around as he saw fit.

"The commitment from the ownership here is absolutely amazing," Tobin said after only a few days on the job. "The Irsays are totally committed to winning. When I interviewed for this job, Mr. (Robert) Irsay at least 50 times wrote the symbol for winning on a piece of paper (a 'W'). He never said how much or told me I can't do this or I can't do that.

"He wants to win, and he's doing everything in his power to see that the Colts are successful," Tobin added. "And that's what our mission is now. We want to do everything possible to bring Mr. Irsay and the city of Indianapolis a winner.

"And we want to do it very quickly."

Tobin's basic philosophy for rebuilding the Colts was cut and dry — you win with defense first and then the running game.

"Teams that have won for any length of time — the Bears, the New York Giants, teams like that — have always had the good, solid defenses in all areas, whether you're talking about points allowed, yardage, whatever," Tobin said. "So improving the defense here is my No. 1 objective. The running game is second and the passing game is third."

But before he could worry too much about his new set of players, he had to get the staff in place.

Tobin realized right away that he had some major — and in many cases unpopular — decisions ahead. But his master plan did not take into account sentimentality. In his words, every decision that was made was done with the best interests of the Colts in mind.

"I'm well-prepared and I'm confident," Tobin said. "I've played the game, I've been in the huddle. I've coached, I've been in personnel the past 23 years. We will win as a team, and we'll lose as a team. There's no one person in the organization that's bigger than the cause.

"These decisions are not being made by Bill Tobin or Jim Irsay or Ted Marchibroda or any other single person," Tobin said. "When we make a decision, it is made by the Colts and it is done in the best interest of the Colts. To me, that's the only way to run an organization."

After the dust had settled and Tobin got knee-deep into his new position, he found out quickly that several immediate changes needed to be made in the coaching staff and front-office personnel. He also learned the Colts were close to $8 million over the $33.9 million salary cap and those cuts needed to be made by Feb. 18.

In his priority order, the coaching staff needed to be taken care of first. While Tobin did decide to retain the services of Ted Marchibroda, many members of the head coach's staff were not as fortunate. Fired was defensive coordinator Rick Venturi, who had been on the staff in some capacity since 1982 including a stint as interim head coach for the final 11 games of the 1991 season. Also let go were longtime secondary coach George Catavolos, defensive line coach Francis Peay and defensive assistant Jay Robertson. Not long after, wide receivers coach Dwain Painter was shown the door as was special teams coach Brad Seely.

"Those were difficult decisions because I have known most of those people for a long time," Tobin said the day after the coaches had been let go. "I thought changes were necessary and I'm happy with the way it's going, but I'm also sad because of the personalities and the people involved.

"But when you're faced with a situation like this, what do you do? You do what's best for the Colts."

But the bloodletting hadn't completely subsided. A few days later, Tobin went to the source of past draft and player decisions and fired personnel director Jack Bushofsky. Bushofsky had been in charge of Colts drafts for 11 seasons, selecting 122 players in that span. But recent drafts had produced more busts than keepers and someone had to go.

And then there were the players. Duane Bickett, the fifth player selected in the 1985 draft, was not retained after a nine-year career as the Colts were unwilling to pay him his steep $2.1 million asking price. At the same time, the Colts also released Reggie Langhorne and Jessie Hester, a pair of wide receivers who had combined for 149 receptions the season before. Two other veterans — defensive lineman Sam Clancy and guard Ron Solt — were told they would not be re-signed.

The big fish came on March 24 when Jeff George was dealt to Atlanta for first- and third-round picks in the 1994 draft and a conditional selection in '96. That pick became a first-round selection when the Falcons won nine games in '95.

George, not surprisingly, was not Tobin's idea of a team player. And it was obvious that the new boss did not want to pay the big bucks for a player he didn't respect.

Tobin sought permission from the Irsays to make the trade, for he knew the somewhat personal nature of their investment in the hometown hero from Warren Central High School.

"It took some talking but Bob told me it was my decision," Tobin recalled in a story in the *Boston Globe*. "I knew it was something I was going to have to do before I got there. (George) had just really hosed them (with his holdout after Irsay had spent millions in free agency to build him a solid offensive line). That was one of the most ruthless things I can remember. This certainly wasn't a team player."

After surveying the conditions in the Indianapolis Colts organization, Bill Tobin immediately saw that changes needed to be made in nearly every area — coaches, players and finances. (Photo by Don Larson)

In a column written by Mike Chappell of the *Indianapolis Star* later that week, Tobin explained how George's holdout from the summer before simply made him someone the organization couldn't completely count on.

"We had no assurance Jeff was going to show up this year," Tobin explained. "I said at (the first) press conference that day I wanted people who wanted to be in Indianapolis. I was speaking to everybody, not just one player. If (George) didn't want to be here, it's best for everybody we let him go and get on with our business with people who do want to be here.

"I have no hard feelings toward Jeff George at all," he continued. "I know his ability. It may be written on my epitaph, 'Here's the dummy that traded Jeff George'. Well, so be it. It goes with sitting in the chair I'm in."

♦ ♦ ♦

When Tobin came on board in January 1994, speculation throughout the NFL centered on a pair of names — one a player and one a coach — who would very likely follow him to Indianapolis.

The coach was Bill's younger brother, Vince, the defensive coordinator for the Chicago Bears from 1986-92 who was out of football for the 1993 season. The player was Jim Harbaugh, a free agent whom Tobin had drafted in his days with the Bears.

The decision to bring in Vince as the defensive coordinator came quickly. Two days after the Colts fired several defensive coaches including coordinator Rick Venturi, Vince Tobin was hired to turn around a defense that had ranked 28th out of 28 teams in the NFL in total defense, rushing defense and sacks in '93, and 27th in points allowed and takeaways.

Bill Tobin insisted that Ted Marchibroda hire his own defensive coordinator, but at the same time said he wanted to review any decision with his coach. Marchibroda claimed Vince Tobin was his No. 1 candidate all along and after his initial meeting believed Vince was the man with whom he wanted to work.

"His record spoke for itself," Marchibroda would say later. "He always had an excellent reputation around the league and after meeting with him there wasn't any doubt in my mind that he was the best person for the job."

In seven seasons as the Bears' defensive coordinator, Vince had headed a defense that finished in the top six in the league five times including three finishes in the top two. Not surprisingly, Bill Tobin rubber-stamped Marchibroda's recommendation but did his best to stay out of the spotlight on the decision.

"I wanted the best man available for the job, and I was never going to let a guy's name keep me from hiring him," Bill would say later, regarding his younger brother. "We hired the best defensive coordinator available, and Vince Tobin's record will stack up against any of them, anytime, anywhere."

As for Harbaugh, Tobin had believed the veteran was a victim of circumstance in Chicago and believed if given a second chance, he could still be an outstanding quarterback in the NFL.

"Just because one team trades a player or releases him doesn't mean his career is over," Tobin said. "It's happened time and time and time again where a guy is resurrected in another city and in better circumstances."

Every time someone would criticize an aspect of Harbaugh's game, Tobin would be there with a quick counter. Mention that Harbaugh didn't have the arm strength to go over the top and Tobin would point to five or six examples in Chicago where his quarterback had made the big throw when needed. Infer that he might not be the player to return a franchise to respectability and Tobin would point to his career record of 35-30 as a starter. Find another quality or two that were perceived weaknesses and Tobin would point to the total package, saying the quarterback possessed all the intangibles.

If nothing else, Tobin is a man of loyalty. Give Tobin a 100 percent effort and he'll never forget it. Give him 110 and he'll champion you forever. Indianapolis has sometimes been referred to — fair or unfair — as Chicago Bears South, because several players have left the Bears for the Colts since Tobin arrived on the scene. The label sticks in Tobin's craw. But the truth is they are all players that Tobin either drafted or believed in completely, to the point where he sincerely felt their abilities would add quality to the roster.

Harbaugh is one of those "Monsters of the Speedway," and he cannot thank Tobin enough for sticking by him during some difficult times.

"A couple of years ago nobody believed in me outside of me, and maybe Bill Tobin and my dad," Harbaugh told the *Chicago Tribune* late in the 1995 season. "I am glad (Tobin) had faith in me. Lindy Infante came in here and I got in a good situation. I had a line that was blocking and receivers who were getting open and catching the ball. That gave me an opportunity to get out and make plays."

Besides bringing in his younger brother and Harbaugh, Tobin also dipped into the free agent market his first spring on the job and picked up a couple of players who would make the defensive coordinator's and quarterback's jobs considerably easier.

On defense, the Colts brought in linebacker/defensive end Tony Bennett, one of the off-season's premier free agents who would add instant credibility to a less than awe-inspiring pass rush. Bennett had started 39 games in three years for the Packers and had 33 sacks to his credit.

Offensively, the Colts filled the void left by Reggie Langhorne by acquiring Floyd Turner, a solid wide receiver who had spent four seasons in New Orleans. He was coming back from a season-long injury that stemmed from a fractured femur, but he showed no signs of slowing down and Tobin believed he made the receiving corps that much deeper.

◆ ◆ ◆

In the high-tech world of the Internet and web sites, Bill Tobin prefers the stone age. The telephone is the most modern convenience in his office at the Colts' West 56th Street complex. A computer? Are you kidding? That's a leap of faith Tobin is not ready to explore.

"I want to make sure computers work for you and you don't work for them," Tobin said.

Tobin believes in a traditional approach of writing everything out by hand, and then being organized enough to sift through his intricate filing system for information. That system — which he brought with him — was said to have taken up an entire wall in his office in the southeast corner of Halas Hall.

"I use an analogy of going to an airport and standing in line, and then being told that the computer is down," Tobin said. "But see, my personnel department has never been down. We've always been up and running. We have no glitches.

"I'm not against computers, but I believe in doing things the old-fashioned way. Call it Smith-Barney or whatever, but it works for me."

In his own words, Tobin is a behind-the-scenes-guy. He's low-key, private in many ways and not one who is going to show his hand prematurely.

"I believe in letting my product do the speaking for me, rather than talk all the time about how I'm going to do things," Tobin said. "I'm from Missouri, the Show-Me State, and I'd rather show you how I'm going to do it rather than tell you how I'm going to do it."

It's those Missouri roots — he pronounces it "Muz-zure-uh" — that are at the center of Tobin's blue-collar work ethic. Reared on a farm near tiny Burlington Junction, the sixth of seven children, Tobin spent his early mornings doing farm chores, including milking the cows.

"Growing up, we had only one bill, really, and that was electricity," Tobin said. "We had our own water, and we burned fuel oil for heat. There was no insurance bill, no cable bill, no telephone bill, no garbage collection bill."

On the 200-acre farm, the Tobin family raised cattle, hogs, sheep and chickens. They also grew corn, soybeans and feed for the livestock, and they had a vegetable garden.

The farm work ethic has carried over to his adult life.

When his title was simply director of player personnel with the Bears, Tobin had the reputation of being a bush-beater, a man who would leave no stone unturned. He would annually visit close to 100 college campuses in search of the kind of talent that could keep his organization on top.

When the *Philadelphia Daily News* polled NFL general managers and personnel heads in 1991 to determine which team does the best job of assessing collegiate talent, the Bears — and Tobin — were head and shoulders above the rest.

"Mike Ditka should get down on his knees every morning and thank God for Bill Tobin," one unnamed general manager told the newspaper.

That opinion has long been shared by those in the know in the NFL. When it comes to the draft, Tobin has few equals. During his stint with the Bears, all 20 of the club's top draft picks were productive, with nine making it to the Pro Bowl. In all, 15 of his draft choices and three free agents earned a total of 51 Pro Bowl appearances in Tobin's 18 years in Chicago.

"Bill did a great job in rebuilding the Bears," said Chicago defensive back Donnell Woolford, a first-round pick of Tobin's in the 1988 draft. "He is a great judge of football talent and he deserves a lot of credit for the success of the Bears."

Added former Bears linebacker Mike Singletary: "When it comes to the Chicago Bears and the success the team has achieved, I think Bill Tobin is a big piece in that puzzle. Bill knows football. He is firm and unbiased in his approach, and he makes good decisions."

Tobin's long stint with the Bears ended in July 1993, after what was characterized as a difference in philosophy with club president Michael McCaskey and new coach Dave Wannstedt. Tobin was with the Bears in some capacity from 1975 to 1993 and was in charge of the personnel department beginning in 1984.

"I left Chicago because of a difference in philosophy and because I said I wanted to give them their reign with the new people they brought in," Tobin said. "My pelts are on the wall. Let's see what happens 18 years from now and see how many pelts are there then."

Bill Tobin quickly established himself by showing his mastery in the NFL Draft. Above, he celebrates the final regular-season victory over New England which clinched the Colts's appearance in the playoffs. (Photo by Don Larson)

◆   ◆   ◆

Tobin didn't waste any time in Indianapolis showing his mastery for the draft.

After Cincinnati selected Dan Wilkinson with the top pick in the 1994 draft, the selection of Marshall Faulk was pretty much a no-brainer. But then the Colts traded up to get the fifth pick overall and selected Trev Alberts. With what many believed to be the second-best quarterback in the draft still on the board — Fresno State's Trent Dilfer — and the Colts QB slots occupied by Jim Harbaugh and Don Majkowski, criticism of Tobin's decision to select Alberts was quick from the national media.

ESPN draft analyst Mel Kiper Jr., who has a history of Colt-bashing, took immediate exception to the pick and lashed out at Tobin on national television. "You can't go with Jim Harbaugh and pass up Trent Dilfer," Kiper said. "That's why the Colts are the laughingstock of the league.

"It was a typical Colts move," he added. "That's why they pick second every year."

But little did Kiper realize as he was saying those words, that a few minutes later Tobin was going to get his own national television soapbox for a rebuttal. When ESPN switched live to analyst Chris Mortensen at the Colts complex, the veteran sportswriter turned broadcaster had no idea the can of worms he was about to open.

Let 'er Rip

Mortensen questioned Tobin regarding his decision to select Alberts over Dilfer, and got a swift response. What was to come was great television, a replay that will likely be played for years on ESPN's draft day coverage.

"Who in the hell is Mel Kiper anyway?" Tobin steamed. "He didn't play college or pro football. I don't know about high school, and to my knowledge he's never put on a jock strap, so all of a sudden he's an expert.

"Mel Kiper has no more credentials to do what he's doing than my neighbor, and he's a postman."

ESPN found a chance to send it quickly back to draft headquarters, and Kiper looked like a guy who's dog had just been hit by a car. But Tobin wasn't finished with his verbal barrage. A few moments later, he walked into the Colts' draft headquarters where the local print and television media were assembled and went off again.

"I just found out a few days ago this guy (Kiper) lives in Baltimore and he used to hang around practices when Teddy (Marchibroda) was there ... he always wanted a job in the NFL but he didn't have any qualifications.

"So every chance that Mel Kiper gets to shoot at the Colts and Indianapolis, he's going to do it," he added. "Mel Kiper has never played the game, never been involved in the game ... never, ever been in a seat of decision-making, other than to second guess.

"We're going to be a good football team and these are going to be good players, and I don't care what Mel Kiper says."

The following Wednesday, Duke Tumatoe immortalized the moment in a special off-season version of *Lord Help Our Colts*.

> *I watched the draft on Sunday*
> *The Colts did very well*
> *I'd like to voice my opinion*
> *Mel Kiper go to hell!*
> *Lord help our Colts. Lord help our Colts.*
> *The Colts will do just fine*
> *Mel can kiss Bill Tobin's behind*
> *Lord help our Colts.*
> *Marshall Faulk will be a superstar*
> *Trev Alberts will be all-pro*
> *Tobin knows what he's doing*
> *That's what the record shows*
> *Lord help our Colts. Lord help our Colts*
> *Mel you might find this a shock*
> *But you're the laughingstock*
> *Lord help our Colts.*

As solid as those two picks turned out to be, Tobin would be the first to admit that anyone can select the right players picking that high in the draft.

"I wanted to enjoy that experience while I had the chance because I never expect to be picking that high again," Tobin said. "I'm content with picks later in the first round and the knowledge that our team is one of the best in the NFL."

But the 1994 draft won't be remembered exclusively for Faulk and Alberts. In the second and third rounds the Colts tabbed Eric Mahlum and Jason Mathews, a pair of offensive linemen that will be counted on big up front in the future. The fourth-round selection was Bradford Banta who immediately occupied the role of long snapper on punts, extra points and field goals. And the seventh-round selection — the 164th pick overall — was truly a gem. The Colts acquired running back Lamont Warren out of Colorado, a player long on potential. Among Warren's many contributions in his first two seasons was a big game against Kansas City in the '95 playoffs that helped lead the Colts to the AFC title game.

Tobin picked up right where he left off when it came time for the '95 draft. Prior to draft day he had acquired speedy wide receiver Flipper Anderson to begin bolstering the Colts' receiving corps, and then swung a draft day trade that brought quarterback Craig Erickson for a pair of draft picks. Though it's believed he wasn't sold on the idea of bringing in Erickson and making him the starting quarterback, Tobin did feel the Colts needed depth at the position, which led him to pull the trigger on the deal.

It also gave him more flexibility in the draft. With their top pick — No. 15 overall — the Colts selected defensive tackle Ellis Johnson, a promising young star of the future. The second-round selection, tight end Ken Dilger, may have been the steal of the draft at the No. 48 spot overall. And then the third-round selection was used to obtain Florida State fullback Zack Crockett, who would eventually pay big dividends in the opening-round playoff victory over San Diego.

In his first two years with the Colts, Tobin quickly proved why the draft is his home away from home. While he's a strong believer in the system, he's also quick to point out the pitfalls.

"Whenever you draft, your chances of being wrong are much greater than being right," Tobin said. "Every time you take a player, you leave 600 or so others, and chances are that some of them will turn out better than the guy you took. No matter how you slice it, the numbers are against you."

Tobin's early rebuilding plan attacked the organization from all angles.

There was the addition of Vince Tobin and a defensive staff that included line coach Greg Blache, linebackers coach Jim Johnson and secondary assistant Pat Thomas. Offensively, Jimmy Robinson took over the receivers, and Hank Kuhlmann coached both the tight ends and special teams.

In the front office, Tobin hired Clyde Powers as the director of pro player personnel and George Boone as the director of college player personnel.

"The key is surrounding yourself with good people," Tobin said on more than one occasion. "That's the key for any successful organization. I've always said that if you treat your employees well, I believe they'll do more for you than you can ever do for them."

After just two years on the job, the Colts had become the team that Tobin built. In '95 alone, the roster had 18 players who weren't there the year before. After two seasons, there were only 20 players still on the roster that predated Tobin's arrival.

But point to Tobin's single biggest acquisition since taking over in January 1994 and one name would consistently rise to the top — former Green Bay head coach Lindy Infante.

All that was accomplished by Harbaugh, Faulk and the rest of the offensive unit in 1995 was a direct result of Infante's offense. And in '96 his role was to increase even more as he took over the head coaching duties handed down when Ted Marchibroda was released.

After the Colts decided to part ways with offensive coordinator Nic Nicolau following the 1994 season, Tobin knew exactly where he wanted to go first in an effort to bring in a top-notch offensive coordinator.

When Tobin called in January, Infante was at the end of a three-year hiatus from football. In fact, when Tobin phoned him, Infante had just informed his wife he was ready to listen to football offers again. Since being let go by the Packers in 1991, Infante had turned down several NFL coaching offers, including one to become the offensive coordinator in Kansas City under head coach Marty Schottenheimer. The timing was just never quite right.

Until the Colts called.

"In this business, timing is everything," Tobin said. "I knew his situation, had followed his career, and I'd heard he was ready to get back into football.

"Picking up Lindy Infante was probably the biggest and most important acquisition we made in the off-season."

In many ways, Infante was the final piece in the Colts' preliminary rebuilding puzzle. Marchibroda had gotten the ball rolling and Bill Tobin had made the major cuts, the tough decisions and the necessary acquisitions. The final two pieces had taken place on the field in the form of Vince Tobin turning up the decibel level on defense and Lindy Infante doing the same on offense.

With those two coordinators in place, Bill Tobin and the organization felt it was only a matter of time before good things began happening with the Indianapolis Colts.

5

Rebuilding the Colts

Step 3: Vince Tobin

As the defensive coordinator in both Chicago and Indianapolis, Vince Tobin sat back and watched as his units became dominating forces in the National Football League within his first two years on the job.

But that's where the similarities end.

With the Bears, Tobin's primary focus was simply not to disrupt a defense that was already in place. In 1986, Tobin was named Chicago's defensive coordinator, inheriting Buddy Ryan's defensive unit that helped lift the Bears to a 46-10 victory over New England the year before in Super Bowl XX.

The Bears defense had been No. 1 in the NFL in 1985, and it was Tobin's job to maintain that level of excellence.

"Vince coached possibly the greatest defense to ever play the game in '86," said Jim Irsay. "It's a combination of a lot of things when you have that much success, but one of them is outstanding coaching."

Filling Ryan's shoes was a tremendous challenge, but one for which Tobin was eager and anxious to assume. And not only did he dot the I's and cross the T's from the year before, but Tobin's defense added an exclamation point in 1986. Once again the Bears were the top-ranked defensive team in the NFL, but they did Ryan's group one better by setting an NFL record for fewest points allowed in a 16-game season at 187.

"They had just come off the Super Bowl and had played very good defense," Tobin remembered during his first press conference as the Colts' new defensive coordinator. "The challenge there was to continue to play good defense, and we played better in almost every phase the following year."

But Tobin didn't rest on his laurels. The next two seasons the Bears continued their dominance, ranking No. 2 in the NFL both years in total defense. After an injury-plagued '89 season dropped them to No. 25 overall, Tobin and the Bears bounced back to rank No. 6 and No. 4 overall the next two seasons.

When he arrived on the scene in Indianapolis in January 1994 within a week of his older brother's appointment as the club's vice president and director of football operations, Tobin found a slightly different scenario.

The Colts' defense was in a league of its own statistically speaking, but it was closer to the CFL than the NFL. The year before, the Colts had ranked last in the league in total defense (352.4 yards per game), rushing defense (157.6 yards) and sacks (21 in 16 games). They were next to last — No. 27 overall — in points allowed (378) and takeaways (21 — 10 interceptions and 11 fumble recoveries). Since 1990, the Colts had never finished above No. 20 in total defense.

After so many seasons looking at the rest of the NFL from the top of the heap, Tobin found himself looking straight up from the depths of a well-dug hole.

"It was as big a challenge as I could have ever imagined," Tobin said looking back on his first days on the job. "Most places you go there are going to be challenges and the Colts' situation was no different. Rarely do people make a change when things are on top.

"This was a team that had its share of injuries and bad things happened to it, but beyond that, the defense just hadn't played that well," he added. "When we first came in we had to decide who to keep and who to replace, and the final tally was definitely weighted toward getting rid of more players than the ones we would keep.

"We knew we had a lot of work ahead of us."

One thing Tobin knew would be in his favor, however, was public opinion. In Chicago, he took over a defense that was expected to be on top for many years to come. In Indianapolis, it was a win-win situation.

"Everything we did was going to be an improvement and we knew that coming in," Tobin said. "In Chicago, there was a different standard in place. It was almost as if winning wasn't enough. But with the Colts they just wanted a defense here that would put them in position to win every week. It was a tall order, but that was what made the challenge that much more exciting to pursue."

From a philosophy standpoint, Tobin wanted a sound defense that wouldn't get the Colts beat as well as one that was attack-oriented and made things happen.

Rebuilding the Colts: Vince Tobin

After many years of success in Chicago, Vince Tobin took over a defense in Indianapolis that could go nowhere but up. (Photo by Don Larson)

"I believe you have to be very aggressive," Tobin said at his first press conference. "You have to set the tone, you can't let the offense dictate to you. You've got to be able to play man-to-man, you've got to be able to blitz, you've got to be able to play zone, and most importantly you've got to be able to do all of them equally.

"If you can do those things you can be respectable again."

If anyone was going to return the Colts' defense to respectability, Vince Tobin was the man for the job.

◆   ◆   ◆

There had been discussion about the time that Vince Tobin took the job as to whether the Colts should revert to a 3-4 defense, or stick with Rick Venturi's experiment of a 4-3 from the 1993 season.

Statistically speaking, the experiment had appeared to be a bust. In their first season with a defense consisting of four defensive linemen and three linebackers, the

Colts had gone from 39 sacks in '92 to 21 in '93, 35 takeaways to 21, and had given up 76 more points than the year before.

Tobin was familiar with both the 4-3 and the 3-4, having used the former in Chicago and the latter while serving as the defensive coordinator for the Philadelphia/Baltimore Stars of the United States Football League from 1983 to 1985.

But Tobin said he never really had any intention of going back to the 3-4.

"When I came here it was pretty much understood that we were going to stick with the 4-3 and I was all in favor of that," Tobin said. "That was the way the league was going and it was really the best way to put the most consistent pressure on the quarterback. I didn't think it was a question of whether we had the talent or not, so we proceeded with the thinking of becoming a better 4-3 team."

It also helped that when Tobin was hired in Indianapolis he was given a pencil that included an eraser.

And erase he did.

Of the 11 starters on defense from '93, five were gone in '94 and one other — Jon Hand — was relegated to backup duty. Among the players who were not retained were linemen Skip McClendon and Sam Clancy, linebacker Duane Bickett, and defensive backs Chris Goode and John Baylor.

"The first thing we did when we came in was to take a long look at personnel," Tobin said. "When we got here this team was close to $8 million over the salary cap and we knew there was going to be some trimming on the defensive side of the ball as well as on offense. So as a coaching staff, we knew we had to sit down and take an intensified look at this team."

Tobin, along with new assistants Greg Blache on the line, Jim Johnson with the linebackers and Pat Thomas in the secondary, decided to tackle the final eight games of the '93 season on film and go through play by play and grade every player. It was a long process but it made the decision process to let people go a lot easier.

It also gave the staff a good idea of how they could turn things around.

One thing that stood out for Tobin was the linebacker position, most specifically a belief that Quentin Coryatt and Jeff Herrod were playing out of position. Coryatt had played middle linebacker in Venturi's 4-3 and left inside linebacker the season before as a rookie. Herrod, the other inside linebacker in '92, had been flipped to outside linebacker in the 4-3 scheme.

Tobin believed Herrod needed to be inside, while Coryatt would be more likely to live up to his potential at an outside linebacker position.

"It really just had to do with body types," Tobin said. "I thought Herrod reminded me an awful lot of Mike Singletary in my days with the Bears. I just thought he had the ability and the instincts to be one of the best in the NFL as a middle linebacker, but he seemed out of place on the outside.

"The opposite was true of Coryatt," he added. "Here was a guy who was built to play the outside. He could rush the passer as well as drop into coverage and he seemed to have the athletic ability to make the transition a smooth one. The difficult thing was that he had been in two different defense schemes his first two seasons and now he was being asked to try a third.

"It took some time but he eventually transformed himself into a legitimate NFL outside linebacker."

Another thing that Tobin and his staff picked up on the tapes of the end of the '93 season had to do with the play of two seldom used players in Venturi's defense — defensive tackle Tony McCoy and linebacker Stephen Grant. In '93, the pair had combined for two tackles. Grant was primarily a special teams player and McCoy had gotten lost in Venturi's doghouse.

"In watching the films closely we saw a couple of guys that really intrigued us," Tobin recalls. "The one thing that stood out about Tony was that the films showed he had the ability to whip a guy at the line of scrimmage. His problem was that sometimes he tended to play out of control and I think the previous coaching staff believed that because of that he was undisciplined.

"What we saw with Tony was a player who had the ability to beat a guy one-on-one on every play," Tobin added. "He was never content to stay down, but rather was always looking to get up and go after somebody. When you have a player with that kind of intensity and ability, you have to find a way to get him on the field. When you have those things working in your favor, suddenly it's the coaches' responsibility to make sure he fits into your defensive scheme."

With Grant, it was a little different story.

"Stephen wasn't flashy like Tony, but instead we were just really impressed with his consistency," Tobin said. "We saw some things we liked the little that he was in there the year before but it wasn't really until training camp that we realized how good of a player we had. He's just one of those guys who over the course of a game and a season is just very consistent. He's not flashy but he gets the job done year in and year out."

And then there was Ray Buchanan. In '93, he played sparingly, coming on to start the last five games at free safety. But when Tobin and his staff saw him play on film they felt he needed to be at cornerback. The idea was to move him to that position in training camp in '94, but an unforseeable problem prevented that from taking place at first.

"We really wanted to move Ray right off the bat but when Jason Belser held out and eventually missed the entire training camp it really handcuffed us as to what we could do," Tobin said. "By the time he got back it was around the fourth game of the season and by then we just needed to let Ray stay where he was at free safety. What really ended up helping us was the progress shown by David Tate at strong safety. That allowed us to move Jason to free and move Buchanan to a corner."

Buchanan stepped up to become one of the most exciting cornerbacks in the NFL. Besides leading defensive backs on his team with 137 tackles, he had eight interceptions, including seven in as many games after a switch to left corner in the fourth quarter of the Miami game in Week 9. Adding to his excitement was the fact that three of the interceptions were returned for touchdowns.

"I think Ray exceeded all of our expectations," Tobin said. "We knew he could be good but I don't think anyone really expected what he was able to do. It was players like Ray that really gave us hope coming back in 1995."

Two other players — Tate and rookie defensive end Bernard Whittington — made their presence known in '94 in their first seasons with the Colts. Tate had 80 tackles and three interceptions from his strong safety position, while Whittington had 54 tackles and 10 quarterback pressures from his left defensive end spot.

"We were getting productivity from several areas and that's important when you're trying to build a defense," Tobin said. "If you have one or two really talented players it helps, but having a whole bunch of guys that can do the job is what makes the difference."

The Colts had a couple of solid players up front. Tony Siragusa, a six-year veteran who originally signed with the Colts as a free agent out of the University of Pittsburgh in 1990, had the best season of his career. He led all defensive linemen in tackles with 108, including 64 solo. He was third on the club with five sacks and 17 quarterback hits, and tied for third with nine pressures. He knocked down three passes, led the team with three forced fumbles and had one fumble recovery.

"Tony was an animal," Tobin said. "He was everywhere. He did a great job against the run, but was also able to get up field and rush the passer. He has deceptive speed for a man his size and some teams that took him for granted paid the price."

Tobin's jewel in the crown in '94, however, was brought in via the free agency route. Needing a pass rusher in the worst way, the Colts spent the big bucks to sign one of the best in the free agent pool, former Green Bay standout Tony Bennett.

"You think of Tony Bennett and you think of what an outstanding football player he is and all of the things he does for you," Tobin said. "But I think what impressed me most were the intangibles. He has a tremendous work ethic and his leadership was something this team was lacking. He was a guy that embodied our defensive philosophy. From the beginning, he was never content with status quo, and those are the kinds of players that can turn a ballclub into a champion."

Overall, the defense took a step forward. They recorded eight more sacks, eight more interceptions and seven more takeaways than in 1993. Total defense was down 20 yards per game, rushing defense was down more than 54 yards from 157.6 to 102.9, and points allowed dropped 58 points from the year before.

But Tobin wasn't satisfied.

"I felt like we had improved but that we still weren't where we wanted to be," he said. "There's only one way to approach a rebuilding process like this, and that's to strive to be the best. We had made an improvement, but I was far from satisfied."

The one area that was most pleasing was the defense's ability to make big plays. In a four-year span from 1990 to 1993, the Colts scored two defensive touchdowns — one on a fumble recovery in the end zone by Jeff Herrod in '93 and the other, Steve Emtman's memorable 90-yard interception return for a TD against Miami in Joe Robbie Stadium in 1992.

On the other hand, the Tobin-led defense proved to be opportunistic. Bennett started things off early with a 75-yard fumble return for a touchdown in the opener against Houston. Two weeks later, Coryatt did him 3 yards better with a 78-yard fumble return for a touchdown at Pittsburgh. And then there was Buchanan picking off three aerials for scores — against quarterbacks Dan Marino, Rick Mirer and Drew Bledsoe. The pick against the Patriots was returned 90 yards.

"Good defenses make the plays, but mediocre ones don't," Tobin said. "It's really that simple. I thought our pressure defense allowed us to make plays but still we didn't make enough. When the season is over and you're not in the playoffs, you have to feel like you could have done more."

The final three home games of the '94 season, however, may have set the defensive tone for 1995. Against division rivals New England, Miami and Buffalo, the Colts went a 12-quarter stretch without allowing a touchdown.

"That was important because it built momentum heading into the off-season," Tobin said. "It gave us a taste of how good we could be. It gave us a goal to shoot for and from that standpoint it couldn't have come at a better time."

◆　　　　◆　　　　◆

The 1995 off-season brought few changes, but the ones that did come about were for the better. Ellis Johnson, a defensive tackle out of Florida, was the Colts' first-round selection and immediately stepped in and made his presence felt. A former college teammate of Tony McCoy, Johnson played with the same fire and intensity.

Another change was having Trev Alberts back in the lineup after the second-year player from Nebraska missed the majority of his rookie campaign with a dislocated right elbow.

The final change was the release of defensive tackle Steve Emtman, a gutsy player who in the Colts' eyes finally lost his ongoing battle against knee and neck injuries. Having only played four games in '94, Emtman wasn't really being counted on in '95 so the staff only had to make subtle changes in his absence.

The biggest advantage for the 1995 Colts on defense was the luxury of all having played together for one season in Tobin's system. Coryatt was at the same position for the second year in a row, an unparalleled accomplishment in his NFL career, Buchanan was starting the season at left corner, and Tobin's problems were more of finding a way to get his best people on the field.

"I thought our players really worked hard in the off-season and they just seemed to have a different kind of fire," he said. "They realized how close they had come the year before and didn't want to feel that way again. They really were beginning to believe in themselves, and I think that showed in the way they were preparing for the season."

One dilemma for Tobin was finding a place for second-year standout Trev Alberts. Tobin had a solid linebacking trio in Grant, Herrod and Coryatt, but had a weakness at left defensive end. He decided to experiment by moving Bennett from right to left defensive end, and Alberts to the right defensive end slot. With Alberts at 245 and Bennett at 242, the Colts likely had two of the smallest ends in the league and that was a concern.

But the reason Tobin would eventually nix the experiment had simply to do with Alberts' inability to get comfortable at the end position.

"I thought Tony did fine in his switch to the left side but the problem was with Trev," Tobin said. "Trev had played linebacker all his life, and he was struggling having to play down at the end position every play. He was OK in pass rushing situations but when he had to be down the entire game it was really wearing on him and his confidence. I really believed I needed to move him back there and just find a way to work him into the defense when I could."

The difference in playing together for a second season in the same system was clearly evident with the Colts. They ranked No. 5 overall in the NFL in total defense allowing 314.2 yards per game and No. 3 in the league against the run at 91.1. In points allowed, they were No. 2 in the NFL with 316 and were No. 6 in first downs allowed at 304.

"I think what was most noticeably different in '95 came from an attitude standpoint," Tobin said. "This team went into games believing they could win. That hadn't happened in the past. Before, these guys would get into the fourth quarter and expect something to go bad. That's the way it had always happened before. But this year they went into the fourth expecting something good to happen.

"That's the difference between a playoff team and one that just misses the playoffs by this much or that much," he said. "That was one of the things I was most looking forward to as far as coaching these guys again in 1996. I knew the attitude was there and when it is you wind up winning a lot of games that maybe you have no business winning. It's not always the team with the best talent that wins in the NFL. Sometimes it's the team that believes in itself and goes out on the field expecting to win.

"That's what is going to be exciting about the Colts defense of the future."

The future does indeed look bright for the Colts defense, though Vince Tobin will have to follow the group from 1,500 miles away. In early February 1996, Tobin opted to take the vacant head coaching position of the Arizona Cardinals, ending his two-season stint in Indianapolis.

"It was tough to leave, especially after all that we accomplished but sometimes when other opportunities arise you have to give them a serious look," Tobin said. "The Arizona situation was too intriguing to let slip by. I'm sad that I won't be a part of what the Colts do in 1996 but I'll be keeping an eye on them from afar."

From up close, too. The Colts and Cardinals were to open the 1996 season against each other in the RCA Dome.

As he took the Arizona job, Tobin said it was almost eerie how many similarities could be drawn between the status of the Cardinals and the way the Colts looked when he arrived in Indianapolis in 1994.

"They both were coming off 4-12 seasons, they both were established franchises that had moved but just hadn't been able to get over the top in their new locale, and the bottom line is that both teams were not very good," Tobin said. "I think Arizona ranked near the bottom in both offense and defense last year, and the Colts were the same in 1994.

"In many ways, that's good because having had my experience in Indianapolis I know we can turn this thing around," he said. "It's just a matter of getting some breaks, making a few personnel changes and then playing good, sound football."

Though he had some memorable years in Chicago when his defense there was on top of the NFL, Tobin said the Colts' 1995 playoff run will always rank near the top of his list in personal accomplishments.

"It was just unbelievable when I look back at all that happened," Tobin said. "I think the excitement of the playoffs and just seeing the town come alive like they did and get behind the team are things I will never forget. Seeing the fans lined up to send us off and then packing the airport when we returned. Those are the things that will never be erased from memory."

He also said he doubts if the excitement will ever be quite the same in Indianapolis again — even if the Colts were to win the Super Bowl.

"Even if they won it all, I'm not sure if the excitement could be any bigger than it was in '95," Tobin said. "I just don't think anything ever again will match up to the intensity of the fans and the love they felt for that football team. There's something about the first year a city experiences something like that which makes it all the more special.

"Every year after this one, the fans will just begin to expect it more and with that you won't see the fanaticism you saw in '95," he said. "For the Colts' sake and the fans of Indianapolis I hope I'm wrong. Because I believe in my heart that there are plenty of good things on the horizon for the Indianapolis Colts."

6

Rebuilding the Colts

Step 4: Lindy Infante

The first time wide receiver Aaron Bailey perused Lindy Infante's offensive playbook, he just stared at the pages as if they were written in Chinese.

After turning page after page and finding the same result, he closed the book, set it on the floor next to him, and shook his head.

"It was incredible," Bailey said. "When I first looked at it I thought maybe I wasn't cut out for this. It took me a while to feel comfortable but once you do, you really feel like you have an advantage."

For wide receiver Sean Dawkins it was much of the same.

"It looked complex and complicated," Dawkins said. "A lot of times the receiver has to make his reads when he's 10 yards down the field. There's a lot of room for error but when you're on the same page the results will be there, too."

Immediate results were exactly what Bill Tobin had in mind when he hired Lindy Infante as the Colts' offensive coordinator in mid-January of 1995. Even though Infante had been out of coaching for three seasons since relinquishing his head coaching duties at Green Bay, Tobin was confident that Infante's brilliant offensive mind could be just what the Colts needed to turn their fortunes around.

As Infante is quick to point out, however, it's all in the system.

Infante first installed his offense as the offensive coordinator with the Cincinnati Bengals in 1980. After working the bugs out of the system in '80, the Bengals went 12-4 in '81 and eventually made it to the Super Bowl before dropping a 26-20 decision to San Francisco. That season, Cincinnati ranked third in the NFL in offense.

The next season Infante was the head coach in Jacksonville in the United States Football League and it was there that the offense really began to take shape.

"Once I was in Jacksonville as the head coach, then I had total control," Infante said. "I didn't have to worry about answering to somebody all the time so I was really able to experiment with it down there. We came up with some things that worked and some things that didn't. And it's been evolving ever since. It's never stayed static.

"Every year you have to almost rewrite the entire playbook," he said. "We added a lot of things (in 1996) that weren't in the playbook when we started here last July. The game is changing all the time. You're always adapting, adding, deleting and fine-tuning so that you can stay on top with it."

From Jacksonville, Infante moved to Cleveland as offensive coordinator in 1986 and '87, before becoming head coach at Green Bay from 1988-91.

"I went to Cleveland with Marty Schottenheimer in 1986 and we put the system in and went 12-4. Bernie Kosar was having great success with it, and actually did the two years I was there," Infante said. "In Green Bay we struggled the first year but a lot of it had to do with the personnel we had. The second year we went 10-6 and (quarterback Don) Majkowski got voted to the Pro Bowl. It all happened within two years there."

With the Colts, Infante saw immediate results in 1995. The team went 9-7 and made it to the AFC title game against Pittsburgh.

"I thought we got it going here to a degree," he said. "But I'd like to think that we've only scratched the surface of what we could do. You hope it keeps getting better because once you've put all those learning adjustments behind you and all the growing pains, there should be a lot of good things to come."

In its most basic form, Infante's offensive system deals with spreading the ball around and getting everyone involved. He believes in diversity and keeping teams off balance. He believes in a strong blend between the running and passing games, something he believes he has with a Marshall Faulk/Jim Harbaugh combo in Indianapolis.

"I told the guys coming in that we're not going to force fit the ball to one guy," Infante said. "You just can't dictate that in the passing game. If you do that, the defense could double cover one guy or have a certain coverage that takes away one-half of the field. If you do that, you limit yourself way too much."

A good example of the unpredictability of Infante's system came the day before the playoff game with Kansas City following the '95 season when the offensive coordinator told a local television station what he believed was going to be the big key for the Colts the next day.

"I told them that I thought for us to be successful our running backs and our tight ends were going to have to catch eight or nine balls between them, and that's where I thought we'd probably end up going with the football most of the day," he said. "I didn't mention that in the meetings though, because I didn't want to put any added pressure on anyone. I would rather we just went out and took what they gave us.

"As it turned out, the two positions caught a total of two or three balls — and we won," he said. "But that's just the way the game evolved."

Infante says individual statistics are not important to him. At the same time, if the offense has been successful, Infante believes the difference between the No. 1 receiver and the No. 4 receiver shouldn't be more than 25 catches for the season.

"I don't sit around worrying about whether I'm keeping a receiver happy because he's catching five balls a game or not," Infante said. "If I start doing that I'm not being fair to the football team. Now I may call a play where I'm thinking the ball is going to a certain guy because of something we've seen, but if that guy isn't open we've got other places to go with the ball.

"In this system I've had guys catch 10 or 11 balls in a game, and the next week not catch any," he said. "That's just something that happens from time to time."

Infante's biggest challenge upon accepting the job with the Colts was getting everyone on the same page. Job One was to teach the system to his offensive staff.

"Unfortunately, in football there's no such thing as a dictionary," Infante said. "The terminologies that we use aren't the same as they are in Chicago, Minnesota or Green Bay. So the first thing you have to do is learn how to communicate with one another as a coaching staff. You can't teach something that you don't understand yourself."

For the first month Infante's job was to acquaint his coaching staff with the system. For sometimes more than eight hours a day the staff of wide receivers coach Jimmy Robinson, line coach Ron Blackledge, running backs assistant Gene Huey and offensive assistant Fred Bruney would pour over the material.

When the coaches had it down, the next step was to teach it to the players. Though he admits that every time he has implemented the system he hears the complaints about its complexity, he personally doesn't think it's that difficult.

"I think what happens on the front end when you get in on the ground floor is it seems complicated because you haven't heard it or done it before," Infante said. "So there's a learning process that takes place. Along with learning a new system, there's unlearning the old system. And unlearning is tougher than learning because you have to get something out of your head and replace it with something else.

"I think it's like learning a new language," he added. "If you grew up in the English language and then were asked to learn Spanish it would seem very complicated. But once you get the system of it then it becomes easy to retain, easy to change, easy to manipulate and easy to move forward with. I think the players that perceived it as a little complicated when they first got started with it will find it is a systematic approach to what we're trying to accomplish.

"Once you learn the system then it becomes very easy, and very easy to change from week to week."

Infante says once you've got the system, it stays with you a long time. He points to a conversation he had with former Cleveland Brown Ozzie Newsome at the NFL Scouting Combine in the spring of 1996.

"I hadn't been around Ozzie since 1987, so it had been a solid nine years," Infante said. "He came up to me and asked, 'Hey coach are you still running duh-da-duh-da-duh-da-duh' and he just rattled off a couple of plays. And we were in one form or another. And he made a comment to the fact that once you learn the system then the pieces fall into place pretty easily.

"This is not a memory offense, it's a system," he said. "And if you learn the system and the way it works, then it's like mathematics or language or anything else. It becomes pretty easy."

Though the players began getting the system in some form during workouts after Infante was hired, the first major push came at the three-day mini-camp in May. That was followed by a rookie camp the following week and another voluntary camp in early June. When training camp opened in July, Infante was eager to spend even longer sessions with his troops in preparation for the 1995 season.

Quarterback Craig Erickson, who came into training camp as the club's starter, struggled in the early going getting the offense down. In fact, as late as mid-August Erickson was still not 100 percent comfortable. But Infante said it was all part of the learning process.

"I find myself thinking a little bit too much once in a while but overall I've been pretty happy with the way things have gone," Erickson said. "When we get out there and things are going smooth you definitely know it. When things are clicking, we're running the ball and we're spreading it around, that's when the offense is working the way it's designed to run."

In a nutshell, that is the essence of Lindy Infante's offense.

Expect the unexpected, spread the ball around, use multiple formations, but most of all don't be predictable.

Jim Harbaugh calls the system "quarterback friendly."

"As a quarterback, the system just gives you every opportunity to be successful," Harbaugh said. "Lindy puts you in position to make big plays. It is not designed for anyone in particular. Anyone can be the feature player at any time."

Infante admits the system does give the quarterback a lot of options.

"We don't go out there and predetermine that one guy is going to get the ball or that we're going to concentrate on one side of the field," Infante said. "We generally have patterns going to both sides of the field. I think Jimmy took advantage of that because if the protection held up good enough he could go from one side to the other and find somebody. If the protection broke down, he went to scrambling to one side or the other and there was generally something working over there, too, someone he could throw the ball to.

"Because there's a lot of people running patterns and because we're playing the whole field pretty much every down, there's a lot of places for a guy to go with the ball."

But this isn't to infer that Infante had forgotten about his bread and butter — No. 28 Marshall Faulk.

"Certainly I'm not going to be ignorant enough to spread the ball around so much that Marshall doesn't have his hands on the ball a great deal of the time," Infante said during training camp. "He's certainly got to be one of the focal points of what we can do, but we need production from other people, too.

"The problem that you have offensively is you only have one ball," Infante said. "If you have 70 plays and you only have one ball on each play you can't have everybody touch the ball on every play. If you have five eligible ball handlers on each play, not counting the quarterback, and your No. 1 guy comes out of the game handling the ball 25 times you've done pretty well."

To those who thought Faulk needed to touch the ball 40 times a game, Infante said he believed that to be excessive.

"I don't think Marshall's carries need to go up but I do think we need to find ways to get him into the open field more," Infante said. "If he stays healthy and we get a couple of holes in the defense, I think Marshall can run wild. But I don't think he needs to have it 50 times a game. I think that's too much. Plus I think you risk shortening a player's career when he handles it that much. You can't take a running back and give him the ball 40 times a game because he gets beat up and then he's no use to you in the playoffs when you need him the most.

"Marshall is a huge asset to our football team and I have no doubt that we'll find a way to use him to his fullest abilities."

As the quarterbacks, receivers and running backs got more comfortable with the system in 1995, the product on the field continued to get better. The fact that the team peaked when it did in the playoffs likely had a lot to do with the system finally beginning to set in with all 11 offensive starters on the field.

"I think that's pretty natural with anybody's offense or defense," Infante said. "I think you can go back and trace our defense under Vince Tobin and see how well they played at the end of the year his first season here. I know his defense was one of the big reasons why I wanted to come here. And that was one of the things I saw on film when I came up here to interview. But personally, I think that's one of the things you find when somebody goes in and puts in a system."

Infante paralleled the Colts' situation on offense to what the expansion teams went through in 1995. What he didn't say, however, was that the Colts were likely playing with a little bit better personnel.

"In '95 I would put us in the same situation as the expansion teams, offensively anyway," Infante said. "We put in a whole new system with a new terminology and that's what the expansion teams went through, too. There, you've got a whole bunch of people going in with a new coaching staff and new philosophies on both sides of the ball that are different than they might have been used to."

Infante said the reason the Colts played better at the end was the offense was becoming more natural to them.

"It's a repetition business and the less you can think and the more you can react the better you're going to be when you hit the field," he said. "I always say if you're out there thinking you're not going to get a whole lot done. You've got to be able to react and that means it's in there to the point where you can respond quickly. I think as the season wore on, we got better and better and more comfortable with the system. When we reached that point, it was easy for us to make changes during the game and in our game planning."

◆　　　　　◆　　　　　◆

As the story goes, Bill Tobin had perfect timing when it came to talking to Lindy Infante about taking over the Colts offensive coordinator position in January of 1995.

Three years removed from being the head coach of the Green Bay Packers, Infante had just told his wife a week before that he was ready to entertain coaching offers again.

He had tinkered around enough with the 4,000-square foot home he had built with his own hands on the beach in St. Augustine, Fla. He had played as much golf as he wanted, had enjoyed an occasional scuba diving or sailing excursion, and spent a considerable amount of time attending to one of his antique cars in the six-car garage behind his property.

"I was ready," Infante said. "I had passed on an opportunity to become the offensive coordinator at Kansas City under Marty Schottenheimer the year before because I still didn't feel like the time was right. But just after the New Year in 1995 I was pretty sure I was ready to get back into coaching football again.

"I just felt like I still had something to offer someone," he said. "I was hoping to find a situation where we could do some good things and then maybe three or four years down the road I could look back and really be proud of the way things had turned out."

When Bill Tobin called, Infante was ready to listen. He immediately boarded a flight to Indianapolis where he spent two days looking over film, before returning to Florida.

"Looking at film, the things I saw were a good stable of running backs and what was a pretty solid offensive line at the time," Infante said. "I think there were a lot of question marks about who the quarterback was going to be. There were a lot of question marks about who the wide receivers were going to be and if anybody was going to step forward out there. And there were some question marks at tight end. But if I had to pick two spots that I looked at from a coordinator's standpoint that encouraged me it was guys like Roosevelt Potts and Marshall Faulk, and the offensive line.

"I figured if you had those components in place, you could definitely build around that nucleus."

After two days he headed back to Florida to think things over, and Ted Marchibroda and his staff headed south to Mobile, Ala., for the Senior Bowl. During that week, he and Marchibroda talked on the phone two or three times. It was during one of those conversations that Infante found out exactly what responsibilities were going to come with the offensive coordinator title. Much like Bill Tobin had received a year earlier, Lindy Infante was going to be given control.

Lindy Infante was given total control of the offense, and that was a big reason he accepted the position. "I really couldn't have asked for anything more," he said. (Photo by Don Larson)

"I didn't make any demands but rather I just wanted to hear what they had in mind," Infante said. "When I asked Ted who was going to call the plays, there was no hesitation. He told me they wanted me to come in, bring in the new offense, install the whole thing and go with it. Ted said, 'You do it. I'm going to go be the head coach. You call the plays. You put in the offense.'

"I really couldn't have asked for anything more," Infante added. "Ted was kind enough to step back and delegate and was just super about everything. His approach really gave us the opportunity as a coaching staff to go do the job that needed to be done."

The season before, Marchibroda had called all the plays in the offense. Even though Infante was pulling the trigger in 1995, he said he never felt like Ted was looking over his shoulder.

"I never felt that way because there was a good understanding from the beginning about the job description," Infante said. "It wasn't like I came here under false pretenses. It was all up front and very honest. Ted's a super guy and he was really good to me. He was supportive and never once did he come in and mandate something. He gave it to us like he did the defense and told us to go make things work. Still, he was supportive and if he saw something that he thought would help us in any way, shape or form, he would give it to us and we'd try to incorporate it. It was a very good working situation between head coach and coordinator."

Though the offense may have needed a fire lit under it, Infante said he doesn't believe "rebuilding" was the correct way to describe it.

"In my opinion I wasn't rebuilding anything because I don't think anything that was done here in the past was anything that needed to be rebuilt," Infante said. "I think that would be a poor choice of words here. It was more like taking a new approach to things and changing some of the things in the passing game. But this wasn't a situation where rebuilding was necessary. I think that becomes a reflection on what was done prior to me getting here. What I'm doing is no different or better or worse than anything anybody else did. I was just taking a new approach."

Though he was happy with the nucleus he inherited, the first major task after beginning to implement the system was making certain he eventually would have the personnel to run it effectively.

"I think we did a good job of picking up (Ken) Dilger in the draft, and unfortunately Flipper (Anderson) got hurt but we did try to go out and upgrade the wide receivers group," Infante said. "And then part of the game plan in the off-season was to go get a quarterback and whether it came out of the draft or free agency it really didn't matter. It's well-documented what happened at that position, but when we signed Craig (Erickson) we pretty much thought he was going to be the guy. How much Jimmy (Harbaugh) wound up evolving was something we really didn't expect and no one could have predicted. We wound up being pretty lucky that we had that kind of depth at that position."

With a group of running backs that included Faulk, Potts, Lamont Warren, Zack Crockett and Ronald Humphrey, receivers such as Bailey, Dawkins, Anderson, Floyd Turner and Brian Stablein, Dilger at tight end, and a quarterback trio of Harbaugh, Erickson and Paul Justin, Infante had a solid offensive group to work with.

Looking back on that first season with the Colts, Infante said he was happy overall with the way the offense played.

"I think the one thing that we did was play what I like to call team offense," Infante said. "I think our defense is the strong suit on our football team and we work pretty hard in several areas to try and make their job easier. Number one, we try not to turn the ball over which makes their job tougher. Number two, to make sure that if we did give it back to the other team that we did so on the other side of the 50-yard-line. Finally, our goal was to keep ourselves in football games and not go out there and take a whole lot of chances that might end up creating a turnover that all of a sudden the scoreboard gets lopsided on you."

Though point No. 3 sounds like a conservative approach to the game, Infante says one thing he's never been accused of is being conservative.

"It's a team approach and I don't think functioning as a team makes you conservative," he said. "I don't think the things we did were conservative. I think the way we did the things was conservative. There's a difference. You can have a play that's willing to take a high chance but if it's not there you're better off dumping the ball to a back or scrambling or whatever. That's the kind of approach we took."

Infante pointed to Harbaugh's five interceptions on the season as the ultimate example of a quarterback not putting his team in bad situations.

"Had Jimmy thrown eight interceptions we might not have made the playoffs," Infante said. "I don't think that's being conservative, that's being intelligent. I'm going to call plays that are bad calls. But if Jimmy, or whoever is the quarterback, tries to make it a great play and goes beyond the scope of what's possible on that play then you have a tragic play. You can recover from a bad play. But those tragic ones where you throw it to the other guy, or run around back there and lose 20 yards or fumble the ball, those are the ones that can get you in trouble."

Infante said it's all part of his offensive philosophy.

"We don't want to go out there and try so hard to win the game early that we lose it late," he said. "It's not that we're against being out there and throwing bombs all over the place and double reverses and things, trying to make the fans get out of their seats. Those are nice, but those are what I call alumni plays. They get people to send in their checks and everything but a lot of times they don't end up winning the games for you. You have to stick to what you think is going to work best. But I don't think that's being conservative."

Lindy Infante swears he never saw the head coaching position of the Colts coming his way. Prior to the release of Ted Marchibroda in February 1996, Bill Tobin had never talked with him about some day becoming Marchibroda's replacement.

In fact, the day Marchibroda's release was announced, Infante didn't know what to think.

"It was interesting because our coaching staff was all over at the Scouting Combine that week that things began to happen," Infante said. "We were all sitting around in the hotel and watching television at about 6 o'clock and they came on with a blip that there was a press conference at the Colts. They said that the club was going to announce that Ted had been let go and they were going to announce the new head coach.

"We were all sitting in the same room and everybody just kind of looked around the room at each other," he said. "And kiddingly, I said 'Who in the hell isn't here?' because if it's somebody on our staff it had to be someone who wasn't there. I knew they hadn't talked to me and within a few minutes I knew they hadn't talked to anyone else. Then came the announcement that Ted had been let go but they hadn't decided on a head coach. That made us breathe a little easier but we still didn't really know what was up."

When Infante returned home around 10 p.m., there was a message on his answering machine from Bill Tobin, asking him to meet first thing the next morning at the Combine hotel. But even that didn't ease Infante's anxiety.

"I didn't know if he was calling me down there to tell me I was being let go, too, or what," Infante said. "Nothing surprises you in this business. I was a little apprehensive about what the conversation was going to be like but I didn't really lose any sleep over it that night."

Let 'er Rip

It didn't take long for Infante to feel at ease after meeting with Tobin the next morning.

"The first thing he said when I walked in the door was that he wanted me to know that I was their first choice to become the new head coach, and that they wanted to talk to me about the job," Infante said. "We talked for a couple of hours that morning and a few days later they made the announcement."

Infante insists he didn't come to Indianapolis bent on one day becoming the head coach.

"When I signed on here I didn't plan on going anywhere else," he said. "I was very willing and content to be the offensive coordinator for as long as they wanted me to be here. I didn't take this job as a stepping stone to go someplace else as a coordinator or whatever. The truth is I missed the game, and I didn't feel like I had to be a head coach again. I really didn't.

"I didn't come here with the idea that I would keep this job for a year but if I don't get a head coaching job I'll quit," he added. "Or if I don't get a head coaching job within two years I'll hang it up. That's not what I took the job for. I came back with the idea that I wanted to coach again. Having lived in Cincinnati, I liked this area of the country and felt comfortable here. I came up for the interview originally and I liked what I saw. I liked the people, I had a lot of respect for Bill and Ted, and I had coached with a lot of the guys on this staff before.

"I really felt like this would be a really good place for me to end my career," he said. "This would have been a good place for me to coach out my career as an assistant football coach. I would have been content to do that. In my wildest dreams, I never expected what happened to happen."

7

Erickson, Flipper and the Marshall Plan

The tattered blue T-shirts with the faded white horseshoe on the front came out of the drawers and became part of the wardrobe around the 12th of July as another training camp in Anderson was about to begin.

Unlike 1994, there was no construction in front of Anderson University and fans found easy access to watch the boys in blue.

But despite an offense that now had Craig Erickson, Flipper Anderson and Marshall Faulk as its primary weapons, Colts fans took a wait-and-see attitude as they anticipated the 1995 season.

Just six months earlier, the Colts had salvaged an 8-8 season when Buffalo kicker Steve Christie's 46-yard field-goal attempt bounced off the left upright preserving a season-ending 10-9 victory by the Colts in the RCA Dome.

The Colts had won three of their final four games down the stretch to get to the .500 mark in 1994, but for the 10th time in 11 seasons in Indianapolis they were out of the playoffs.

For Colts fans, the '94 season had a familiar ring. Close but not close enough. Faulk had injected the offense with some life and Vince Tobin's defense had been impressive, but it wasn't quite enough to get the Colts over the top.

As Ted Marchibroda prepared to take his troops to Anderson in the final days before the beginning of training camp '95, the veteran coach could barely sleep at night because of the anticipation of what might lie ahead. With all his heart he believed this was the best of his four teams in Indianapolis since 1992 and he was anxious to see where this team might go.

Director of football operations Bill Tobin was confident, too. His second year of tinkering with personnel and combining that with a solid draft class had provided reasons for optimism.

After all, Lindy Infante was now running the show on offense and figured to add a more unpredictable element to the club's offensive play calling. When things had gone south in recent years, Marchibroda's play calling and that of offensive coordinator Nic Nicolau had often come under fire. With Infante on board, the consensus opinion was at least the Colts should be more fun to watch.

Then there was Erickson, a player many believed was the upgrade at the quarterback position that the Colts sorely needed. Jim Harbaugh was adequate, the so-called experts proclaimed, but he would likely never get the team past the first round of the playoffs. Erickson had played on some bad Tampa Bay teams but many believed if surrounded with a good supporting cast, that the former University of Miami signal caller could take the Colts to the next level.

One of the reasons for the optimism with Erickson was the addition of speedy wide receiver Flipper Anderson. The speed element was something that had always been lacking in the Colts' game plan. And with Marshall Faulk in the backfield, it was believed that Flipper could stretch defenses to the point where they could not sit at the line of scrimmage and wait for Faulk to take a handoff.

With Erickson, Flipper and the Marshall Plan working in Infante's new offensive system, many believed this was finally going to be the team that could bring the Colts back to respectability.

There were other additions, too. Former Green Bay tight end Ed West, a 12-year veteran, was expected to battle Ken Dilger for the starting job and in the meantime serve as his tutor to prepare him for future NFL battles.

The kicking game had a pair of new faces with Bill Tobin bringing in former Bears punter Chris Gardocki, known for his ability to angle the ball inside the 20, and gambling on former 49ers placekicker Mike Cofer, who had been out of football for a full season.

And there were the rookies. Ellis Johnson was expected to add instant stability to the defensive line, Dilger was seen as a promising young tight end and Zack Crockett was being counted on to push Roosevelt Potts at the fullback position.

There was also a new No. 4 for the first time in 10 seasons. Harbaugh, who wore No. 12 in his first season with the Colts in '94, reclaimed the No. 4 jersey he wore with the Bears and at the University of Michigan. The number came free when long-time Colts kicker Dean Biasucci opted to sign with Pittsburgh during free agency.

"Yeah, I've got my number back," Harbaugh said with a big smile, a few days into camp. "I saw Dean (a few nights ago) and I was giving him a hard time about it. I told him it hadn't even cooled off and I snatched it out of his locker."

As a collective unit, the new faces — and new uniform numbers — brought with them new reasons for optimism as the 1995 season was about to get underway.

Just before training camp kicked off, *Indianapolis Star* reporter Mike Chappell wrote of the enthusiasm that was shared by fans and players alike.

"Optimism and expectations are engaged in a frenetic foot race at the Indianapolis Colts West 56th Street complex," Chappell wrote two days before the start of camp. A quote in the story from veteran center Kirk Lowdermilk seemed to sum up the club's feelings.

Many believed that Craig Erickson was the upgrade at quarterback that the Colts sorely needed and would be the one to take them to the next level. (Photo by Paul Sancya)

"Stepping back and taking an honest look at things, there are enough good players here for us to be a legitimate playoff contender," Lowdermilk said. "If we aren't (contenders), we should be ashamed of ourselves.

"The expectations should be high. If we can stay focused and stay healthy, I don't see any reason this team shouldn't win 10 games. The people are here."

For the most part, the people were indeed there. The few exceptions that had exited via free agency in the off-season included both veteran kickers (punter Rohn Stark and Biasucci), defensive end Jon Hand, tight end Kerry Cash and tackle Zefross Moss. Stark, the final original Indianapolis Colt that had moved with the team from Baltimore in 1984, was the one player who seemed conspicuous by his absence. But that was primarily because he had been there for every dog day in Anderson in the club's first 11 seasons in Indianapolis.

As the quarterbacks, receivers, rookies, free agents and players who had spent the end of the '94 season on injured reserve began arriving in Anderson, Marchibroda was as upbeat as he had been in his second stint as the head coach of the Colts.

"I'm just anxious to get started," Marchibroda said. "I think this is the best team we've put on the field in the four seasons I've been here and I truly believe our players now know what it takes to be successful.

"I think we're heading in the right direction, and I know our players can't wait to get on the field and show what they can do," he said. "It's not enough to talk about what you can do, you've got to go out and do it as well. I expect more from this team. We are expecting the playoffs."

That alone was a monumental change in Marchibroda's attitude of just a few seasons before when he inherited a team that had finished the 1991 season with a 1-15 record. Before, he was hoping to win; now he expected it.

Bill Tobin expected it, too. In an 18-month span that included several personnel changes, the front-office veteran believed he had assembled a team that was ready to turn the corner.

"I said last year that we wanted to address the defense, running game, special teams and then the passing game," Tobin said. "That was our blueprint, and we worked it with a good amount of success. It was reflected in our draft, and it was reflected on the field. We doubled our win total last year. We were competitive in each game and I think we did things the right way.

"Our aim is to build on last year's successes," he added. "I feel very strongly that we have the appropriate coaching staff in place to help us reach our goals. On the field, we have good people in key places. We have the quality of talent and the type of character needed to win. We have upgraded the talent level of our team from last year, and we hope to achieve week-to-week consistency in our play."

For the most part, everything heading into training camp was upbeat. It had only been two summers since Jeff George staged his training camp-long holdout, but No. 11 was rarely mentioned — if at all. The talk concerning this team centered around a new quarterback, the Pro Bowl most valuable player in the backfield and a new offense designed to exploit their strengths.

But training camps with the Colts never come and go without at least a hint of controversy. And this would be no exception.

Just days before the team made the trek up I-69, 30 miles northeast of Indianapolis to Anderson, the club pulled an end around in contract negotiations with Steve Emtman, the first player chosen overall by the Colts in the 1992 draft.

In short, they waited until the last possible moment to offer him an ultimatum. The message was clear: Agree to a drastic pay cut or find your name on the waiver wire. Eventually, an angry Emtman stuck to his principles and left the club he had grown to love and respect.

At the heart of the problem was Emtman's contract — particularly his $3.025 million salary cap number. Emtman was in the final year of a four-year, $9.165 million deal that included a $4.165 million signing bonus. The Colts wanted Emtman to accept a salary reduction to $700,000 per season which would represent a major relief toward the salary cap.

The contract did, however, contain several incentives that could have enabled Emtman to come close to the $2 million per season number he had come to expect.

The difference though was that for him to make the money this time he would have to earn it, a fact that through no fault of his own had not been the case in his first three injury-plagued years in the NFL.

Emtman balked at the offer, saying he felt the Colts' timing was incredible. Not only had they waited until the last possible second, they had ignored his offers earlier in the spring to reduce his contract to help relieve the cap situation.

"We talked in April and we told them we would have no problem restructuring (the contract) or working with them," Emtman said. "I don't think it's right for them to wait until two days before training camp opens to throw this at me. And there really weren't any negotiations. All of a sudden it's take it or leave it."

Not surprisingly, though, the story had two sides. Having seen the effort that Emtman had made to battle back from a series of debilitating injuries in his four-year career, Colt fans had to have some sympathy for what the defensive tackle had gone through. He was a fan favorite, someone that represented the good things about today's professional athletes and a player who had always taken "pride in the horseshoe."

But take the emotion out of the equation, and the facts were pretty lopsided in favor of the Colts doing whatever they felt was necessary.

Fact: In his first three seasons in the NFL, Emtman suffered three season-ending injuries, two involving torn ligaments in each knee and the other a herniated disc in his neck.

Fact: Of a possible 48 regular-season games, Emtman had played in 18, starting 14.

Fact: The Colts paid Emtman $7.165 million of his contract. For that investment, they had received 77 tackles, seven quarterback pressures, five sacks, one highlight film interception against Miami his rookie season, one forced fumble and one fumble recovery.

In the end, after a day in which it appeared the two sides were about to patch up their differences, Emtman decided to walk and take his services elsewhere.

The Colts, owner Robert Irsay and son Jimmy in particular, were disappointed.

"I don't know what happened," said Jim Irsay. "There was zero contact and communication. It was very strange because (Emtman's agent Demoff) Marvin wouldn't call me back and ... we had to rustle up Steve (Saturday morning) and when we finally got in touch with him, he told us he didn't want to talk.

"It was obvious they didn't want to make a deal and stay," he said. "The whole thing is frustrating and disappointing. We did a lot in the last three years in terms of incredibly fair treatment, and I'm disappointed in the way it ended."

Emtman ended his chapter with the Colts with criticism for his perception of the way he was treated the final days before camp was to begin.

"This has nothing to do with money and everything to do with the way I was treated," Emtman said. "I've busted my ass for this organization. I've given them blood, sweat and tears, and what happens? They back me into a corner. For them to come to me two days before training camp with a take-it-or-leave-it offer gave me no leverage.

"The one thing I wanted was to play football and prove I'm worthy of my contract," he said. "I think this was a good business move for (the Colts), but I certainly think it should have been handled in a more respectful manner.

"I bleed Colt blue," he said. "I believe in Colt pride and I believe in pride in the horseshoe. I wanted to be here because I've been through an awful lot as a Colt. I have an awful lot of respect for some people in the organization ... Jimmy Irsay, Ted Marchibroda, Tom Zupancic. And my teammates are a bunch of great guys who are on the verge of doing some great things. I wish I could be a part of that.

"But a long time ago, my dad told me I had to stand for something," he said. "Well, right now I'm standing up for what I think is right."

Emtman eventually would sign with Miami and see limited action as a reserve for the Dolphins in '95.

One week after the Emtman mess, the Colts almost stepped in it again. This time, however, cooler heads prevailed.

On the day the veterans reported to Anderson, the Colts terminated the contract of linebacker Jeff Herrod, one of the club's most consistent defensive players in recent years. Again a salary cap move, this time the Colts were able to get him back under a new contract within 24 hours. Almost appearing to learn from previous mistakes, the communication between management and Herrod's agent was admirable.

Two other veterans — Ray Buchanan and Tony Siragusa — reported to camp and eventually walked out, seeking changes in their contracts. One other unhappy camper was fullback Roosevelt Potts, who reported a few days late to camp as a protest over his current contract. His two-day holdout cost him $8,000 in fines.

But as the contract situations began to weed themselves out, the real on-the-field football issues for the '95 Colts began to surface.

The biggest was at quarterback where Craig Erickson had been named the starter just a few days after the Colts acquired him in a draft day trade with Tampa Bay. Jim Harbaugh, the '94 starter, had been demoted to a backup role, and World League most valuable player Paul Justin was the Colts' No. 3 quarterback.

The first week of camp, Erickson's arm looked dead, but both he and Marchibroda passed that off to just being tired and sore from a long off-season of work. After five days, however, the arm appeared to be back at full strength.

"He's now throwing the way we expected him to throw," Marchibroda said two weeks into camp. "And I don't think there's any question he's going to throw even better. He's got more zip on the ball, and he's making the proper reads.

"One thing I was impressed with was that he told me three or four days ago that his arm was back. A lot of times when you're dealing with a young quarterback they really don't know their arm that well. But this guy does and that's a big plus."

Erickson's momentum in camp built right up to the preseason opener against Cincinnati in the RCA Dome. Though the Colts dropped a 34-21 decision to the Bengals, Erickson was impressive. In one half of play, he completed 12 of 18 passes for 152 yards and one touchdown. In the four drives he engineered, the Colts scored a touchdown, a field goal and drove inside the Bengals' 20 on another drive. He mixed up his passes and found eight different targets in his 12 completions.

"The first couple of series I think the speed of the game caught me a little bit by surprise," Erickson said. "It's not that I haven't been there before, but being in a new offense I felt myself thinking a little bit. I think I settled down in the second quarter and felt a little more comfortable out there."

Paul Justin played the fourth quarter and threw for 167 yards on 15 of 26 passing and one touchdown.

Meanwhile, Harbaugh played a series or two in the third quarter of the opener but was scheduled to play the second half in the second preseason contest, a road game against the Seattle Seahawks. Though being a backup was an unfamiliar role, Harbaugh was doing his best to take it all in stride.

"This is a different situation for me," he said prior to the game with the Seahawks. "But I'm comfortable with it. I couldn't have asked for a better working relationship than I have with Craig and Paul. I pull for them to do well in practice and in games, and they in turn support me.

"Sure I'd like to be the starter, but that's not the way it is," he said. "At the same time you have to know you're going to get your chance at some point."

His first real chance came in the preseason matchup with Seattle. Trailing 17-13 with three minutes to play in the Kingdome, Harbaugh rallied the Colts to a 20-17 victory.

He looked impressive on the game-winning 11-play, 78-yard drive that ended with a 4-yard touchdown pass to rookie Marvin Marshall with 45 seconds to play. On the drive, Harbaugh completed seven of 10 passes for 75 yards and the score. Playing the entire second half, he completed 13 of 20 passes for 142 yards. He also gained 28 yards on three carries, including a 7-yard touchdown run on a quarterback draw.

"I thought Jimmy did a great job of throwing the ball and I felt like our quarterbacking has really been excellent overall in the first two games," Marchibroda said. "It's good to see Jimmy playing that well off the bench. I'm sure it has been a difficult adjustment for him but he seems to be handling it very well."

Erickson had another solid showing, completing 10 of 14 passes for 88 yards in the first half.

In preseason game three at Lambeau Field against the Green Bay Packers, won by the Colts 20-17, Erickson had his first noticeable slip. He completed just seven of 18 passes for 31 yards, fumbled twice, and overall, the entire first unit offense struggled.

"Obviously, I didn't take a step forward today," Erickson said. "But it's still a good victory. A lot of guys put in a lot of effort and they should be commended for it."

For the second week in a row, Harbaugh came on strong in his relief role. This time he rallied the Colts back from a 17-9 deficit by completing 15 of 24 passes for 187 yards and a touchdown. He also hit Lamont Warren on a two-point conversion pass play and scrambled four times in the game for 30 yards.

In the final preseason tune-up, a date with Harbaugh's old team the Chicago Bears in the RCA Dome, all three quarterbacks shined in a convincing 29-7 Colts victory.

Erickson, Harbaugh and Justin combined to complete 22 of 29 passes for 297 yards and three touchdowns. Erickson was 10 of 14 for 132 in the first half including a 53-yard touchdown pass to Floyd Turner. Harbaugh was 7 of 9 for 97 yards including a blitz-beating 25-yard touchdown toss to rookie Ben Bronson. Justin hit on five of six passes in the fourth quarter for 68 yards including a 21-yard touchdown pass to running back Ronald Humphrey.

Coming out of the preseason with a 3-1 record, Marchibroda was particularly excited about his quarterback situation. In a column written by Wayne Fuson in the *Indianapolis News* following the preseason finale, Marchibroda talked about the Colts' depth at the QB spot.

"We are deep," Marchibroda said. "I've never had this many good quarterbacks. Ever. And I don't think anybody else has either — especially the way we're using them. We have a veteran in starter Craig Erickson, a veteran backup in Jim Harbaugh and a promising young kid in Paul Justin."

◆   ◆   ◆

A week after he stole the show in Honolulu and was named Pro Bowl most valuable player, Marshall Faulk was asked about the significance of the award.

Did this firmly establish him as one of the top running backs in the game? Was it the ultimate honor to be named the MVP of the NFL's all-star game? Was this the crowning accomplishment of an already star-studded rookie season?

Faulk just flashed his sheepish grin.

"It's nice," he said. "But the individual honors are not what I'm playing for. The only thing I care about is winning and that's the only thing that really makes me happy."

Therein lies the true Marshall Faulk.

Sure, the 22-year-old lives to get locked up with a linebacker one-on-one, or hit the line of scrimmage and find a hole big enough to drive any of his 10 automobiles through.

But given the choice of rushing for 2,000 yards, leading the league in scoring, or having his team make the playoffs, the Colts' second-year back would not hesitate in his reply.

"You can get 2,000 yards and not make it to the playoffs," he said. "You can score a lot of points but still be on a losing team. The only thing that matters to me is helping this team make it to the playoffs.

"And I don't just want to make it there: I want to win," he said. "I don't play this game for the money. I play because I love it and because I want to make it to the Super Bowl. I don't see any reason why that dream can't come true."

With Craig Erickson at quarterback, solid receivers such as Flipper Anderson, Floyd Turner and Sean Dawkins as targets, and Lindy Infante's new offensive system in place, Faulk was excited about the prospects.

"We have a lot of talent on this team," Faulk said in an interview in late August. "Everybody talks about the new offense with coach Infante and how I should benefit from it. But it's not just me, it's everybody.

"What this offense does is it spreads out the defense and makes it so they can't just stop one thing. I think we have a lot of offensive weapons and that's what is going to make us successful."

Still, Faulk remained the No. 1 weapon in the arsenal. His rookie numbers told the story the best:

- He rushed for 1,282 yards on 314 carries with 11 touchdowns.
- He tied for the team lead in receptions with 52 catches for 522 yards and one touchdown.
- He had four 100-yard rushing games with a high of 143 in the season-opener against Houston.

The most-asked question of Faulk heading into his second regular season was what could he do for an encore?

"I don't really get caught up in all of that," he said. "I just want to go out and give 110 percent. That's basically it. If I do that, whatever it is that people are expecting me to do, it will happen."

The expectation was obviously for Faulk's career to begin to parallel those of the elite active running backs in the league, players like Emmitt Smith, Barry Sanders and Thurman Thomas.

Smith rushed for 1,563 yards and 12 touchdowns in his sophomore NFL season, which was 600 yards more than his rookie campaign. Thomas rushed for 1,244, up nearly 400 yards from his first year. Sanders slipped from a 1,470-yard rookie season to a very respectable 1,304 his second year but still managed to average more than 5 yards per carry.

"My second year is going to be a challenge but I don't see it as any more pressure than I had last year," Faulk said. "And the way I look at it, all the pressure that's applied isn't near the amount that I put on myself to perform. That's the ultimate pressure. The self-inflicted kind that drives you to be the best you can be."

Ted Marchibroda wasn't worried about his running back having to contend with a sophomore jinx. In his view, that jinx is reserved for a different kind of athlete.

"To me the sophomore jinx is when the ballplayer has a pretty good first year and thinks he's a pretty good football player and then doesn't have to work the second year in order to have a good year again," Marchibroda said. "Marshall has not been in that category. He came into camp a week early and he's worked hard every day that he's been in camp. I just don't believe in the sophomore jinx in Marshall's case."

That may be because of the amount of times Marchibroda hoped to get his franchise running back the ball. As a rookie, Faulk accounted for 40.9 percent of the club's net offense and there was little reason to expect a significant drop-off.

"I really don't expect to get any more opportunities than I did last year, but I'd like to think the ones I do get will be better ones," Faulk said. "I think my chances this year will be better as far as the production or the quality that we get out of it."

As for the ultimate goal of leading his team to the playoffs, Faulk remained supremely confident.

"We will be in the playoffs," Faulk said. "We can only stop ourselves in that regard. I think we're on the verge of big things and I can't wait to be a part of that."

♦ ♦ ♦

As Marchibroda and Infante perused their stable of skill players early in training camp, one fleet-footed receiver kept catching their eye.

Even though he was slowed early in camp with a sore knee, Flipper Anderson had a God-given talent that the Colts had seen very little of in their 12 seasons in Indianapolis.

Walter Murray could move, Andre Rison looked like a jet on AstroTurf and Clarence Verdin could motor, but Anderson belonged in their company. Even at age 30 — middle-aged in professional football terms — it was apparent in July that Flipper could fly.

"When I was a rookie I could do the 40 in about 4.3, but now I've slipped to about 4.4," Anderson said with a big smile. "All I know is that I still have enough speed to beat most guys."

In his first seven NFL seasons, "most guys" did indeed have trouble keeping up with Anderson. He ranks fifth in Rams history with 5,246 yards on 259 catches. His most amazing statistic, though, was his career average per catch — 20.3 yards.

By contrast, the Colts as a team in 1994 had averaged just 11.6 yards per catch. Sean Dawkins had led all receivers with a 14.5-yards-per-catch average.

In one game in 1989 against New Orleans, Anderson caught 15 passes for an NFL record 336 yards. But now he had a horseshoe on his helmet and Marchibroda and Infante could only dream about the possibilities.

"Flipper has that deep speed and he has that reputation around the league that he can get behind you," Infante said. "You really need to get behind people in this league. He has excellent hands, he's not going to make many mistakes and when you get the ball around him he's going to go get it.

"He's a very complete wide receiver."

With a wide receiving corps that included Floyd Turner and Sean Dawkins, Anderson was being counted on right away to become the Colts' go-to receiver.

"I've been the go-to guy since I was 11 playing Pop Warner football in New Jersey," Anderson said. "Everybody thinks there's all this pressure but this is what I do. I play football and I think I'm pretty good at it."

Early on in training camp, Anderson had a scare after a collision with safety Derwin Gray during a drill. Anderson and Gray collided at the knees and Anderson was slow getting up. Tests later showed no structural damage but the receiver had to sit out 10 days before returning to practice.

"I was scared at first because I thought it was a major injury," he said. "But my reflex was to jump right up and when I did I felt a lot better. After I jogged a little bit I knew I was going to be OK."

With Anderson on board, the Colts hoped to be able to stretch defenses to make room for Marshall Faulk. With the Rams, Anderson had a similar experience with running back Jerome Bettis but few people put Bettis and Faulk in the same class.

"Jerome was pretty much just a straight forward, tackle-to-tackle type of guy, while Marshall is a lot flashier and defenses have to worry about him more," Ander-

Despite a sore knee that slowed him early in training camp, it was evident that Flipper Anderson, shown here in a game against the New York Jets, had the God-given talent that the Colts had seen very little of in their 12 years in Indianapolis. (Photo by Paul Sancya)

son said. "I think it's going to take a lot of pressure off of him that I'm here, and vice versa.

"Because teams are going to have to cover Marshall coming out of the backfield, I think that's going to leave some solid single coverage for me," he added. "And if that happens, that's going to make it tough on a lot of defenses."

One of the big transitions a receiver has to make when he comes to a new team is to feel comfortable with the quarterback. Anderson said that wasn't a problem with quarterback Craig Erickson.

"He's a good quarterback," Anderson said. "I can't wait to get the season started and get things going with him. I told him the other day he's really putting some zip on the ball. He throws a real easily catchable ball."

◆   ◆   ◆

Preseason records mean very little. Preseason production, however, is something else entirely.

Though Colts fans were able to gloat over a 3-1 preseason record, the players and coaching staff were positive about the upcoming regular season for other reasons.

The offense was running smoothly, the defense was applying pressure and making big plays, and the special teams were showing improvement. The staff believed it could be a formula for a playoff contender.

"I think a lot of our guys are anxious for the regular season to start because we feel like we have a good thing going here," Erickson said. "I think we've worked hard as a group throughout the preseason and now we're ready to see some of that hard work pay off."

In many ways it was difficult to digest the Colts' preseason performance. The starters played mostly just the first half each week, and the Colts' backup players dominated their opponents in the final three games.

But regardless of who was playing, it was apparent that offensive coordinator Lindy Infante's much-ballyhooed offensive system was sinking in. Receivers ran the correct routes, quarterbacks made the proper reads and running backs found the holes.

In four games, the Colts averaged 376.5 yards. And the performances were consistent. The Colts rolled up 409 against the Bengals, 366 against Seattle, 384 against Green Bay and 347 against Chicago.

The three quarterbacks combined to complete 81 of 120 passes (67.5 percent) with seven touchdowns and just one interception. Twenty receivers made preseason receptions, and nine players had at least one run from scrimmage.

"The thing I like about this offense the most is that you really have a chance for success with it," Harbaugh said. "Especially at the quarterback position. You just have a lot of ways to do good things. He puts you in a position to make big plays. It's an offense that's not designed to get anybody in particular the ball but rather anyone can catch the ball.

But it wasn't just the offense.

The defensive front seven applied a great deal of pressure in the preseason, with tackles Tony Siragusa, Tony McCoy and rookie Ellis Johnson coming up with a consistent push up the middle.

Defensive ends Tony Bennett and Trev Alberts, though small compared with the prototypical NFL ends, made up for the lack of size with their quickness to the outside and their overall athleticism.

The linebackers were steady and the secondary gave up few big plays.

"I'd have to say I've seen some encouraging things defensively in the preseason," said defensive coordinator Vince Tobin. "We're not there yet, but we're getting there."

The kicking game was one of the real surprises, especially considering placekicker Mike Cofer hadn't kicked in a game in more than 18 months. But if anything, his leg appeared well-rested and alive. He made 11 of 14 field goals, including six of eight beyond 40 yards.

"I think we're moving in the right direction as a football team," Marchibroda said in late August. "I think we're heading into the regular season on a high note and now it's time to go to war."

8

Same Old Colts?

Same Old Colts.

To some it's a harmless three-word phrase used to describe more than a decade of mediocre play by Indianapolis' boys in blue. Show some excitement, get people's hopes up, but finish around the .500 mark and always just out of the playoffs.

Same Old Colts.

To Bill Tobin, it's like a dagger that pierces the heart.

For Tobin, you may as well spit in his face, drag the flag through the mud or sit during the national anthem if you're going to denigrate his team in that way. For Tobin, *Same Old Colts* is ancient history, something that took place light years ago in football terms by a group of players who for the most part no longer wear a horseshoe on their helmet.

Same Old Colts.

To the players, it's the ultimate insult. Not only do these Colts know very little about what happened before, they know even fewer of the parties responsible. To the group of Colts that opened the 1995 season against Cincinnati in the RCA Dome, *Same Old Colts* was a phrase with which they simply couldn't identify.

And yet sometime late in the afternoon of Sept. 3, after dropping a disappointing 24-21 overtime decision to the lowly Bengals, the *Same Old Colts* references were being tossed around the home team's locker room by members of the media.

Ted Marchibroda was the first to nip any *Same Old Colts* talk at the bud. When asked by a television reporter if this was the *Same Old Colts* revisited, the veteran coach fired a salvo at his critics during his opening comments following the loss to the Bengals in the postgame press conference room. "I know what you guys have written and for the first ballgame you can say whatever you want. But I'm glad I'm playing with these Colts and not the old Colts. We're one down but it's a long season.

"I'll remember what you said and I may remind you what you said."

Less than 24 hours later, Marchibroda still hadn't cooled in his opinions.

"I guess I can understand why you're saying it because it's been happening before," Marchibroda said at his weekly Monday afternoon press conference with the

Let 'er Rip

local media. "I've been here four years and this is the best football team I've had in that time. We've improved it over four years, our players work hard and there's no doubt in my mind that they're going to play well before it's all over.

"It's a good football team and what we've got to do right now is put it behind us. We got beat but we can't dwell on it. The important thing is not that you got knocked down. The important thing is whether or not you bounce back. For that we'll have to wait until next Monday."

◆   ◆   ◆

For players and management alike, the season opener got off on a bad note long before the opening kickoff. As the players came out an hour before kickoff they couldn't help but notice more empty seats than usual. By the time the noon kickoff rolled around, the situation hadn't changed much.

Nearly 20,000 seats were empty in the RCA Dome at kickoff, meaning only 42,445 fans showed up despite the fact the Colts went 3-1 in the preseason and appeared to be riding a wave of momentum into the regular season. Ticket manager Larry Hall said he believed some of the problem with selling the game had come from Labor Day weekend and also from the fact the Bengals had never been a good draw in Indianapolis. Still, the bottom line was the crowd was the smallest opening day gate in the history of the Indianapolis Colts — by close to 5,000 fans.

Things went downhill from there. The Colts trailed 13-10 at half and fell behind 21-10 late in the third quarter following a pair of Doug Pelfrey field goals and a safety when quarterback Craig Erickson could not handle a shotgun snap from center Kirk Lowdermilk near the Colts' own end zone.

A 40-yard field goal by Mike Cofer got the Colts to within eight at 21-13 early in the fourth, and then backup quarterback Jim Harbaugh came on to work some magic in a 14-play, 78-yard drive in the final three minutes of regulation. A 5-yard touchdown pass to Flipper Anderson with three seconds remaining got the Colts to within two at 21-19, and then Harbaugh hit Floyd Turner with a two-point conversion pass to send the game into overtime.

In OT, the Bengals won the toss and the Colts never got the ball. Ray Buchanan was flagged for a 34-yard pass interference penalty and four plays later Pelfrey kicked a 47-yard field goal that lifted Cincinnati to the season-opening victory.

Prior to the win, Cincinnati had lost an NFL-record 20 straight games in September and October.

The Colts didn't need to look far to figure out the reasons why they had lost their 10th season opener and ninth home opener in 12 seasons in Indianapolis. Marshall Faulk was limited to 49 yards on 19 carries, the defensive line did not register a sack on quarterback Jeff Blake and the secondary did not allow a deep ball but gave up way too much underneath.

But Craig Erickson shouldered the brunt of the blame. In his first regular season start as the Colts quarterback, Erickson completed 19 of 31 passes for 196 yards but threw three interceptions and mishandled the snap for a safety. The three intercep-

Same Old Colts?

Indianapolis Colts quarterback Craig Erickson did not get off to a great start with the Colts. He had three interceptions and mishandled a snap that led to a safety in a 24-21 overtime loss to Cincinnati in the opening game of 1995. (Photo by Paul Sancya)

tions led to 10 points and overall the former Tampa Bay quarterback just seemed to play the majority of the game behind the eight-ball.

"That wasn't one of my more memorable games," Erickson said at game's end. "There's obviously three balls I would like to have back. It was just a combination of some pretty good plays by them and some bad decisions on my part.

"When you throw one interception in a game, you can't let it ruin you for the rest of the game," he said. "If you have one bad game, you can't let it ruin you for the whole season."

Eight minutes into the game, fans appeared to be voicing their approval over the April trade that brought Erickson to Indianapolis for a pair of draft choices. He had completed his first five passes for 49 yards, including a 16-yard touchdown toss to Flipper Anderson to give the Colts an early 7-0 lead.

"It almost seemed like things were too easy that first drive," Erickson said. "We were making the big plays when we needed them. After that it was almost as if I was trying to force the action too much."

Erickson actually completed 10 of his first 11 passes. Unfortunately two of the completions were to the Bengals. On the first one, he simply didn't see linebacker Andre Collins on a pass intended for Anderson. The second pick was off a bootleg on a ball he admitted should never have been thrown.

"There was no excuse for the first one," he said. "He was the intercept guy on that play and I just didn't find him. I guess I was just feeling a little too good about myself. Things were really clicking right away but that brought me back to reality pretty quickly.

"The second one was a play-action that the guy just got on me too quickly and I should have thrown it away," he said. "Instead I tried to force it in to the tight end and the safety was just there. It was just a bad decision."

The safety was the back-breaker. On third-and-8 at the Colts' 3, Erickson was in the shotgun formation and couldn't get a hand on Lowdermilk's snap. The ball bounded out of the end zone to give the Bengals an 18-10 lead with 3:56 to play in the third quarter.

Lowdermilk said later the snap was "high and hard" but Erickson claimed he still should have come down with the ball.

"I've got to come up with it ... it was probably just a combination of a lot of things," Erickson said. "Maybe the crowd noise got to us a little bit down there or something. But there's really no excuse for it. We do that all the time. We did it a couple of dozen times today. To have it happen and be the difference in the game, it's pretty tough."

From the moment Erickson arrived in Indianapolis, there had been no quarterback controversy. A few days after the trade was consummated, Marchibroda named Erickson his opening day starter. Following the Bengals game, Marchibroda insisted that status hadn't changed but there was no hiding the fact the pressure had been turned up a notch on Erickson.

"A quarterback is going to have games like that," Marchibroda said. "We can't judge him by just one ballgame. He made some poor decisions out there today but all the games we've ever seen on him he hasn't done that in the past.

"Craig is the starter and maybe we've found a role for Jimmy," he said. "I know Jim would like to be the starter but you can't make a change based on one performance."

As for Erickson, he knew right then he couldn't afford too many more outings like that one.

"My job is to go out and do the best I can do," he said. "That wasn't one of my better efforts but I have to bounce back and play well next week. I know what I can do and I think my teammates know that as well."

The second week in September is a little early to be talking about must-win games in the National Football League. In a 16-game season that usually carries with it huge emotion swings not to mention the ongoing threat of injury to key personnel a lot can happen to affect the outcome of a season.

Same Old Colts?

Still, for a team on the rise to drop its opening two games to two teams that many consider among the worst in football could be almost too much to overcome for a young football team.

As the Colts took their show on the road to the Meadowlands to face the New York Jets, this had to be part of the mind-set.

Not surprisingly, Erickson took the heat for most of the week. Though Marchibroda and Infante continued to support their quarterback, national media critics — on ESPN in particular — attempted to dissect Erickson's problems and basically accused him of having tunnel vision. On a Monday night program prior to *Monday Night Football*, ESPN reported that Erickson appeared to be locking in to his primary receiver and telegraphing where he was going to throw the ball. The network cited several Bengals players who said film had showed that Erickson would tip his hand before throwing the ball.

Infante basically called the reports nonsense.

"I didn't see it and I don't believe it," Infante said. "There were a couple of occasions, I believe, where he may have made a bad read. I think he's made it clear that the three balls that were intercepted he would like to have had back but there's other quarterbacks in the league that threw some interceptions, too."

But Erickson's problems would continue in Week 2.

In the first half against the Jets, Erickson and the offense could get nothing started and New York, behind the passing of Boomer Esiason, led 17-3 at intermission. Three plays after Erickson lost a fumble at his own 24-yard line, Esiason hit rookie Wayne Chrebet on a 5-yard touchdown pass to make it 24-3 with 13:14 remaining in the third.

With one foot in the grave, the Colts called on Jim Harbaugh to work some of his comeback magic for the second week in a row. The last time the Colts had rallied from a 21-point deficit, the coach was Ted Marchibroda but the year was 1975, when they rallied to beat Buffalo 42-35.

If they were to do it again, Harbaugh was going to have to come up big. The first two drives netted nothing. On the first, Marshall Faulk fumbled while attempting to dive into the Jets' end zone and the home team recovered. On the next drive, Harbaugh moved the Colts into position but Mike Cofer missed a 38-yard field goal.

But this time, the defense would provide the initial spark. Defensive end Tony Bennett jump started the Colts with a recovered fumble and a 32-yard sprint for a touchdown that made it 24-10 late in the third quarter.

It turned out to be just what the doctor ordered for the Colts and Harbaugh. Suddenly, a 14-point deficit didn't seem that insurmountable. The next time the Colts touched the ball Harbaugh marched them 80 yards on 12 plays with the quarterback hitting Sean Dawkins for a 15-yard touchdown pass to cut the lead to 24-17 with 8:46 remaining.

It appeared as if the Jets, however, were going to pad their lead on the ensuing possession as they marched to the Colts' 20. But an attacking defense caused Esiason to fumble with Stephen Grant coming up with the recovery at the Colts' 25 with 5:40 remaining in regulation.

Let 'er Rip

Mike Cofer (3) and holder Chris Gardocki celebrate after Cofer's game-winning 52-yard field goal against the Jets in the second game of 1995. (Photo by Paul Sancya)

    This time Harbaugh moved down the field quickly, marching 75 yards in seven plays for the score. The game-tying touchdown came when Harbaugh beat the blitz and hit a wide-open Faulk for a 14-yard score.

    Still, the Jets had two chances to win the game. The first at the end of regulation and the second to start the overtime period were hampered by a series of dropped balls by Jets receivers. Esiason was frustrated as were the 65,134 fans in attendance who at one time were of the belief they were on hand to witness a rare blowout by the Jets.

When the Colts did get the ball back in overtime, they would not be denied. Harbaugh came through on a third-and-10 play with a 24-yard pass to Dawkins that moved the ball to the Jets' 39. Following a 4-yard run by Faulk and two Harbaugh incompletions, Cofer came on to split the uprights from 52 yards out to give the Colts a most improbable 27-24 victory.

Cofer, who had missed a 42-yarder against Cincinnati and then missed from 36 and 38 earlier against the Jets, said later he believed his job was on the line.

"I'm not going to lie to you, I kind of felt like I was kicking for my football life," Cofer said. "The way I look at it, the offense did a hell of a job battling back to give me the opportunity to save my job."

Harbaugh completed 11 of 16 passes for 123 yards, two touchdowns and no interceptions. Faulk gained 81 yards on 21 carries and caught eight passes for 58 yards. Erickson completed 12 of 18 for 141 and threw his fourth interception of the young season.

"This might be the best feeling of all time," Harbaugh said following the victory. "I'm so happy that I'm numb. It was a tremendous victory and nobody gave up. When we got the running game going, I felt good about our chances. We started making plays and we were right back in the fight. It was good that the comeback effort produced a win. This is an incredible natural high. I'm really enjoying myself."

Said Marchibroda of his "backup" quarterback: "Jimmy has the hot hand and he's done extremely well. I will have to take that into account for this week. I have said before that Jim is like a great relief pitcher, sort of like a Goose Gossage or a Dave Righetti. He is a battler who never quits."

Duke Tumatoe summed up the first two weeks this way the following Wednesday in his version of *Lord Help Our Colts*:

> *Do we have a starting quarterback?*
>
> *Or just a finishing one*
>
> *I'll bet the real fun this season*
>
> *Has not yet begun*
>
> *Lord help our Colts. Lord help our Colts.*

The glow of equaling the greatest comeback in Colts history was tempered the next day with some disheartening news for the remainder of the '95 season.

Wide receiver Flipper Anderson, who had caught eight passes for 111 yards in the first two games, suffered tears in the medial collateral and posterior cruciate ligaments in his left knee and would be lost for the season.

"Now the others are going to have to step up," Marchibroda said.

Once again, however, Marchibroda's big decision during the week prior to the Buffalo game was who to start at quarterback. He waited until Saturday evening to make his decision, hoping to force the Bills to have to prepare for both Erickson and Harbaugh. For most of the week, the two quarterbacks shared the practice load equally.

Let 'er Rip

But when game time rolled around, it was Jim Harbaugh who emerged as the Colts' starter.

"I felt this would be best for the ballclub," Marchibroda told Mike Chappell of the *Indianapolis Star* on Saturday evening. "I don't think this shows a lack of faith in Craig, although to this point he hasn't performed as well as we had hoped he would."

The truth is the move was to show faith in Harbaugh's abilities. His two-game statistics — 20 of 29 passing, 209 yards, three touchdowns, no interceptions and an NFL-best 124.1 quarterback rating. In addition, he had engineered two splendid comebacks, one which resulted in the victory over the Jets.

Harbaugh looked forward to the challenge that lay ahead in Orchard Park, N.Y., the next day. He told the *Indianapolis Star* on Saturday "I've got a chance to play and I'm going to play with that same aggressive style. There's no reason to be tentative or to worry. I think (Marchibroda) looks at this as a case of I'm playing well and maybe I've got a hot hand. He's going to run with it and see where it goes. We'll see how long it lasts."

Cinderella's slipper didn't fit the veteran quarterback in his first start but a lot of the problems were out of his hands. Buffalo posted a hard-fought 20-14 victory in Week 3 in a game the Colts felt as if they gave away.

Trailing 17-14 midway through the fourth quarter, the Colts had a chance to tie but Cofer's 39-yard field-goal attempt was wide left with 8:01 remaining in the game. On the Bills' next possession, it appeared as if the Colts received new life when Steve Christie missed from 43 yards out which would give the Colts the ball and decent field position for Harbaugh to work his magic for a third time this season.

But new life turned into a slow death when it was revealed cornerback Eugene Daniel was offside on the attempt, allowing Christie to kick again from 5 yards closer. He made the 38-yarder with 2:07 to play to give Buffalo the 20-14 edge.

Harbaugh came back to march the Colts 46 yards to the Bills' 34, but then threw four incompletions and Buffalo was able to run out the clock.

Harbaugh was 19 of 33 for 241 yards with one touchdown and no interceptions.

But it was penalties that killed the Colts. Indianapolis was flagged 11 times for 111 yards. Besides Daniel's costly offside call, second-year guard Eric Mahlum was flagged for holding in the fourth quarter on what would have been a 15-yard Marshall Faulk run to set up first-and-goal at the Bills' 3. The Colts trailed 17-14 at the time.

The defense also missed opportunities to make a pair of huge plays. The first came when Quentin Coryatt could not cover a Thurman Thomas fumble in the end zone in the first quarter that was eventually recovered for a touchdown by Carwell Gardner. Later Damon Watts dropped an easy interception right in his mitts near the goal line midway through the fourth quarter.

At 1-2 the Colts limped to the week off in their schedule, hoping there would be good things on the horizon.

"I told the team after the Buffalo game that if we played with the same effort, that we would win our share of games this season," Marchibroda said. "I do know that our execution needs to reach a higher level, but there were many signs during the Buffalo game that we are finding ourselves as a team."

At 1-2, Duke Tumatoe continued to marvel at Harbaugh's play.

> *Harbaugh was bruised and battered*
> *Buffalo beat the hell out of him*
> *And Erickson's counting his millions*
> *saying, "Go get 'em Jim."*
> *Lord help our Colts. Lord help our Colts.*
> *Harbaugh carried the load*
> *He looked like a squirrel trying to cross a busy road.*
> *Lord help our Colts.*

Coming off the bye week in the schedule, director of football operations Bill Tobin was asked to sum up where he felt the team was.

"We had time to reflect on our three performances, as well as a chance to mend a little bit," Tobin said. "Though we are not satisfied with our record, there are indicators that we are on the right track. We have played well enough at times to win, but there have been individual breakdowns. What we are doing is working from within to correct our mistakes.

"We want, at this point, to avoid change because a team can get worse if injudicious decisions are made. The football staff shares the feeling that we can win with the personnel on hand. I can vouch that I feel good about the roster quality, and I like the attitude in the locker room."

Finally, Tobin made it clear that even though the Colts were 1-2, they were not the *Same Old Colts*.

"We all had a very sour feeling after the Buffalo and Cincinnati games, and we aim to do something about it," Tobin said. "I have said all year that we are not the same team that has struggled for years. We have different coaches and players and we will have a different result.

"We want our fans to know this, and we have 13 games left to make our statement."

9

Jim Harbaugh: Captain Comeback

Early in training camp in 1995 at Anderson University, *Chicago Sun-Times* columnist Dan Pompei was in town specifically to do a story on Jim Harbaugh.

Harbaugh claims Pompei had used him as a punching bag in his final seasons with the Bears, and with the quarterback listed as No. 2 on the depth chart behind Craig Erickson, the sportswriter had likely made the trek to Anderson to write Harbaugh off once and for all.

In an interview one afternoon between practices, Pompei began to dissect Harbaugh's current backup status. As the interview progressed, Harbaugh noted a hint of sarcasm in Pompei's questions. When Pompei inquired about how things were going overall, Harbaugh replied, "Well, you know, same old thing. Just back here at training camp. Some things never change."

As Harbaugh tells it, Pompei kind of got a smirk on his face and said, "What do you mean, same old thing? You're the backup quarterback, you're over 30, I mean your career is on the downslide. It seems like things have really changed for you."

Harbaugh could only smile.

"I said, 'Well you never know, there may still be a little glory for me out there somewhere. You just never know about these things'."

Although Harbaugh proved prophetic with his answer in training camp, it's unlikely that even he could envision what was to come for him and his teammates.

The calendar year 1995 would produce some of the finest moments of his NFL career — and some of his deepest frustrations. And in between, there was a time when Harbaugh was able to step back and look at the total picture and attempt to have some fun.

When the new year dawned, Harbaugh was one of three quarterbacks on the Indianapolis Colts roster heading into the 1995 season. Don Majkowski was an unhappy free agent and most people believed he would wind up somewhere else. Browning Nagle, also a free agent, was more up in the air, but his start in 1994's season finale against Buffalo left a bad taste in the mouth of management. So Harbaugh believed at the very least he would have an opportunity to battle for the starting job come training camp.

His first year with the Colts in 1994 had been a roller coaster ride from beginning to end. He started the first eight games and enjoyed moderate success, but following a bad first half against Washington in week 8, it's believed owner Robert Irsay lost his patience. The owner reportedly told Ted Marchibroda and Bill Tobin, "I want us to give that Majkowski guy a chance to start."

(The owner pronounced the name MUH-JOW-SKI, rather than it's proper pronunciation with a silent 'J'. But this wasn't a big surprise coming from the elder Irsay. This is the same person who earlier in the season was happy with the play of HAR-BRO. The next season he would refer to quarterback Paul Justin as JUSTINE.)

Harbaugh sat the next six weeks, before coming back to start against Miami in the Dome in week 15. The Colts won the game 10-6 to improve to 7-8 on the season. His reward for getting them closer to .500 was a baseball cap and clipboard for the season finale against Buffalo, as the coaching staff wanted to see what Nagle could do in a starting role.

The next week was a humbling one for Harbaugh. One week he was the starter, the next he was running the Bills' scout team in practice against the Colts' No. 1 defense. How quickly the mighty had fallen.

"I'm on the scout team and Roosevelt Potts comes up to me and says, 'Just look at ya. One week you beat Dan Marino, the next week you're Rudy'."

As it turned out, the experiment with Nagle only lasted a half. Trailing 6-0 at intermission, Marchibroda turned to Harbaugh for the final 30 minutes. He threw a 13-yard touchdown pass to Floyd Turner to get the Colts the lead and then helped his team hang on for a 10-9 season-ending victory over the Bills.

When 1995 began to unfold, Harbaugh was getting vibes that some changes might be in the air. The Colts had talked about either looking for a quarterback in the draft or trying to trade for one that could step right in and upgrade the position. In either case, Harbaugh still was of the belief he would get a chance to battle for the starting spot in training camp.

"I had so many detractors in the past, that my mind-set at that time was this was going to be a positive thing for me," Harbaugh said. "The way I looked at it if they brought in the best possible free agent and then I beat him out for the starting job in camp, people would at least have to say 'He's got a little bit of talent,' or 'He's not as horrible as everyone thinks.' So I guess I was pretty excited about that."

But that's not the way things worked out. The Colts obtained quarterback Craig Erickson in a trade with Tampa Bay on April 22 and gave him a big contract with a salary cap number of $2 million per season. Two days later Ted Marchibroda named Erickson the No. 1 guy heading into a camp that was still more than two months away.

Needless to say, Harbaugh was a little taken back.

"As soon as they traded for Craig, Ted sat me down and said, 'Jim, we're going to go with Craig'," Harbaugh recalled. "He said, 'We wouldn't have gone out and paid him what we did if we didn't think he was going to start. So we're going to make him the starting quarterback. We still like what you can do. You're a veteran, we know what you can do, we feel comfortable with you in there, but we want to go in a different direction.'

"And then he said, 'We just feel like you didn't have the fourth-quarter production. You just didn't get the job done in the fourth quarter'."

Harbaugh claims that one came out of left field.

"That was a blow," Harbaugh said. "I would just have soon he had taken a two-by-four out from underneath his desk and hit me over the head with it. When someone tells you that you can't get the job done in the fourth quarter, I guess it was just difficult for me to deal with."

Difficult enough that Harbaugh contemplated retirement.

"I didn't know what I wanted to do," he said. "I didn't know if I wanted to keep playing or maybe go into coaching. That was my thought at the time. It was just tough for me to accept."

But accept he did — almost to a fault. As training camp drew nearer, Harbaugh was beginning to look forward to his backup role.

"As the weeks went on I really got a great attitude about it," Harbaugh said. "I tried to look at things in a different way. I just felt that whether I'm a backup or a starter, I'm sure there's a lot of people in the world that in their own jobs would like to be the boss. I'm sure some would like to be the head coach, or would like to be the No. 1 guy but not everybody can. So I just wanted to take pride in my work, and do my job, and have fun with it."

Harbaugh said it was simply a matter of looking at the total picture.

"I just wanted to treat football as the game it is, and it's a fun game," he said. "I don't know how many more years I have to play but I'm going to go out there and have fun while I still have a uniform. Nobody really talked to me in the media and there was no more of 'This team can't win because they have Harbaugh.' I didn't have to deal with that or fight with any critics. It was great.

"I went back to my old style," he said. "If I wanted to run around and scramble around I could do it, and nobody really paid that much attention to me."

Because of his commitment first and foremost to having fun, Harbaugh has fond memories of his preseason '95 experience. Instead of playing with the first unit, Harbaugh found himself battling with a bunch of guys who very likely wouldn't be on the final roster. He admits there were several times he would walk into a huddle and not know everyone's name, but it didn't make it any less fun.

"I really was able to bond with guys like Tyronne Jones and Ben Bronson, and guys like that," he said. "We were just out there winging it and having fun. Guys like Bailey and Stablein, and those guys were having fun playing football, too. They were just basically happy to be out there and I could sense that, and I fed off of that.

"It was the same way I had played in high school, and at Michigan and for most of my career with the Bears," he said. "They were good memories and they were all coming back, and it made football a lot more fun for me."

And that fun was translating into a much more optimistic Jim Harbaugh.

Indianapolis Colts quarterback Jim Harbaugh accepted his role as a backup with a professional attitude. After leading a comeback to force overtime in the first game of the season then sparking a rally to beat the New York Jets, he was given the starter's job. (Photo by Paul Sancya)

"I needed to look at it on the bright side and say, 'Hey, I'm 30 years old and glad I still have a uniform'," he added. "I just wanted to have fun playing football again."

◆ ◆ ◆

At the end of his seven-year stint with the Bears, football was a lot of things for Jim Harbaugh but it wasn't fun.

The Bears had lost their final four games of the season to finish 7-9 under new head coach Dave Wannstedt. Bears fans needed a scapegoat and as the starting quarterback, Harbaugh was the most likely candidate.

But Chicagoans took it way too far. Harbaugh wasn't simply the scapegoat, but more like the sacrificial lamb. Every call on every sports talk show around town seemed to center on Harbaugh and the comments weren't flattering. The stories in the paper placed the blame on his shoulders and everyone wanted a piece of him. No matter what he did, it just wasn't good enough.

Harbaugh found that he couldn't even go out to eat because someone at the booth next to him would recognize him and begin making disparaging comments. It happened in the grocery store, at the bank, pretty much everywhere he went.

The bottom line — Harbaugh had worn out his welcome.

Jack Harbaugh, Jim's dad who is the head football coach at Western Kentucky University, knew things had gotten bad for his son during the 1993 season but he didn't realize how bad. In the season finale, a home game at Soldier Field against Detroit, the elder Harbaugh got to witness it all first hand.

"I've never experienced anything like it and I've been in this business 33 years," Jack said in an interview in the summer of 1994. "First, it was the talk shows with people calling in and venting their frustrations, and that was bad enough. But then to go to the ballgame and listen to the fans, well it was just cruel and brutal. It wasn't the least bit fun."

The quarterback didn't like it but had almost come to accept it.

"I think too many people used me as the scapegoat," Harbaugh said. "It was convenient. As far as the coaching staff, they're not going to blame themselves and the fans aren't going to blame a new coach. They needed someone to blame and I was a convenient target."

Harbaugh said he learned to deal with it.

"As bad as it might have seemed from the outside, to me all the criticism and all the negativity ran off of me like water off a duck's back," he said. "The hard part was the losing, and the frustration that I wasn't playing like I wanted to play."

Harbaugh completed 61.5 percent of his passes for 2,002 yards in '93, but he had just seven touchdown passes and 11 interceptions. He was also sacked 43 times for 210 yards.

"I've always been one who has expected an awful lot out of myself when I'm on the football field. In many ways, I'm a perfectionist," he said. "But when I look back on (1993), after getting some perspective, I don't think anyone could have flourished in that situation. Sometimes you get in a situation where no matter how hard you try it's not going to be good enough.

"It was hard for me to see that then, but it's much easier now."

One of the things that made '93 particularly difficult for Harbaugh was a lack of support from his offensive line. In one three-game stretch, he was sacked 25 times. By contrast, the '93 Colts allowed 29 sacks in 16 games.

"I got into a lot of bad habits because I was trying to get rid of the ball too quickly, because I knew I was about to get hit," Harbaugh said. "That's a bad mentality for a quarterback to get into. If you're constantly thinking about something bad that is about to happen, chances are it will."

Harbaugh wasn't thinking he was about to lose his job in Chicago following the '93 season, but he did.

Wannstedt decided the club needed an upgrade at the quarterback position. He convinced management to go and sign Detroit's Erik Kramer and a few days later made it clear to Harbaugh that the club had decided to go in another direction.

Harbaugh was given his walking papers and immediately began looking into where he might play next. The two teams that interested him the most were the Los Angeles Raiders and Indianapolis. What turned out to be the deciding factor was that with the Raiders he would have been brought in as the backup to Jeff Hostetler, while with the Colts Harbaugh would have a chance to challenge for the starting job.

"All I wanted was a chance," Harbaugh said. "A lot of people figured I was done, that I might get a backup job somewhere but I would never amount to anything again. I figured in Indianapolis I might get a chance to prove some people wrong."

◆   ◆   ◆

Two games into the '95 regular season, Harbaugh's backup role was on the brink of change. He had engineered two incredible comebacks against the Bengals and Jets, and Craig Erickson had faltered in both games.

On the flight home from Newark International Airport following the 27-24 overtime victory over the Jets, Ted Marchibroda summoned Harbaugh to the front of the plane.

It was during this conversation that the expression "Let 'er Rip" was born. It was also during that conversation that Harbaugh almost fought to stay as the backup.

"We were on the plane on the way home, and you've got to remember that game was like one of the highlights of my career, and Ted calls me over and I knew what he was calling me over for," Harbaugh recalled. "He said, 'I don't know which way I'm going to go next week. I'm kind of leaning one way, but it's a tough decision whether to stay with Craig or to put you in because you have the hot hand.' Then he asked me what I thought about that.

"And I said, 'To be honest with you I kind of like this backup role'," Harbaugh said. "My feeling was I kind of liked just coming in and it was fun. It was a good gig. It's all upside. You come in with your team behind and there's only one way to go. I told him I kind of enjoyed that. At the same time, I didn't want to see Craig get benched after only two games but Ted said he wanted to think about it a little bit more."

About half an hour later, Marchibroda called for Harbaugh again.

"He said, 'I'm going to go with you next week, but I just want you to keep the same frame of mind that you have as a backup.

"Just go out there and let 'er rip'."

Harbaugh's genuine dilemma was that in consciously deciding to make the most of his situation, whether as the starter or as the backup, he had come to totally support Erickson.

"Craig was the No. 1 quarterback and I wanted to support him," Harbaugh said. "I played with plenty of backup quarterbacks who were always trying to get your job, always maybe undercutting you to your other teammates or to the press or whatever. I never wanted to do that. I wanted to make Craig as comfortable as he could be and encourage him to do the best he could do.

"I was hoping that he would have a great year and hoping that he would do well," Harbaugh said. "I remember being in the Cincinnati and the Jets games and hoping that he would pull it out, hoping that we would win and he'd have a great game. I was right there behind him."

Where some backups might wish the worst for the guy ahead of him, Harbaugh said that was never the case. And he believes Erickson felt the same way when the roles were reversed.

"Never once did I hope he would throw an interception so I would get a chance to play," Harbaugh said. "That was never the way I was thinking. There were even times early when Ted would look at me and I'd say, 'Craig is doing fine, it's not his fault' or 'Just let him go, he'll be fine.'

"I really wanted him to succeed."

But things didn't work out for Erickson. When Marchibroda opted to go with Harbaugh in the third game of the season, it was a decision that would last the whole year. Paul Justin would get a start at New Orleans and Erickson would start against Jacksonville, but both times it was because Harbaugh was nursing a nagging injury.

As for Harbaugh's numbers there was simply no way to get him out of the lineup. By season's end, he had thrown for 2,575 yards with 17 touchdowns and just five interceptions. His quarterback rating of 100.7 was tops in the NFL. He also rushed for 235 yards on 52 carries.

Interestingly, he had an answer for Marchibroda's claim of lack of fourth-quarter production as well in '95. In the fourth period, he ranked second in the NFL, completing 60.7 percent of his passes for 916 yards with seven touchdowns and just one interception.

His 100.7 QB rating marked only the 21st time a quarterback had eclipsed the 100-point rating barrier in NFL history. The only other Colt to do it was Bert Jones at 102.5 in 1976.

The crowning achievement for Harbaugh was when he was named to his first Pro Bowl played in Hawaii in February.

He said a big reason for his success was that he always believed in himself, even when many others had given up on his abilities.

Let 'er Rip

Jim Harbaugh went back to playing the way he liked to play after being named the backup quarterback. His ability to run or pass made him a dangerous offensive weapon coming off the bench. (Photo by Paul Sancya)

"I always believed in myself but it took me a while to identify my style," Harbaugh said. "I'll never look as fluid as Joe Montana or Dan Marino. I used to try and copy Montana. I'd be thinking I was starting to look like him and I'd look at it on film and it was me again.

"I don't have the big arm like Marino or Troy Aikman," he said. "I don't have the ability to read defenses like Steve Young. I can't scramble like John Elway. I have a style all my own and it's ugly.

"But I think I proved this year that you can be ugly but still be effective."

With his late-game heroics and the fact he led the Colts to three fourth-quarter come-from-behind victories, Harbaugh earned the nickname of "Captain Comeback." Asked once what he thought of the name, Harbaugh broke into an ear-to-ear grin.

"That's fine," he said. "You can call me anything you like because after all the things I was called in Chicago, there's no way it could be any worse."

Harbaugh said when the Colts defeated St. Louis, Miami and San Francisco in an early-October run in 1995, someone called him "Mr. October."

"When I was asked what I thought of that I said, 'Mr. October' is just fine with me," Harbaugh said. "When I was in Chicago, they called me, 'Miss October'."

◆ ◆ ◆

The day Jim Harbaugh was drafted in the first round by the Chicago Bears he was sick in bed with a 103 temperature. To make matters worse, he had the chicken pox.

"The Bears had never talked to me and I really thought I was going to be taken by Green Bay with the fourth pick of the second round," Harbaugh said. "The Bears thing came out of the blue.

"I was just watching the draft and right before the Bears were to pick, the phone rang and it was Michael McCaskey calling," Harbaugh recalls. "He said they were going to take me and did I want to come there, and I said 'Sure.' Then they called back about a half-hour later and said they wanted me to fly to Chicago, and I told them I couldn't because I had a 103 fever and the chicken pox. It wasn't good, it wasn't pretty, I mean I was totally broken out all over my face."

But as Harbaugh tells the story, the Bears told him not to worry about it, that they just wanted him to come in and meet the coaches so everyone could put a face with the name. But Harbaugh wasn't excited about having his chicken-pox face permanently engraved in their memories.

"I went up there that night, and they ended up having a press conference, and I had to go on three television stations live before the night was over," he said. "I'm sure everyone in Chicago thought I had the worst acne they'd ever seen.

"I remember meeting with Ditka and I became aware of the fact that Ditka didn't really want me there, at least not with that first pick," Harbaugh said. "I think that was Bill Tobin and Mr. McCaskey's idea. So I was already right in the middle of something before I ever started there.

"Then I come strolling in about 15 pounds lighter than they thought and all broken out in chicken pox," he added. "It wasn't a good start."

Things improved between Harbaugh and Ditka, at least for a while.

"Coach Ditka came to appreciate me and he was glad they had picked me," Harbaugh said. "And we had a great relationship — right up until the audible. But then we have a great relationship now, which is just as good."

When many people think of Harbaugh with the Bears, it's the infamous audible against the Vikings that comes to mind. It was 1992 and the Bears were leading Minnesota 20-0 in the Metrodome and Harbaugh had been totally on his game.

"Ditka called a deep pass and I had been coached that week that if I got a certain coverage to audible," Harbaugh said. "And it was kind of a gray area because it was 'If you see this look, you can audible to this play.' And that was what I was thinking. Anyway, our receiver, Neal Anderson didn't hear the audible. He ran a streak route.

Let 'er Rip

I was throwing a hitch route and all of a sudden Todd Scott was sitting there waiting for it and he returned it for a touchdown.

"I came over to the sideline and just got laid into, just like everyone has seen on that replay a million times," Harbaugh added. "To make a long story short we go on to lose the game and that was that."

Harbaugh re-learned a valuable lesson that day.

"It's just one of those things in football. If you make an audible you need to be right about it. It needs to work. If it doesn't work then it's a bad audible and you're going to be held accountable."

From 1987-93, Harbaugh put up some big numbers in Chicago. When he left following the '93 season he held Bears' career records for completions (1,023), attempts (1,759), completion percentage (58.2), interception percentage (3.18) and consecutive passes without an interception (173). He was also second in total yards passing with 11,567. His career record was 35-30.

When he thinks back at how low he was in '93 and then the success attained in the '95 season, Harbaugh can hardly believe it all happened in just a two-year span.

"I never would have believed it," he said. "Maybe if I had a genie, or if I had been granted that one wish, this would have been something I would have wished for. To go from constantly getting booed and criticized to everybody patting you on the back and telling you how great you are, it's like the antithesis of that whole situation in Chicago."

And while he was enjoying the good times following the '95 season, he was happy in the fact he would never forget how he felt in '93.

"I think I'm thankful for having had those bad times because, put it this way, my head will never swell," he said. "That will always keep me humble to know that everything is so fleeting. You can have money, you can have fame, but none of that lasts very long. People can be cheering you one day and booing you the next.

"Since I've already seen that happen, and because I know what that's like, I appreciate what I have now," Harbaugh said. "I look back on those hard times as being a blessing, because now I know both sides of the equation."

That reality hit home with Harbaugh following the 1995 season, when he made his first trip to the Pro Bowl in Hawaii. He remembers having a conversation with San Francisco quarterback Steve Young.

"Steve came up to me and congratulated me on having such a great season, and I said 'Thanks Steve and gosh you had a great year yourself. Congratulations'," Harbaugh said. "And he was like 'Oh, I don't know.' And I said 'What do you mean? You had a great year. Personally you battled back from injury and got your team in the playoffs' and all this and that.

"And he said, 'Well Jim, if we don't go to the Super Bowl, it's just not a good year. And I get compared to Montana all the time. You'll find out, you'll see how it is next year. Just wait until your rating dips below 100 and everybody is saying where's the old Harbaugh?"

Having seen both sides of midnight in the NFL, however, Harbaugh believes he'll be ready for whatever happens.

"I would like to think I'll be able to hold my head high no matter what happens," he said. "Hopefully things will continue on a good note, but if they don't I'm just going to have to deal with it."

His exposure to both sides of life in the NFL can also be traced to his relationships with the coaches he's played for during his career.

In his college and pro careers, Harbaugh has played for some interesting head coaches including Bo Schembechler at Michigan, Ditka and Wannstedt at Chicago, Ted Marchibroda for two seasons in Indianapolis and currently Lindy Infante beginning in 1996.

"With Bo and Ditka, I knew where they were coming from," Harbaugh said. "They would yell more, but that's how they got their point across. That was their coaching style. But I also had great relationships with both of those guys because I knew what they wanted was in the best interest of the team. I always sensed that they wanted me to do well and they wanted the team to do well.

"Ditka and Bo were very honest, very straight forward and they were going to tell you exactly how they feel," Harbaugh said. "Sometimes it's good, sometimes it's not, but they're going to tell you how they feel. Ted is the same way, he's exactly the same way. He'll tell you what's on his mind. He has a little different approach as to how he gets the message across to you but the message is the same. And Lindy is a person who I've always had the greatest amount of respect for, too."

The mention of Wannstedt, however, was almost like hitting a nerve with the veteran quarterback.

"I didn't leave (Chicago) with the feeling that Wannstedt was honest," Harbaugh said. "He could be telling you one thing and be thinking something else. I saw it with me and I saw it with other players. So I don't have as much respect for Dave Wannstedt as I do for the other guys.

"I would much prefer to play for Ditka, Bo, Ted or Lindy than to play for Dave Wannstedt," he said. "I couldn't play for Dave Wannstedt anymore because I lost that respect. I could never again believe what he was saying. There's just no comparison."

◆   ◆   ◆

With two games to play in the 1995 season and the Colts sitting at 8-6, Harbaugh became aware of a bonus clause in his contract that would enable him to get a significant bonus if the team won 10 games.

He relayed that point to his offensive linemen and told them if they won the final two games, he would buy them all Rolex watches.

As it turned out, they split the last two, but since the club enjoyed so much success in the playoffs, Harbaugh decided to buy the watches anyway as a token of his appreciation. The final bill for the 12 watches — he even gave them to the practice squad players — came to more than $30,000.

It was the second time he had bought Rolex's for his linemen, the other time coming in the early 1990s in Chicago.

Let 'er Rip

Jim Harbaugh bolts through an opening in the Kansas City line during the Colts' 10-7 victory over the Chiefs in the AFC playoffs. (Photo by Paul Sancya)

"It's kind of funny, too, because Will (Wolford) and Joe (Staysniak) and maybe Kirk (Lowdermilk), and other guys I'm not sure if they're going to be here (in 1996) or not," Harbaugh laughed. "It was like I bought a Rolex for them and now they're all gone.

"But the good thing is all the guys I bought Rolex's for in Chicago, they're starting to come back now. I see Troy Auzenne is wearing his, and Jay Leeuwenberg still has his. So, it wasn't too bad of an investment.

"Who knows, maybe I'll play with Will again sometime."

The saying "Art imitates life" may have been written with Jim Harbaugh in mind. When things went bad in Chicago for Harbaugh professionally, it spilled over into his personal life. His girlfriend broke up with him, his dog, Wrigley, got sick and nearly died, and his future in professional football was very much in doubt.

Eighteen months later he had gotten back together with his girlfriend and they were engaged to be married, his dog had made a full recovery, and his future with the Colts was bright as he led them down the stretch toward the AFC title game.

"My life was like a country western song," Harbaugh said.

As good as Harbaugh's life has turned out in regards to football, he'll be the first to admit that things couldn't be better personally.

He said it has gotten to the point that when people come up to him and say 'Congratulations', he has to stop and think of which one of many things he was being congratulated for. Was it his February 1995 marriage to longtime sweetheart Miah Burke? Was it his selection to the Pro Bowl following the '95 season? Was it the Colts' success in the playoffs? Was it his wife's recent news that a child was on the way with a due date of late September?

"I can't imagine things being any better," Harbaugh said. "I just feel so blessed with all of the good things happening in my life. I just want things to continue like this always but you know that it usually doesn't work out that way."

A new baby on the way is something which is particularly exciting for Harbaugh. He loves children and for the past five years has been a father figure for Miah's son Jay from a previous marriage. Jay, now 6, looks up to Jim as the only father he's ever known.

"He's called me dad for a while now," Harbaugh said. "I don't know if that was good or bad. Still, my relationship with Jay is that he's a son to me and I'm a dad to him. That's worked out great. He didn't have a dad before and now he does. I didn't have a son before and now I do. What more could two people ask for?

"I feel like there's not many things I'm really good at, but I feel I'm really good at being a dad," he said. "For some reason I just have infinite patience with kids. And I love that role. I just love being around kids."

The fact that Harbaugh came from a very loving home is evident in everything he does. He makes mention of his upbringing often in casual conversation, and says he hopes to be for his children what his parents were to him.

"I come from great, great parents who just always gave us love and were always there for us," he said. "I know my parents were always around when I was growing up and always interested in what the kids were doing. That's not easy these days. I think about it even with Jay. Sometimes we'll want to go on vacation as a family but it's tough to do. Our lives are just too fast-moving.

"And the kids are the same way, if not more so," he added. "You've got to drop them off at this soccer game or take them to gymnastics. It's always something. But I wouldn't want it any other way. I feel blessed."

Harbaugh hopes he can always imitate the role models his parents were for him.

"As a parent, I just want to be like my parents were to me," he said. "With Jay, I just try to take him every day and kiss him on the face, and hug him, and tell him that I love him. Because I know there will come a time when he won't want me kissing him and hugging him and telling him that. I believe you can't tell someone too many times how much you love them."

Let 'er Rip

♦ ♦ ♦

As he came off the field following the 35-20 wildcard playoff victory over San Diego in early January, Harbaugh was overflowing with emotion. He felt tremendous joy and thankfulness for the position he had been in and what both he and his teammates had accomplished.

When an NBC crew shoved a camera in front of his face and asked him how he felt, Harbaugh's emotions spewed forth in millions of homes coast-to-coast.

"They asked me how did I feel, and all those emotions just came pouring out," Harbaugh said. "I said I just wanted to thank God, thank Jesus Christ my Lord and Savior for this blessing. That's what came out. It was nothing that was planned. I never said to myself that if we were to win I was going to get this message out. It was nothing like that at all. I was just filled with the Holy Spirit and with all of that joy and it just came out."

What Harbaugh wasn't prepared for were the hundreds of cards and letters he would receive in response to that one shining moment. People wrote him and said that they were having a bad day or a bad year, but what he said after that game had just lifted them out of their doldrums. In a 60-second interview on national television, Harbaugh felt as if he had made a tremendous difference.

"That was overwhelming," he said. "The response I got was unbelievable. At the same time it was very encouraging to me. It was nice to let it all out and feel that people were right there with me in those feelings."

Harbaugh traces his personal relationship with Jesus Christ to August of 1991. "That's when I turned my life over to Christ," Harbaugh says. "It just didn't happen overnight."

He says it really blossomed in Chicago in 1993, when Bears fans were making life miserable for both he and his family.

"Every time I would walk on the field I would get booed," he said. "Every time they would say my name on the loudspeaker I would get booed. I'd come home from the game and I could tell my mom had been crying because of what people were saying in the stands. I'd hear that dad almost got in a fight in the stands today because some guy was saying something about me and they almost went to blows.

"You feel bad that your family is put through that, and I felt bad that I was put through that, too," he said. "All the boos every time you turn around, and having to listen to everything that is said about you or written about you. But I think it was because of my relationship with Christ that I was able to put that all in perspective."

Had he not had the inner strength which he said he found in God to get him through '93, Harbaugh honestly doesn't know how he would have handled it.

"It probably would have devastated me to the point where I wouldn't have been able to function," Harbaugh said. "Who knows what would have happened to me? My life could have been over. Who knows what I would have done? It would have been devastating. But because I had a relationship with Christ, I knew it was more important what God thinks of you than what the cheering masses think."

The playoffs hadn't even come to an end and the letters were flooding into the *Indianapolis Star* and *News*. One after another, someone was extolling the character of Jim Harbaugh.

"Jim Harbaugh is everything that is good about professional sports," read one letter. Another said that Harbaugh "was a terrific role model for the young people of today." One other said that "there was no better representative for the people of Indianapolis on a national level than Jim Harbaugh."

Before long, Harbaugh's face graced the cover of *Indianapolis Monthly* magazine, in its annual "Best of Indianapolis" issue.

Like it or not, Harbaugh had become an instant role model to the young people of Indianapolis, as well as throughout the country.

Fortunately, Harbaugh was comfortable with the role.

"I feel like we all should be role models by the way we live," Harbaugh said. "And I strive for that, and unfortunately I fail every day from where I want to be. But it's just all about trying to do the best you can.

"But anybody who thinks that because of my success on the football field that I'm somehow any different than anybody else, I'm not," he said. "I'm just a person who makes a lot of mistakes just like anybody else, and who constantly strives to be better."

Being a role model comes naturally for Harbaugh. Being put on a pedestal, however, is something else entirely.

"I don't think any human being should be put up on a pedestal," he said. "The only person that should be put up on a pedestal is God. He's the only one who walked around this earth without making any mistakes, without any sins."

Harbaugh says there's times when kids will ask him for autographs, and while he signs, say something like, "Gosh, Mr. Harbaugh I want to be just like you."

When that happens, Harbaugh says he'll smile, continue to sign, and then look down and say, "You're selling yourself short. You're selling yourself way short. You can try to be like me, but then try to be something even better."

10

Giant Killers

When the 1995 schedule was released in May, a formula seemed to exist by which the Colts could win nine or 10 games and have a solid shot at making the AFC playoffs.

The "smart" thinking seemed to suggest the Colts needed to get out of the gate at least 3-1 and possibly 4-0. Games against Cincinnati and the New York Jets appeared to be must-win matchups, while Buffalo on the road would be tough and it was too early to get a clear gauge on St. Louis.

It was imperative, though, that the Colts have early success. That's because a three-game stretch loomed early in the season that included back-to-back-to-back games with Miami on the road, San Francisco at home and Oakland on the road.

That same "smart" thinking was the Colts needed to find a way to come out of that trio of games with at least one victory. But by the time the Murderer's Row stretch arrived, Goliath had grown in size and stature.

Instead of a rugged three-game stretch to contend with, the Colts would have to play the role of giant killer four times. Suddenly, the St. Louis game was big because the Rams had opened 4-0 and had yet to turn the ball over in the first 16 quarters of the season. The Rams were no longer the lambs of season's past and at 1-2 the Colts had their work cut out for them.

The upcoming stretch now was against opponents with a combined late September record of 13-2. The writing was on the wall for the Colts and a definite downside existed. Now, if the Colts didn't win at least two of those games, they would be 2-5 at best and Ted Marchibroda's job would be very much in jeopardy.

Yet as the Colts prepared for the Oct. 1 matchup with St. Louis, Marchibroda was quietly confident. He believed his club had shown signs of life in the first three games and the future was still bright.

"The pressure to win is always on in this league," Marchibroda told *Indianapolis News* sports editor Wayne Fuson a few days before the Rams game. "I know you have to win. But I really think we're ready now to play our best football. It's a long season ahead ... We need some success.

Marshall Faulk proved his worth against St. Louis. He rushed for 177 yards, scored two touchdowns and caught five passes for 45 yards. (Photo by Paul Sancya)

"After the Buffalo game you should have seen how hurt the players were," he added. "When they worked as hard as they had, it was really tough to lose one like that. We went into that game expecting to win."

One thing that made the game with the Rams in the RCA Dome a strange one was that the 1-2 Colts were favored by 2½ points to beat 4-0 St. Louis. Apparently the oddsmakers didn't believe the Rams were that good or the Colts were that bad.

"I think this is an indication that people believe we have enough talent on this football team to be competitive," Marchibroda said. "And since I know that we believe that, I just hope the oddsmakers are right."

In an article in the *Indianapolis Star* the day of the game, Jim Harbaugh said the upcoming schedule put the Colts in a unique position.

"This is a challenge and an opportunity for the Indianapolis Colts to make a statement," he said. "We have a chance to show that we can play against the best teams the NFL has to offer."

Tackle Will Wolford basically said it was time to put up or shut up.

"We're going to find out what kind of team we have," he said. "Ever since we started in July or even before that, we've been thinking we had a chance to be a pretty good football team. Over the next few weeks, we're going to find out."

Driving to the RCA Dome the first day of October, it was as if the Cleveland Browns had come to town instead of St. Louis.

Over the years, home games against the Browns had become quite troubling to Colts players and management. That's because with routinely 15,000 or so available seats to be had at every game, die-hard Cleveland supporters would make the five-hour trek south to cheer on their beloved Browns. At the same time, a large number of "Browns Backers" resided in Central Indiana and would always crawl out of the woodwork for a game in the Dome.

With St. Louis off to a 4-0 start and Rams fans just getting acquainted with their new team, fans came over by the thousands to show their support and cheer them on to what was being looked at as an easy fifth victory of the season. An estimated throng of more than 12,000 Rams fans packed the RCA Dome, wearing their brand new, just-out-of-the-plastic blue and gold paraphernalia, and making the home field atmosphere seem much more St. Louis friendly.

If you closed your eyes, you would have bet the Browns were in town. There was no sea of orange, no one wearing dog masks and no one barking in the end zones. Other than that, it was a Browns-like scene in Indianapolis. They took over the food court in Union Station. They mulled around in the new Circle Centre Mall. And they told anyone who would listen about their premature Super Bowl plans.

And it only took one play in the game for Rams players to make themselves feel at home as well. On the first play from scrimmage, quarterback Chris Miller went deep down the right sideline and hit Isaac Bruce for 72 yards to the Colts' 5. Two plays later, Miller hit Bruce from 4 yards out for a touchdown and St. Louis had a quick 7-0 lead with 13:13 to play in the first quarter.

It was a rather inauspicious start for the boys in horseshoes.

But then Marshall Faulk took over.

Ever since the Colts made Faulk the second selection overall in the 1994 draft, they had dreamed about a day like this one. A day when the fleet-footed back would take over a game ala Emmitt Smith or Barry Sanders. A day when the holes were all there and Faulk was finding every one of them. A day when no one would be able to stop him.

October 1 was that day and the Rams were simply reduced to the role of innocent bystanders.

In the first three games of the season, Faulk had rushed for 177 yards and three touchdowns.

Against the Rams he duplicated the feat — in a three-hour time span. The play of the day was the sprint draw and the St. Louis defense acted as if it had never seen it executed before. The Rams defense came into the game allowing just 71 yards rushing per game, but Faulk beat that number by more than 100 yards by himself. As a team, the Colts rushed for 235 yards.

Final score: Indianapolis 21, St. Louis 18.

Faulk had touchdown runs of 32 and 33 yards, and gained 125 yards in the first half alone.

Offensive guard Joe Staysniak explained the effectiveness of the sprint draw.

"The sprint draw is used to make a defense's enthusiasm work against them," Staysniak told *Indianapolis Star* columnist Robin Miller. "Jim (Harbaugh) has the ball for quite a while and the Rams are licking their chops as they close in on him.

"We get in behind them and push 'em wide and, at the last second, Jim makes a quick handoff to Marshall," he added. "And everyone knows Marshall only needs a little bit of daylight."

Along with the career-high 177 yards rushing, Faulk also caught five passes for 45 yards giving him 222 all-purpose yards.

"That's the kind of game we knew we would one day see when we drafted him two years ago," Marchibroda said. "He has all the tools to be one of the great ones and that's what the fans in attendance saw today."

Speaking of the crowd — there were more than 58,000 in attendance — Colts fans seemed to take the St. Louis crowd flavor almost as a personal affront. Many people who have attended every Colts game in the Dome since 1984 said it was the loudest they have ever heard Colts fans yell. (They would eventually change their minds two weeks later against San Francisco).

As for the Rams fans, who had quieted down considerably by game's end, Faulk said he didn't think they were really that much of a factor.

"This is the Colts' stadium, and no visiting fans can change that," Faulk said. "After all, one end zone has the Colts' name on it and the other reads 'Indianapolis.' They can't bring enough fans to change that."

◆   ◆   ◆

Everything wasn't totally positive for the Colts coming out of the St. Louis game. Bill Tobin's patience with kicker Mike Cofer finally ended, and the veteran was released after missing a 39-yard attempt against the Rams.

After making 11 of 14 field goals in the preseason, and then hitting his first two in the regular season, Cofer had proceeded to miss seven of his next nine attempts. Five of those misses were from within 42 yards, including four under 39 yards.

"It was time," Tobin said. "He went into a slump where he lost total confidence in himself. With that he lost the rest of us. We couldn't afford to allow his slump to pull the rest of the team down and that's what was happening."

Duke Tumatoe, in his weekly version of Lord Help Our Colts, viewed Cofer's demise like this:

> *Mike Cofer lost his job*
> *Do you think that's kind of mean?*
> *Mike, if the Colts wanted an erratic kicker*
> *They would have held on to Dean*
> *Lord help our Colts. Lord Help our Colts.*

The next day, the Tuesday following the St. Louis game, the Colts held a kicking tryout and former Jets kicker Cary Blanchard was the winner. Blanchard kicked for the Jets in 1992 and '93 but was out of work in '94. He had many tryout stops prior to landing the job with the Colts, and heard plenty of flattering remarks, but was handed no contract offers.

"I was just happy to get it behind me," Blanchard would say later. "The whole process was driving my wife crazy and I was getting pretty frustrated, too. This was a great opportunity for me and I just wanted to go out and make the best of it."

As it turned out, Blanchard would waste very little time getting in the Colts' good graces. The following week against Miami, he would split the uprights from 27 yards away in overtime to give the Colts a most improbable 27-24 victory over the Dolphins at Joe Robbie Stadium.

It wasn't that surprising that Blanchard was the hero, but rather that he ever had a chance for heroics in the first place. The Colts trailed 24-3 at halftime and appeared to only have a faint pulse. Four weeks before, the Colts had rallied from 21 down to beat the New York Jets, but this wasn't the Jets. This was the Miami Dolphins, a team many expected to be a Super Bowl contender before the 1995 season would come to an end.

But the Dolphins were far from magical on this day, and the Colts were as close to perfect over the final two quarters and overtime as an NFL team could be.

This was supposed to have been a day reserved for Dolphins quarterback Dan Marino. Early in the game, Marino broke Fran Tarkenton's NFL record for completions in a game, and the veteran QB appeared in sync. But Captain Comeback had other ideas.

Jim Harbaugh threw three second-half touchdown passes and did very little wrong. He completed 20 of 24 passes for 278 yards in the second half. Overall, his numbers were 25 of 33 for 319 yards. He would later be recognized as Miller Lite's NFL Player of the Week.

Said Duke Tumatoe the following Wednesday:

> *By halftime I had written the song*
> *But I made my judgement in haste*
> *The Colts and Harbaugh changed my tune*
> *As they laid Miami to waste.*

As good as Harbaugh was, the usually reliable Pete Stoyanovich was equally as bad. The former Indiana University placekicker missed a pair of field goals that could have put the game away. Stoyanovich first missed a "chip shot" 27-yarder wide right with 9:56 to play that could have put the Dolphins on top 27-10. Later he missed a much tougher 49-yarder with 12 seconds to play in regulation that could have ended the Colts' comeback attempt on a sour note.

It was immediately after Stoyanovich missed the gimme that Harbaugh got the Colts within striking range. He directed a six-play, 80-yard touchdown drive that was capped by a 47-yard touchdown pass to Floyd Turner to make it 24-17 with 6:37 remaining.

Following a Dolphins punt, Harbaugh marched the Colts 76 yards in 12 plays for the game-tying score. This time, he hit Aaron Bailey on a 21-yard TD catch, with the young receiver making a diving catch in the right corner of the end zone. Suddenly the score was 24-all with 1:09 to play in regulation — and the sun-baked crowd of 68,471 fans in Joe Robbie Stadium sat in stunned silence.

In overtime, the Colts won the toss and proceeded to march to the Dolphins' 18. Harbaugh was perfect on the drive, completing all five of his passes for 47 yards. From the 18, Marshall Faulk carried the ball twice to get it to the 10 before Ted Marchibroda called for the field-goal unit and Blanchard kicked the game-winner.

Harbaugh said the key for the Colts was remaining focused, despite the 21-point deficit.

"We were told at halftime to go out like we were tied and just work on executing our offense," Harbaugh said. "We did what Ted Marchibroda said and we won."

Linebacker Jeff Herrod summed it up best in a quote in the next day's editions of the *Indianapolis Star*.

"I'm sure everybody counted us out," Herrod said. "I'm sure folks back home turned off the television at halftime and went out and mowed the lawn. I probably would have, too."

Again Duke Tumatoe summed it all up the best in the following week's version of *Lord Help Our Colts*. Actually this version was the more upbeat, "Go Colts" lyrics.

> *Marino set the record*
> *But Harbaugh got the prize*
> *I couldn't believe what was happening*
> *Right before my eyes.*
> *Go Colts. Go Colts. Beat the crap out of the NFL.*
> *The weather was hot and nasty*
> *But the Colts came jamming back*
> *The last drive in the fourth quarter*
> *About gave me a heart attack.*
> *Go Colts. Go Colts. Beat the crap out of San Francisco.*
> *San Francisco is full of sissies.*
> *But their football team is not.*

If the Colts are going to beat them
They're going to have to stay real hot.
Go Colts, Go Colts, Beat the crap out of the NFL.

◆   ◆   ◆

The victory over the unbeaten Rams was a good step, but no one knew just how good St. Louis was going to be.

The win over Miami, especially because it was at Joe Robbie Stadium, was significant but it was still only an AFC team and everyone knew the NFL's power curve was weighted heavily toward the NFC's side of the ledger.

Plus, as *Indianapolis Star* columnist Robin Miller would point out, "in the incredible comeback against 4-0 Miami, the Dolphins got as much credit for flopping as Indy did for fighting back."

It was that respect thing rearing its ugly head once again.

But next came San Francisco, the defending Super Bowl champions, in a game that presented the Colts with an incredible opportunity. A victory over the 49ers, and they would earn instant credibility. The critics could say anything they pleased but the fact of the matter would be they had knocked off the defending world champion.

Steve Young would be there. So would Jerry Rice, George Seifert and the San Francisco Super Bowl gang.

Lay an egg and everyone would say, 'What did you expect? They were playing the 49ers?' or 'See, I told you the Colts hadn't played anybody'. But find a way to win and the public would be forced to sing a different tune.

Later in the season, the Colts would look back at the Oct. 15 matchup with the 49ers and refer to it as the day the franchise grew up.

The growing process was put in fast forward in particular on the 49ers final drive of the first half. Leading 7-6, San Francisco marched to the Colts' 6 where it had a first-and-goal with less than a minute to play.

On the first play, Young tried to run and gained a couple of yards. On second down from the 4, he tried to run again and linebacker Quentin Coryatt stopped him at the 1. The next play, Young was forced to scramble and again Coryatt stopped him and was credited with a sack for no yards with less than 20 seconds showing on the clock. Next a mad scramble ensued as the 49ers, out of timeouts, tried to bring on their field goal team but appeared to be just a second too late.

Just as the clock expired, the officials blew their whistles and after much discussion decided to put two seconds back on the clock. Referee Gary Lane, speaking to an NFL-appointed pool reporter following the game, explained the controversy this way: "There were 17 seconds remaining (following the previous play) which went toward the sideline. There was an extra ball on the field in the secondary. Indianapolis had picked the ball up, I believe from Steve Young, who was near the goal line. Another guy threw off his gloves. We were trying to get the stuff out of there and go get another ball. By the time we got the ball and got it back in, we were delaying the

Let 'er Rip

As disappointed players for the San Francisco 49ers leave the field Indianapolis defender Ray Buchanan jumps for joy after the Colts defeated the defending Super Bowl champions 18-17. (Photo by Paul Sancya)

start of the snap. My head linesman called an official's timeout with two seconds to go. We put two seconds back on and would have wound the clock, but Indianapolis called a subsequent timeout."

The Colts called timeout to figure out what had just transpired. Marchibroda was visibly upset and had to be physically restrained on the sideline. In the meantime, given an extra minute to think about it, Seifert ordered his team to go for a touchdown instead of a field goal, a decision that would eventually come back to haunt him.

Tony McCoy called the decision an insult and said it fired his team up. Safety David Tate inferred that the 49ers simply had no respect for the Colts. Linebacker Jeff Herrod said San Francisco was "throwing it right in our face."

With a capacity crowd at first booing the official's decision to put time back on the clock and now screaming louder than ever before, Young handed the ball off to Derek Loville who tried to get around left end. But Trev Alberts beat the tight end who was trying to block him and forged his way into the San Francisco backfield. That drove Loville farther to the outside where safety Jason Belser slammed him to the ground at the 3-yard line.

"I think we grew up on that series," Belser would say later. "That gave us an incredible amount of confidence and made us feel as if we could play with anybody at any time."

Duke Tumatoe wondered about it, too:

But what was that stuff before halftime
What were the officials doing?
It seemed to me like the Colts almost got
One gigantic screwing.
Lord help our Colts (2 seconds my ass). Lord help our Colts.
Hey, I looked but I couldn't see
Was Homer Simpson the referee?
(I thought it might be a FOX thing) Lord help our Colts.

The Colts went on to win 18-17 on four Cary Blanchard field goals. Trailing 17-15 late in the fourth quarter, Blanchard made a 41-yarder with 2:36 remaining to give the Colts the 18-17 advantage. San Francisco drove down the field but Doug Brien missed a potential game-winning 45-yard field goal with 50 seconds remaining.

The offense on this day was adequate with Harbaugh completing 12 of 18 passes for 175 yards including a 15-yard touchdown pass to rookie Ken Dilger in the third quarter. It was Dilger's first NFL touchdown.

But this game belonged to the Colts' defense. Just ask Steve Young who came to know the Colts up front on a first-name basis. Young was sacked six times, knocked to the turf on numerous other occasions and knocked from the game for one play in the fourth quarter on an incredible hit by rookie defensive tackle Ellis Johnson.

The defense employed a new look in the second half, going with five backs, three down linemen, two linebackers and Alberts who bounced back and forth between the line and a linebacker slot.

"Our coaches said 'Let's cut down what we do and smack them in the face,'" Alberts said. "We didn't think they wanted a war, but that's what we gave them."

With the Colts 4-2 for the first time in their 12-year history in Indianapolis, Ted Marchibroda said he believed his club had finally learned what it took to win in the NFL.

"I think we have crossed that bridge, and now we need to learn how to keep on winning," Marchibroda said. "For the first time since my return to coach the Colts (in 1992) I felt like we entered (the San Francisco game) expecting to win, and we did.

"We have a couple of reminders in our locker room," Marchibroda added. "One is never forget to fight. Another is to play with maximum effort from the starting bell

Let 'er Rip

to the final gun. We have typified that over the last three games, and we have achieved some great things. Not many people thought we would be 4-2 after we opened 1-2, but we have believers within our organization.

"I think we're a team to be reckoned with," he said. "When you've accomplished what we have over the past three games, somebody has to take notice. If they don't that's fine with us. We'll just keep on playing our game. One thing you must realize is that our last two wins came over an eight-time Pro Bowler in Dan Marino and a two-time Pro Bowler and Super Bowl MVP in Steve Young."

Suddenly, the only Goliath that remained standing was the silver and black Oakland Raiders.

Even though the Colts had to travel more than 2,000 miles to the left coast to take on the 5-2 Raiders, the task didn't seem quite so insurmountable following the three-game winning streak.

Then there was the quarterback situation in Oakland. Injured Jeff Hostetler was out, and the ageless, 40-year-old Vince Evans was scheduled to lead the Raiders against the Colts.

Marchibroda warned his team prior to the game about how dangerous backup quarterbacks can be. The Colts had seen it in past seasons from the likes of Washington's Gus Ferrotte, New England's Scott Zolak and Doug Flutie, and New Orleans' John Fourcade.

Colts opponents had seen it recently from Jim Harbaugh.

But still ... Vince Evans? Going into the game he had completed only eight of 18 passes for 143 yards and one touchdown. Over the last two seasons he had thrown a total of 50 passes.

But as the Colts would soon find out, none of what had happened in the past would make any difference to the ageless one. All he did was complete 23 of 35 passes for a career-high 335 yards and a pair of deep touchdown passes to Rocket Ismail as the Raiders brought the Colts back to reality with a 30-17 victory at the Oakland-Alameda Coliseum.

It was a game of big plays — and Oakland made them all.

Evans threw nine completions of 17 yards or more, including 46- and 75-yard touchdown tosses to the Rocket.

The Colts special teams in a word "weren't".

Napoleon Kaufman had an 84-yard kickoff return for a touchdown. Eugene Daniel was flagged for offside on a punt late in the second quarter that gave the Raiders new life with a first down. They would eventually get a field goal by Jeff Jaeger from 28 yards to tie the game at 10-10 at halftime. Ronald Humphrey and Lamont Warren had a mixup on a kickoff return, allowing the ball to hit the ground between them. Humphrey was pinned at the 8 and Oakland was able to cash in on field position. Finally, Ben Bronson had a big fumble on a punt return in the fourth quarter that also led to a Raiders field goal.

"This was a team loss, just as our wins over the past three weeks were achieved as a team," Marchibroda said. "I thought our intensity was fine but we did not make the plays. To win, a team must make the big play on offense and avoid it on defense. We did neither. This loss should be a lesson to us. We know what it takes to win in this league, and we are a good enough team to compete with anyone in this league if we play to our ability. We do not need career efforts from each player to be successful, but we must have solid efforts from every man on the field.

"We will correct our mistakes."

11

Up and Down

After watching the Colts come out of their grueling stretch of the schedule alive and well, many hometown fans expected the remainder of the schedule to be a relative cakewalk.

With a 4-3 record following seven games, the "smart" thinking once again was that there was no reason the Colts couldn't finish 11-5, with 10-6 being almost a gimme.

The reasoning had merit. Five of the final nine games were at home including four against AFC Eastern Division foes New York, Buffalo, New England and Miami. At the very least the Colts should beat New York and New England, and a split against the other two would mean a 3-1 home mark against the division. The fifth home game was against San Diego, who had gone to the Super Bowl the year before, but was struggling through an up-and-down season in 1995.

It was the road games, though, that really gave the Colts reason for optimism. Of the four road opponents the toughest game looked to be against New England in Foxboro, an opposing stadium that had given the Colts fits through the years. The other three games — against Carolina, Jacksonville and a very average New Orleans team — all appeared to be very winnable.

Ted Marchibroda, for one, did not expect his team to have a letdown. He believed it was all part of the maturation process he had seen the club undergo since he first returned to coach the Colts in 1992.

"I would be very surprised," Marchibroda said in a story in the *Indianapolis Star*, when asked if he was concerned about a letdown. "You can talk all you want about how you have to approach these games, but you have to go through the experience. You have to live the trials and tribulations before you fully realize what it takes to have a winning team."

As they approached the halfway mark in the season, the Colts' first test would come from a New York Jets team that was riding a high. The week before, after dropping four games in a row, the Jets had stunned Miami 17-16. The victory improved their record to 2-6 but the Jets saw a victory over the Colts as being a major step toward credibility.

The Colts on the other hand, had to make sure it didn't happen. Jim Harbaugh said he believed the game was particularly tough because of the parity in the NFL.

"Everybody is tough and everybody is capable of beating everyone else," Harbaugh said. "More so this year than any year I can think of. It's not a cliche anymore.

"We have to realize there are no homecoming games in this league."

If they didn't realize it before, it didn't take the Colts long to see that the rematch with the Jets was not going to be any easier than the first game of the season when they had to rally from a 21-point deficit to win in overtime.

With the scored tied 3-3 with less than five minutes to play in the first half, Harbaugh put the Colts in the end zone on a 4-yard run around the left side. Unfortunately, as he dove for the cone, Harbaugh would suffer a pulled groin that would nag him in the weeks to come. He would play sparingly in the second half, with Craig Erickson leading the team.

The big play for the Colts came on the final play of the first half with Jets quarterback Bubby Brister attempting to tie the score with a pass toward the end zone intended for rookie Wayne Chrebet.

But veteran Eugene Daniel stepped in front of the pass and raced 97 yards down the sideline to give the Colts a 17-3 advantage. It was the longest interception return for a touchdown in Colts history and the 34-year-old Daniel was feeling it afterwards.

"I don't know if I could have run another yard," Daniel said in an article in the *Indianapolis Star*.

Instead of a 10-10 tie, the Colts led by 14 and would eventually hang on to win 17-10.

But this victory belonged to the defense. The Colts' offense managed just 114 yards, the lowest total ever in a victory. In the second half they managed just 3 net yards.

Duke Tumatoe's version of *Lord Help Our Colts* the next week came with a different refrain. It went like this:

> *Jimmy, Jimmy, Jimmy, Jimmy Harbaugh pulled his groin.*
>
> *Jimmy, Jimmy, Jimmy, Jimmy Harbaugh pulled his groin.*
>
> *He pulled his groin.*
>
> *It hurt so much.*
>
> *He pulled his groin.*
>
> *You must not touch.*
>
> *Jimmy, Jimmy, Jimmy, Jimmy Harbaugh pulled his groin.*
>
> *Jimmy, Jimmy, Jimmy, Jimmy Harbaugh pulled his groin.*
>
> *That wacky Bubby Brister.*
>
> *Threw a pass right to Eugene.*
>
> *The longest intercepted touchdown*
>
> *The Colts have ever seen.*

However, Jimmy, Jimmy, Jimmy, Jimmy Harbaugh pulled his groin.
Jimmy, Jimmy, Jimmy, Jimmy Harbaugh pulled his groin.
The Colts are tied for first.
This week they play Buffalo.
The Colts are in deep trouble.
If Jimmy's groin cannot go.

◆   ◆   ◆

As the 5-3 Colts prepared for a first-place battle with Buffalo in the RCA Dome, there was plenty of reason for optimism from the boys in blue.

First, quarterback Jim Harbaugh practiced during the week and it appeared he was going to play against the Bills, a team he had played well against in his first three meetings as a Colt.

Next, the Colts had been playing well at home with consecutive victories over St. Louis, San Francisco and New York.

Beyond that, the Colts had experienced moderate success against the Bills in recent years. After losing 18 of 25 games to Buffalo from 1981-93, the Colts had won two of the last three meetings and three of the last six.

Add to all of that the fact that running back Thurman Thomas and wide receiver Andre Reed were not expected to play for the Bills, and it appeared as if the Colts had a solid opportunity to head to New Orleans the following week with a 6-3 record.

"For a lot of us it was the first time in a long time that we had experienced a lot of success," said veteran linebacker Jeff Herrod, who was drafted by the Colts in 1988. "It was almost one of those cases where you had to teach yourself how to win and how to go into games expecting to have a chance at winning. In the past the mentality was always to keep in a game and have a chance to win late.

"With this team it was different," he said. "We were going into games expecting to win. It was like a completely new concept."

As good as the Colts were feeling about themselves, reality came like a slap in the face as Buffalo posted a 16-10 victory before just under 60,000 in the Dome.

Nothing was more frustrating for Marchibroda and his staff than to lose games that an opponent was basically dangling in front of you like a carrot. And this was one of those games. After tying the game at 7 midway through the first quarter on a 4-yard run by Marshall Faulk, the Colts self-destructed. Four subsequent possessions inside the Bills' 25-yard line netted only three points.

"You can't win in this league when you have numbers like that put up on the slate with your name next to them," Marchibroda said. "This was a tremendous opportunity that we somehow let slip by. Both of our games with Buffalo this season are games that we will look back at in December and wish we had found a way to get at least one of them in the win column."

The missed opportunities were the rule rather than the exception.

For example, the Colts had a second-and-2 at the Buffalo 3 late in the third quarter. Three times they gave the ball to Faulk and each time the Bills stuffed him. Indianapolis would turn the ball over on downs and not get any points out of the drive.

Marchibroda defended his decision to keep the ball in Faulk's hands.

"When you need a yard and you have a talent like that in the backfield you should be able to find a way to get into the end zone," Marchibroda said. "We didn't this time but there will be other times."

The game was also interesting from a quarterback perspective. Harbaugh started but left late in the first quarter after aggravating his groin injury. Paul Justin came on in relief but he left in the second quarter with a bruised right shoulder after a nasty — but clean — hit by Bills linebacker Bryce Paup.

Erickson came in late in the second and played the remainder of the game. He completed nine of 15 passes for 122 yards with no touchdowns or interceptions.

Tumatoe saw it this way the following week on the *Bob & Tom Show* in Indianapolis:

> *Jimmy, Jimmy, Jimmy, Jimmy Harbaugh pulled his groin.*
> *Jimmy, Jimmy, Jimmy, Jimmy Harbaugh pulled his groin.*
> *Jimmy played.*
> *But not too long.*
> *Paul Justin came in.*
> *And now his head feels like a gong.*
> *Jimmy, Jimmy, Jimmy, Jimmy Harbaugh pulled his groin.*
> *Jimmy, Jimmy, Jimmy, Jimmy Harbaugh pulled his groin.*
> *Craig Erickson.*
> *Had his chance to play.*
> *He tried to throw completions*
> *But the ground got in the way.*

Next up was New Orleans, a game the Colts felt they should win. The Saints were struggling on the season, but the equalizer appeared to be the fact that Harbaugh was not going to be able to start. Justin started in his place, and completed 10 of 13 for 90 yards but simply couldn't get the offense going.

The game was a struggle from the get go, and New Orleans led 14-7 when Harbaugh limped into the game to try to rally his teammates. All he did was march the Colts 73 yards in five plays to tie the game at 14-14, with Roosevelt Potts coming down on the receiving end of a 40-yard TD pass with 13:14 to play in the game.

The Saints went ahead with 6:33 remaining on a 25-yard field goal by Doug Brien, but Harbaugh brought the Colts storming back. He took them 57 yards in 11 plays.

In fact, when he hit Brian Stablein on an 18-yard pass to the Saints' 1 with 13 seconds to play it appeared as if Captain Comeback had done it again. But there was another costly flag on the play. Harbaugh had been penalized for stepping over the line as he threw the pass and the ball came back to the 24.

Quentin Coryatt wraps ups a New Orleans receiver in a game the Colts felt they should have won. The Saints held on for a 17-14 victory. (Photo by Paul Sancya)

On the next play, Cary Blanchard tried to put the game into overtime with a 41-yard field goal attempt, but the kick sailed wide left with eight seconds remaining.

Final Score: New Orleans 17, Indianapolis 14.

Suddenly, the giant-killing Colts were 5-5 and the future did not appear nearly as bright.

Ted Marchibroda, as was his custom during his four-year stint in Indianapolis, attempted to accentuate the positive in his postgame remarks.

"We're still in the thick of this thing," Marchibroda said after watching his team drop back-to-back games for the first time that season. "Anytime you play as hard as we did ... there is no shame in losing."

Marshall Faulk had a big game for the Colts in his first return to New Orleans since when he lived there in high school. Faulk rushed for 98 yards on 17 carries and scored one touchdown. He had another 30-yard run negated by a holding penalty, on a call that was clearly made long after Faulk had burst through the line of scrimmage.

Another mysterious call that went against the Colts was a taunting foul against Roosevelt Potts after he scored the fourth-quarter touchdown that tied the game at 14-all. It appeared as if Potts made a routine touchdown spike, but the official who threw the flag said Potts had thrown the ball toward a New Orleans player.

"That was a bull---- call," said center Kirk Lowdermilk.

Harbaugh described it this way. "It was horrific," he said.

Even Duke Tumatoe addressed it in rhyme the following week:

> *The penalty against Roosevelt Potts*
>
> *Can we get the officials' names?*
>
> *They must be the same guys*
>
> *Who have been working the Pacers games.*
>
> *Lord help our Colts, Lord help our Colts.*
>
> *Do you officials get my gist?*
>
> *Go visit an optometrist.*
>
> *Lord help our Colts.*

Foxboro, Mass., has never been a place where the Colts look forward to playing.

Prior to the meeting in mid-November of '95, the Indianapolis Colts were 5-17 against New England, including a pathetic 2-9 mark at Foxboro. For whatever reason, it just seemed as if Murphy's Law ruled the roost every time Indianapolis took the field in New England.

In '94, the Colts intercepted four passes including a 90-yard TD return by Ray Buchanan but the Patriots won easily 28-13. The year before, the Colts were limited to 136 total yards in a 38-0 Patriot drubbing.

But some of the games have been downright incredible. In 1991, the Colts led 17-3 in the fourth quarter and 17-10 with less than two minutes to play. With Eric Dickerson needing to gain 1 yard on second or third down, the Colts could have ran out the clock. Instead he was stuffed both times, and the Patriots rallied to tie the score at 17-all and force overtime. In OT Hugh Millen hit Michael Timpson on a 45-yard touchdown pass to give the Patriots a 23-17 win.

On and on the games have gone in Foxboro. But the bottom line was usually the same — the Colts would find a way to lose.

In '84, New England won 16-10 with the winning touchdown being set up when a Colts' punt hit linebacker Gary Padjen in the back and was recovered by the Patriots inside the Colts' 10. In '88, Doug Flutie fooled Duane Bickett on a naked bootleg touchdown run with 23 seconds to play to lift the Pats to a 21-17 victory. In '89, the Colts led 16-15 with less than two minutes to play, before John Stephens scored the game-winning touchdown from 10 yards out with 25 seconds remaining.

As the 5-5 Colts went to Foxboro in '95, the ghosts were coming out hoping to work their magic one more time.

Working for the Colts, however, was the fact Harbaugh was expected to start which would give the offense a big lift. The Colts also signed Vince Workman during the week to bolster a running attack that had been slowed by injuries to Lamont Warren and Ronald Humphrey. Workman would be used to back up Faulk.

"We've talked about big games, but this is the biggest," Marchibroda said prior to the game. "It's a must game for us. It's a divisional game and a conference game and one that our players know the importance of. But we've played our best football when we're healthy and we're as close to being 100 percent as we have been all season. When we beat St. Louis, Miami and San Francisco, we were healthy."

For one game in Foxboro, anyway, the Colts not only knocked the monkey off their backs, they slammed him to the turf.

Harbaugh completed his first 11 passes, and wound up 20 of 26 for 232 yards and two touchdowns. Faulk rushed for 96 yards on 24 carries and a touchdown, while also catching eight passes for 71 yards. The Colts led 17-3 at halftime and rolled to a 24-10 victory.

The offense rolled up 370 yards, while the defense limited Drew Bledsoe and company to 202 total yards. Patriot phenom running back Curtis Martin, who had rushed for 520 yards in his last four games, was held to 48 yards on 16 carries.

"It was a great win for the Indianapolis Colts," Marchibroda said in the postgame press conference. "Before the game I told the guys in the coaches' room that we've gotten respect in the National Football League, but that now we've got to take that next step. Today, we took that next step.

"The Colts are back."

The weekly *Lord Help Our Colts* offering was another upbeat affair.

Jimmy, Jimmy, Jimmy, Jimmy Harbaugh played real well.

Jimmy, Jimmy, Jimmy, Jimmy Harbaugh played real well.

Jimmy's back.

He played very well.

I'm willing to bet.

Jimmy has pissed off Bill Parcells.

Foxboro Stadium is an awful dump.

Foxboro Stadium is an awful dump.

It's such a dump.

It's cold and wet.

Drew Bledsoe had a game

Let 'er Rip

> *He'd like to forget.*
> *Oh the Colts defense they played fantastic*
> *And it was really great.*
> *Siragusa was outstanding and he's got a lot to work with*
> *He sure knows how to throw around his weight.*

As big a game as New England was on the road, the get-over-the-hump contest loomed the next week with Miami at home. The Dolphins would still be smarting from the 21-point lead they blew the first time and Dan Marino would be ready to take it to the boys in blue.

Both teams were 6-5 and tied for second place in the division coming into the game. The Dolphins had lost five of their last seven after the Colts burst their bubble and snapped an early four-game win streak.

On paper it looked like it could be a down-to-the-wire contest left to be decided by either Cary Blanchard or Pete Stoyanovich, the two main players in the outcome of the first meeting in October.

But someone forgot to tell Harbaugh.

The veteran quarterback went wild. He threw three touchdown passes in the first half and scored on a quarterback sneak later in the game. The Colts jumped out to a 24-0 lead and Harbaugh was unstoppable.

The Dolphins would get a couple of late scores to make it respectable but Indianapolis claimed a 36-28 victory before 60,414 at the RCA Dome.

Over the final two quarters of the first Miami game, and the first two quarters of this one, Harbaugh put together an incredible string of numbers. In a total of eight offensive possessions, Harbaugh led the Colts to six touchdowns and two field goals. His NFL-best quarterback rating improved to 108.4 and his rating for the game was 138.9.

"We're not going to go away," Harbaugh said following the game. "People have put too much into this. Everybody has talked about getting this team into the playoffs and we're trying to make it happen.

"With six games to go, we knew it was gut-check time. We wanted to be one of those teams that historically makes that run at the end of the year, gets the momentum and gets into the playoffs."

Faulk had another solid game with 95 yards rushing on 22 carries and was on the receiving end of one of Harbaugh's TD throws.

And the defense came up big as well. After Miami had trimmed the Colts' lead to 24-14, defensive end Tony Bennett sacked Marino in the end zone for a safety to make it 26-14 with 1:54 to play in the third. It was one of three Bennett sacks on the day.

Marchibroda summed it up this way. "We're in a great position," he said, "and we're playing our best football right now."

The Colts' Tony Bennett breaks through the line and dumps Miami quarterback Dan Marino in the end zone for a safety in a 36-28 Indianapolis victory. (Photo by Paul Sancya)

Duke Tumatoe's weekly song poked fun at not only the Dolphins but the upcoming game with the expansion Carolina Panthers. It went like this:

Dan Marino's got the record

But bless my soul.

Jim Harbaugh will be the one

playing in the Pro Bowl.

Lord help our Colts. Lord help our Colts.

Bob Trumpy you are so sad.

The best he could say all day was "These Colts aren't bad."

Lord help our Colts.

The Colts play in Carolina

Men, remember you're in the South.

Be ready if you hear somebody say

"Hey, you've got a pretty mouth."

Let 'er Rip

Lord help our Colts. Lord help our Colts.
This game is real big.
Make the Panthers squeal like a pig.
By the end of the game let's see
A resemblance between Kerry Collins and Ned Beatty.
Lord help our Colts.

12

Expansion Foes

The Carolina Panthers and Jacksonville Jaguars.

They were supposed to have been the weak sisters on the schedule, a pair of expansion teams making their inaugural run through the National Football League. Good enough to compete, but not deep enough to do a whole lot of damage.

From a player and management perspective, the expansion teams were a group that you pulled for, much in the same way you would pull for any underdog to knock off a higher-rated team. You rooted for them — until you had to play them. Then, for 60 minutes of Sunday afternoon football, you tried your darndest to not go down in history as a team that lost a regular-season game to an expansion team.

Still, getting a chance to pick up a couple of victories with the expansion teams on your schedule was better than not having that opportunity at all. And very likely that was the way the Colts approached it when they found out they would play both Carolina and Jacksonville during the 1995 season.

When specific dates were released, the Colts had to feel even better. Both games were in early December, and both on the road. Somehow, trips to South Carolina and Florida in December seemed a lot friendlier than where the Colts were accustomed to playing.

December for the Colts had always been like a nagging toothache with an exposed nerve. To anyone who has ever felt that kind of ache, the one sensation that takes it to another extreme is cold.

And December for the Colts was always paved with frigid road trips to New England, Buffalo or the New York Jets. Since 1987, the Colts had played 19 December games on the road and 11 were in cold-weather cities. Nine of those games were either in Foxboro, Mass., or New Jersey's Meadowlands.

The 1993 season had been the worst, as the Colts played three December road games — against the New York Jets, the New York Giants and Philadelphia.

It was almost as if the NFL gods were punishing the Colts for being a dome team by making sure they played a few subfreezing games each year as well.

Let 'er Rip

But 1995 was different. The Colts opened December with back-to-back dates against Carolina and Jacksonville, followed by a pair of home games to close out the season against San Diego and New England.

If nothing else, the Colts figured they had a very competitive final stretch of the schedule. The truth is they hoped a sweep of the expansion teams and at least a split of the two home matchups could give them sufficient momentum heading into the playoffs.

The early feeling on the expansion teams was that although the salary cap and free agency system in the NFL had allowed both teams to be competitive from day one, many wondered if the December timing would play strongly in favor of the Colts. The thinking was the two teams, which had opened the season with little to no depth, would likely be pretty well beat up by the time the Colts arrived in town in December.

As the month of December arrived though, it was apparent that the Colts were going to have to fight hard in order to win one, much less two of the games against expansion foes. Carolina (5-7) in particular, the team the Colts would meet Dec. 3, had exceeded early expectations and was playing a pretty solid brand of football. Jacksonville was 3-9, but even at that, three victories by an expansion team was considered a positive performance.

At 7-5, the Colts were still in the hunt not only for a playoff spot but for the AFC Eastern Division title. Buffalo led the division at 8-4, but because they beat the Colts twice would win the title if the two teams finished in a tie. One game back of the Colts was Miami at 6-6, but in that head-to-head scenario the Colts had the edge. Indianapolis had beaten Miami in both regular-season meetings.

In a story in the *Indianapolis Star* the week of the game, Ted Marchibroda provided his usual line when it came to looking ahead at the schedule. His message: We're not worrying about anyone other than ourselves.

"If we continue to play football like we have the last two weeks, everything should look very promising for the Colts," was Marchibroda's canned response. "But we haven't accomplished anything yet. It's what we do from here on in that determines what we accomplish this season."

But what about winning the AFC East?

"If it happens, it happens and that would be great," Marchibroda said. "But right now our goal is the playoffs and we'll keep it that way.

"The important thing is (the playoffs) are in our hands and that's where you like to have them," he said. "We don't have to worry about anybody on the outside. If we don't do the job that's necessary, then we don't deserve to be there."

It's a good idea in theory, but how many of the players figured expansion competition would be less than they were used to facing? The next two weeks would tell a big part of that story.

Before the Colts traveled to Carolina, the club was hit with some shocking news. Owner Robert Irsay suffered a stroke on Wednesday night, Nov. 31, and was conscious and in stable condition at Indianapolis' St. Vincent Hospital.

With Jim Irsay unavailable for comment, Marchibroda went on record for what the news had done to the ballclub.

"We're certainly sorry for what happened to Mr. Irsay," Marchibroda said in a story published in the *Indianapolis Star*. "He's the guy who has put this team together. It means more to him and he's done more to bring this football team together than anyone else."

Marchibroda said he informed the team of Irsay's condition just prior to the Thursday practice.

"We mentioned it to the team," he said. "But that's the extent of it. I know he wouldn't want it to be a distraction. I'm sure what he wants more than anything else is a victory on Sunday and we certainly hope we can provide it for him."

Irsay would wind up missing the final four regular season games of 1995, plus all three playoff games. Prior to the stroke he had only missed two Colts games since they had moved to Indianapolis in 1984. The first was the season finale of the 1-15 debacle in 1991 when the Colts lost on the road at Tampa Bay. The other had been two weeks prior to the stroke when he did not attend the New England game because he was ill.

In the months to come, very little was reported concerning the Colts owner. Speculation abounded as to whether he would ever leave the hospital, until the family announced in February that plans were underway to convert a good portion of Irsay's Carmel estate into what amounted to a rehab center. The target date for the elder Irsay to return home was set for sometime in mid-May.

By late April, Jim Irsay said he still believed his father could have a good quality of life.

"He's doing decently," Irsay said of his father. "He's in bed sometimes, he's in a wheelchair sometimes. He has times of good clarity, while other times he's lost and he's whispering out words. It's hard to understand.

"I think the key thing is that he's got a good attitude and a good disposition," said Jim. "He seems to be accepting his condition, even though he doesn't fully understand the realm and the permanency of it.

"There are smiles, there's not a lot of anger and not a lot of frustration — and that's good," he added. "We're hoping to get him home in May. It's just very fragile. He gets a cold and most people go to the drug store for over-the-counter stuff and he has to go to the hospital. It's a day-to-day thing that we're just addressing. I think there's some quality of life for him to be had there and that's what our hopes are."

◆   ◆   ◆

The Carolina team the Colts would go up against in the first weekend of December was one that had been assembled solidly by former Bills general manager and now Panthers G.M. Bill Polian.

Polian's first major decision had been to bring in former Pittsburgh Steelers defensive coordinator Dom Capers as head coach. Polian had always believed in building a strong defense first and as a tandem, he and Capers made some early moves to shore up that side of the ball.

They used a good chunk of salary cap change to bring in Carlton Bailey, Sam Mills, Brett Maxie, Gerald Williams, Mike Fox, Lamar Lathon and Darien Conner, all defensive starters.

As they entered the game against the Colts, the Panthers were tied with the Colts defensively in the NFL at No. 7 in total yards, allowing 307.5 yards per game. Most impressively, though, Carolina was leading the league in takeaways with 31. Two weeks previously, the Panthers had beaten Arizona at home 27-7, and the defense limited the Cardinals to 94 yards of total offense.

And then there was the offense.

Polian believed a solid quarterback was the other part of the equation that had to be addressed right away. In this vein, he brought in former Bills backup Frank Reich and former Colts signal caller Jack Trudeau. Both were given the task of nurturing first-round draft pick Kerry Collins out of Penn State.

With five victories, Carolina came into the game already possessing two more wins than any expansion team in NFL history. The Panthers had won five of their last seven, including road wins over San Francisco and New England. At 5-7, the Panthers still believed they had an outside shot at a playoff berth with three consecutive home games against Indianapolis, San Francisco and Atlanta, before closing on the road at Washington.

After 60 minutes of football at Clemson Stadium, they would be clutching victory No. 6 and playoff fever was high in Carolina.

Once again, the Colts battle cry looking back on this one would be it had been another one that got away. The Colts had plenty of opportunities to win but critical mistakes continued to hamper them.

In the closing minutes, with the score tied 10-10, the Colts had a second down-and-2 situation at their own 19. The give went to Marshall Faulk who gained the necessary yardage for an apparent first down. But an illegal shift penalty was called on a wide receiver, and the Colts eventually had to punt.

Carolina got the ball back and marched to the Indianapolis 38 where it was faced with a third-and-5. Kerry Collins threw a pass over the middle that was deflected by Derwin Gray for an incomplete pass. But instead, the official ruled that Gray's hand had glanced against the receiver's face mask and the Panthers were the recipients of a 15-yard penalty. Instead of sending John Kasay in for a potential game-winning 55-yard field goal, four plays later Carolina was the beneficiary of a 38-yarder that split the uprights and gave the Panthers the victory.

The Colts led 10-0 after one period and appeared to be in control. But the Carolina defense shut them down the final three quarters. In fact, both defenses did a masterful job. The Colts held Carolina to 255 yards of total offense.

The big difference for Carolina, however, was its sack attack. The Panthers recorded seven sacks — six on Harbaugh — to consistently disrupt the offensive flow.

"They had a good scheme and we couldn't stop it," offensive tackle Will Wolford said a few days later. "It wasn't anything fancy, it's just that they kept winning the guessing game. They gambled a lot on defense and on this day they were very successful."

Indianapolis Colts defender Derwin Gray clutches the ball after apparently breaking up a pass to a Carolina receiver. Instead, it was ruled that Gray's hand hit the receiver's face mask. The penalty set up the Panthers' game-winning field goal. (Photo by Paul Sancya)

Let 'er Rip

Indianapolis defenders Jason Belser (29), Ashley Ambrose (33) and David Tate (49) knock the ball away from a Carolina receiver. (Photo by Paul Sancya)

The loss hurt even more when the Colts realized they could have moved into a tie for first place in the AFC East with a victory as Buffalo lost in a Sunday night game at San Francisco.

Fans continued to struggle with the Colts up-and-down ways. In a letter to the editor that appeared in the *Indianapolis Star* on December 10, Bob Hensley of Plainfield, Ind., wrote: "Anyone else feel like pulling their hair out after last Sunday's Colts-Panthers game? How can the Colts look like a playoff team against Miami, then turn around and play like the Colts of seasons past at Carolina?

"Every time this team works into position where it can control its own destiny, it loses a game that all of us penciled in as a victory before the season started. Don't blame ownership, management or coaching — it's the effort being made out on the field. One week there's a pass rush and the QB is well protected. The next week one or both is missing. The special teams look good, but the next game it's poor decisions and sloppy tackling. Playoff contenders play hard, smart football every down. Our Colts have a long way to go."

Even more difficult than the loss to an expansion team which dropped the club's record to 7-6, the Colts also were worried about Harbaugh's knee, which he sprained in the second half. Management, players and fans were on pins and needles overnight as they waited for the results of the next day's magnetic resonance imaging test.

"I'll get an MRI tomorrow and see what it shows," said Harbaugh in an article the next day in the *Indianapolis Star*. "At worst, it's a tear in the meniscus, I'll get (arthroscopic surgery) and have to miss a week or two.

"At best it's a bad bruise and I can be back for Jacksonville."

Back for a game against Jacksonville, that all of a sudden had slipped into the must-win category.

◆   ◆   ◆

When the Colts showed up for work the day after the Carolina game, they received some frightening news. Harbaugh had just undergone surgery to repair torn cartilage in his right knee and would be out at least one and maybe as many as three games.

With just three games left in the season, the Colts were well aware that their playoff hopes might just fall in the hands of either Paul Justin or Craig Erickson.

Ted Marchibroda had the same choice facing him Monday. Should he start Erickson, who had struggled early and lost his job, or go with Justin who had shown glimpses of good things but still lacked the experience to be an every down player in the National Football League?

After two days of thinking about it, Marchibroda opted to go with Erickson, basing his decision on the player's veteran leadership.

"Craig is a veteran, and this is a big ballgame for us, a must ballgame," Marchibroda said. "When I decided to go with Jimmy (Harbaugh) as the starter, I felt it was important that Craig sit back and take a look. Now, he's ready to play."

Having spent the majority of the season holding a clipboard and wearing a baseball cap, Erickson was definitely ready for the opportunity. While the media tried to stir up problems with the quarterback and get him to vent his frustrations about the way things had worked out, Erickson would have none of it.

His only reply was that he wanted to do whatever he could to help his team win a big game.

Much like Harbaugh had shown class throughout the season, Erickson was in the same boat. Harbaugh had supported him through a tough time, and Erickson was not about to show any disrespect for Harbaugh.

He made it clear from the first day of practice that week that he wasn't going to take the attitude of "I'll show you." Instead he tried to remain even-keeled.

"Going out and trying to do too much and trying to prove something that may or may not need to be proven is only going to get you in trouble," Erickson told *Indianapolis Star* reporter Mike Chappell. "I've got to play a little smarter and not turn it over as much as I did the first couple of weeks. I've got to play within myself and play my game. If I do that, things will fall into place."

Unlike their expansion colleagues in Carolina, Jacksonville was looking to play out the run. They were 3-10 going into the game with the Colts and had lost five in a

Let 'er Rip

row. The Jaguars had struggled on defense in particular, ranking 25th against the run and 26th against the pass. The most dismal statistic was sacks where they had produced just 11. The Jacksonville offensive line, on the other hand, had allowed 51 sacks, the most in the league.

It looked like a potential mismatch on the schedule but the Colts knew they couldn't treat it that way.

All of a sudden they were in a position, not only to seriously mess up their playoff hopes, but to go down in history as the first team to lose to both expansion teams in one season.

This team wanted very much to go down in history, but not if it meant historical preservation accompanied by a black smudge.

What they would eventually find as the game with Jacksonville unfolded was something they had lacked on a consistent basis the entire season — solid special teams play.

Yet it was the special teams that had a lot to do with the Colts riding into Municipal Stadium and coming away with a hard-fought 41-31 victory.

Consider:

- Aaron Bailey returned the opening kickoff 95 yards for a touchdown.
- On Jacksonville's first possession, the Jaguars marched to the 10 but were forced to settle for a 27-yard field-goal attempt by Mike Hollis. But Tony Siragusa came in up the middle and blocked it, keeping the Colts lead at 7-0.
- Later, Derwin Gray recovered a fumble on a punt return that gave the Colts the ball at the Jacksonville 2. Three plays later Marshall Faulk scored a touchdown to make it 21-7.

As important a role as the special teams played, Erickson had a solid outing as well. He completed nine of 16 passes for 129 yards and two touchdowns. He hit Aaron Bailey on a 14-yard first-quarter touchdown pass to give the Colts a 14-0 lead. In the fourth quarter, Erickson hit Dilger on a 16-yard touchdown that upped the lead to 34-17.

The Colts would eventually get the lead up to 41-17 before two late Jacksonville touchdowns made the score look closer than it really was.

"It probably wasn't the prettiest win," Ted Marchibroda was quoted as saying the next day in the *Indianapolis Star*. "But it was a win. Now, we're right where we want to be."

Where they were was in a position of controlling their own destiny heading into the final two games of the season. They had split with the expansion teams, and winning a game with their starting quarterback on the sidelines. Confidence was high but a big challenge loomed in an RCA Dome matchup with 7-7 San Diego.

Win their final two and they'd be in the playoffs for the only the second time in 12 seasons in Indianapolis.

It would be a wild final two weeks of the regular season.

13

Controlling Their Own Destiny

Colts play-by-play announcer Bob Lamey has been teased for years by other members of the Indianapolis media about his yearly list of playoff scenarios that he compiles sometime early in December.

He always has it on hand at the Colts' West 56th Street practice facility and is quick to show it to whoever would inquire, or pull it out as evidence to a point he was trying to make.

The only problem was that often times, Lamey's scenarios involved five or six other outcomes that would have to occur in order for the Colts to sneak in to the playoffs with an 8-8 or 9-7 record.

In 1992, the Colts needed to win the season finale against Cincinnati and then have Pittsburgh beat Cleveland, Denver beat Kansas City, and Buffalo beat Houston — in order to back into the playoffs. The Colts rallied to defeat Cincinnati, but not surprisingly the rest of the scenarios failed to play out.

Still, Lamey had figured on his home computer just what had to happen during each of the last few weeks for the Colts to get in.

In 1995, things were much more cut and dried for the veteran announcer and the Colts.

If the Colts could beat San Diego in the second to last regular-season game, they would qualify for the playoffs. If they could beat both San Diego and New England, they would be in a strong position to host a first-round playoff game. If they split with San Diego and New England, and both Miami and Denver were to lose one more game, the Colts could even get in at 9-7.

But the bottom line remained simple — beat the Chargers and begin making playoff plans.

At his Monday morning press conference, Marchibroda set the tone for the week.

"This isn't just another game," Marchibroda said. "We're approaching it like this is a playoff game. This is the biggest game in the history of the (Indianapolis) Colts. ... This is the reason you're in the National Football League, to get into the playoffs."

Unfortunately for the Colts, three time zones to the west, the San Diego Chargers were also looking at the game in the same vein. San Diego had won three in a row to improve to 7-7 and found itself in the thick of the playoff race.

Kansas City and Pittsburgh were the only two teams that had clinched playoff spots heading into week 15. As for the final four spots, Buffalo had the inside track with a 9-5 record, followed by Oakland, Miami and the Colts at 8-6. Denver, Seattle and San Diego were in the next group at 7-7.

As the Colts headed into the week, there were two interesting developments — one positive and one negative.

On the positive side, Harbaugh had made a swift recovery from arthroscopic knee surgery just seven days before and was ready to start against the Chargers. The Colts weren't complaining. Even though Erickson had put up representative numbers in his start against Jacksonville, there was just something about the way the team played when Harbaugh was behind center.

Harbaugh said in a story in the *Indianapolis Star* early in the week that he expected no problems with the knee in the San Diego game. He also said the week off helped to heal his nagging pulled groin injury.

"When I go on Sunday, this will be the healthiest I've been since way back," Harbaugh said. "There's no problem with the knee, the groin is healed and I can run 100 percent."

On the negative side of the ledger was the fact that Colts fans still had yet to embrace their team.

When the Colts moved to Indianapolis, the season ticket base was 57,500 for the 60,000-capacity RCA Dome. Over the years the number had dwindled to the low 40,000-range, and in 1995 was believed to have slipped under the 40,000 mark for the first time in history.

The problem? The product on the field had simply not been good enough to warrant Colts fans shelling out $30 a pop to see the home team play. In the movie *Field of Dreams* Kevin Costner's character hears the voice that whispers, "If you build it, they will come." With the Colts, the voice would have said, "If you build a winner, they will come." Everyone involved in the organization always believed that Colts fans would once again pack the dome if they could get a consistent winner.

Victories at home over St. Louis, San Francisco and Miami in particular had increased interest in '95, but losses to Cincinnati, New Orleans and the previous week to Carolina, just hit home the underlying belief that these Colts were not that different from teams of years past.

Colts fans had long taken a wait-and-see approach, and the truth is it was likely going to take more than just a first-game exit from the playoffs to begin to fill seats in the RCA Dome once again.

The disturbing number that management faced this week as the team prepared for what Marchibroda called the biggest game in Indianapolis Colts history, was that as of Tuesday more than 15,000 seats were still available for the "big game" with the Chargers. Despite a radio plea by Bill Tobin on his Wednesday night program with Bob Lamey, Thursday's deadline would come and go with another game blacked out locally and eventually more than 5,000 seats empty on game day.

Though the Colts controlled their own destiny on the field, they still needed to do a little bit more to gain a spot in the hearts of Colts fans.

◆   ◆   ◆

While Harbaugh was on his way back, the Colts now had a new player to worry about — Marshall Faulk.

Faulk suffered a knee injury late in the game against Jacksonville, but an MRI on Monday came back negative. According to Marchibroda, it was only a bruise and Faulk would be ready for action against the Chargers.

But the underlying problem with Faulk was more on-the-field related than off. Simply put, Faulk was not having the kind of year he had hoped and he was beginning to point fingers at some of his linemen up front.

The problem hit its boiling point in the Jacksonville game, when Faulk screamed at guard Joe Staysniak after a block was missed and Staysniak's man had come free to make a tackle on Faulk. What Faulk didn't realize at the time was that an audible had been called and it was actually tackle Jason Mathews who had missed the assignment, not Staysniak. Cooler heads prevailed, but the tension that had been growing throughout the season between Faulk and his linemen still remained.

Marchibroda attempted to pass it off as no big deal.

"It was nothing out of the ordinary," the head coach said. "That happens on the sidelines in every game. So this was nothing unusual ... nothing to be concerned about."

It was concerning enough, however, that Marchibroda called several of the linemen in his office to try and get to the bottom of the problem. He also called in both Faulk and fullback Roosevelt Potts. A couple of the linemen said they just wanted an apology from Faulk over his public outburst. They felt if he was going to publicly criticize, then he should publicly apologize.

The apology never came.

Faulk's frustrations were easy to understand. As a rookie, he had four 100-yard games, had rushed for 1,282 yards and had numerous big plays. Overall, he had 10 runs of 20 yards or more. In addition, his yards-per-carry average was 4.1.

In his sophomore season in the NFL, everything was much more of a struggle. For the entire 16-game regular season, Faulk still got his 1,000 yards (1,078 to be exact) but nothing was coming easily. The most telling statistic was the lack of big plays. He only had four runs of more than 20 yards in 1995 and two of them had come in his game-breaking 177-yard performance against St. Louis. The other two were a 30-yarder against New Orleans and a 40-yard run versus Miami in the RCA Dome.

Still, there just seemed to be a whole lot more runs of less than 3 yards than there had been in the past.

Let 'er Rip

    The game against Jacksonville was a good case in point. Because the Jaguars ranked 25th in the NFL against the run, many expected Faulk to be able to run wild. And for the first five carries he did just that. He gained 35 yards and appeared well on his way to his second 100-yard outing of the season.

    But when it was all said and done, he nearly failed to reach even half of the century mark total. Over his next 17 carries, Faulk gained just 19 yards. On 15 of those carries, he was held to 3 yards or less.

    Not surprisingly, the linemen did not want to get pulled into the fray and tried their best to keep their comments out of the media. Still, more than one offensive starter on the line said they questioned how hard Faulk was hitting the hole.

    Then later in the season, when Zack Crockett would have a big game in Faulk's place in the first round of the playoffs, gaining more than 100 yards against the Chargers, the linemen would look at each other and say 'That's what happens when you hit a hole hard.'

◆   ◆   ◆

    To a man, Colts players will tell you that they were as emotionally charged as humanly possible when game time rolled around Sunday afternoon against the Chargers in the RCA Dome.

    "Some guys took intensity to a new level," said tackle Will Wolford. "I've never seen these guys as pumped up as they were the last few days."

    Center Kirk Lowdermilk agreed.

    "We gave it everything we had — and then some," he said.

    But it wasn't enough.

    An electric crowd of 55,318 in the RCA Dome went through a plethora of emotions as the Colts fought for the right to dine at the AFC playoff table.

    The fourth quarter alone was one emotion swing after another. Entering the period, the Colts trailed 14-10, but got to within one on a 42-yard field goal by Cary Blanchard to make it 14-13 with 13:16 to play.

    But San Diego came right back. Stan Humphries hooked up with wide receiver Tony Martin on a 38-yard touchdown pass, with Martin badly beating free safety Jason Belser on the play. The score gave the Chargers a 21-13 edge. It was the second long touchdown catch of the game for Martin, and the second time Belser had been beaten badly.

    "I feel like I was responsible for 14 points today," Belser would say later. "That's something I'm going to have to live with, but something where I hope someday soon I'll get a chance to show my true colors."

    Trailing 21-13, Captain Comeback worked his magic once again. Harbaugh drove the Colts 85 yards in 10 plays and Faulk eventually scored on a 1-yard run with 6:58 remaining in the game. The TD came following a pass interference call in the end zone by Chargers safety Bo Orlando that gave the Colts a first-and-goal. The Colts then tied it on a floating two-point conversion pass from Harbaugh to Floyd Turner.

And then the Colts caught a break. On the ensuing drive, Humphries was intercepted at midfield by Quentin Coryatt, and the linebacker returned the ball to the Chargers' 25-yard line.

Suddenly, things were looking up for the Colts and fans were on their feet in anticipation of good things on the horizon.

But it would only last three plays. Harbaugh, who had thrown only four interceptions the entire season, returned Humphries' favor by underthrowing receiver Brian Stablein down the right sideline. The ball was picked off by Willie Clark.

San Diego moved the ball down the field and John Carney hit a 33-yard field goal with 1:59 to play to give the Chargers a 24-21 lead.

Instead of being up by at least three, the Colts were down three. But Captain Comeback, the man with the 'S' on his chest, still had something left. He again marched the Colts down the field to the San Diego 33, where they were faced with a third-and-10. Harbaugh went back to pass and found a wide open Aaron Bailey over the middle at the 15, but the second-year receiver dropped the ball. It was in his mitts, but he simply dropped it.

But Blanchard reached back to salvage something out of the drive as he hit a career-best 50-yard field goal with 48 seconds to play in regulation.

Though overtime looked like a strong possibility, Humphries was not to be outdone. Unfortunately, once again it was the Colts that failed to make the big play. This time it was a pass over the middle intended for Ronnie Harmon that went through his hands and right into the waiting arms of Coryatt.

But he dropped it.

Three plays later, Carney would kick a game-winning 43-yard field goal with eight seconds to play to lift San Diego to a dramatic 27-24 victory.

"You win as a team and you lose as a team," Marchibroda said following the game. "You can go through life and say 'If, if, if.' In the final analysis, we lost and that's what matters. This loss hurts, there's no doubt about it. The guys gave us everything they had and that makes it hurt even more.

"We spent everything we had today," he said. "Now we have to reach a little deeper for (New England). Now, that's the only one that counts."

Marchibroda knew he had a monumental task on his hands to lift the Colts back emotionally in a week's time to play the Patriots in the season finale on Sunday night football.

Within 24 hours, the Colts would learn that they still controlled their own destiny. A win versus the Patriots would send them to the big dance. It was simply a matter of whether they could stir up those incredible emotions one more time.

Even with so much on the line, it wasn't going to be easy.

As he sat in the locker room following the game and calmly answered every question, Harbaugh tried to put a positive spin on the situation that the Colts found themselves in.

"It's disappointing, but at the same time we're still in a position to make the playoffs by winning next week," Harbaugh said. "Sure it's frustrating when we had it in our grasp today and let it slip away. But at the same time there's a lot of teams out

Let 'er Rip

there that would like to be in our situation today. Talk to the Jets. Talk to the Patriots. Talk to Jacksonville.

"At least we can still have a successful year if we can find a way to win next week."

Second chances don't come along very often in any walk of life.

Yet that's exactly what the Colts had when they woke up Monday morning, Dec. 18 — a second chance.

For the second week in a row the Colts' mission was simple — win and you're in.

What was even crazier, though something Colts players and coaches didn't even want to think about, was that scenarios still existed by which the Colts could back into the playoffs with an 8-8 record. If the Colts lost to the Patriots, Seattle lost to Kansas City, and either Miami or Oakland fell to St. Louis or Denver respectively, the Colts could still sneak in.

At the same time there was still a scenario that existed by which the Colts could host a wildcard playoff game. If they beat the Patriots, and San Diego and Oakland both lost, the Colts would host their first playoff game in the franchise's Indianapolis history.

But none of that mattered to what Jim Harbaugh and strength coach Tom Zupancic had labeled the "50 men on 56th Street." The only thing that mattered was finding a way to get past New England and get in the playoffs the honest way.

Ray Buchanan said it was time to put up or shut up.

"We have to go out and take care of business," Buchanan said. "You can't be depending on other people. It's up to us."

The game marked the third time in Indianapolis Colts history that they had entered the final weekend of the season controlling their own playoff destiny. In 1987, the Colts secured a playoff spot with a 24-6 decision over Tampa Bay in the dome. In 1989, the Colts needed a victory over New Orleans to make the playoffs but were ripped 41-6 in the Superdome.

As they prepared for the Patriots, the Colts were not worried about Curtis Martin, or Drew Bledsoe or whatever Bill Parcells was saying about how badly the Patriots wanted to close the season on a winning note.

The only thing the players were talking about was worrying about themselves and how they played against New England. If they played their game, and made the big plays instead of letting the opportunities slip away, they felt they could win.

The Colts would also have to win without big fullback Roosevelt Potts blocking for Marshall Faulk or catching swing passes out of the backfield. Potts tore the anterior cruciate ligament in his right knee against San Diego and would be lost for the year. Rookie Zack Crockett was going to have to grow up in a hurry.

The 54,685 fans on hand for the Sunday night regular-season finale on national television came with one thought in mind — to celebrate a berth in the playoffs.

Floyd Turner cradles a pass from Jim Harbaugh for a touchdown that tied the game against New England in the final contest of the 1995 season. (Photo by Paul Sancya)

And while a victory over the Patriots seemed so much within their grasp, the Colts had to have some serious questions on their minds as they hustled off the field and into the locker room at halftime, trailing New England 7-0.

The Colts had all of 74 yards in total offense in the half. Marshall Faulk had reinjured his knee and did not play in the second quarter. The club was badly in need of a wake-up call.

The call came and was delivered by nose tackle Tony Siragusa. Siragusa had seen enough in the first half and when everyone was settled in the locker room, the Goose let loose.

First he threw a table with food on it against a row of lockers. Then he threw another. Then he proceeded to kick and punch a wall a few times, letting all of his frustrations pour out into the open.

"It was something to watch," said linebacker Jeff Herrod. "It was right out of the World Wrestling Federation. But you looked around the room and a lot of the younger players in particular had their eyes fixed right on him.

"It was one of those halftimes when Ted would give the soft-spoken message and then 'assistant coach' Siragusa would make his feelings known," Herrod said. "All I know is that the WWF had nothing on the Goose."

Some of the veterans just rolled their eyes and looked the other way. One said it was out of character for Siragusa. "That's the first time in Tony's life that he's ever turned over a table of food without first eating its contents," said the player who requested anonymity.

For the most part though, those on hand thought Siragusa's antics served their purpose.

Veteran safety David Tate enjoyed the halftime fireworks.

"I thought he blew a gasket," Tate said. "He went nuts. But it had the desired effect. I looked around at some of the younger players and they were downright scared. They didn't have any idea what Tony might do next."

What he did was make it perfectly clear what he thought about the 7-0 halftime deficit. All of his frustrations from the San Diego game the week before and now the first 30 minutes of the Patriots game came bubbling out and the Goose reminded his teammates of one simple fact. If they lost this game, everything they had worked for would be down the drain.

"I don't know what I did," Siragusa said later. "All I know is there were things flying all over the place. I told them we had 30 minutes left to play, and I wasn't ready to pack it in, yet. I wasn't going home a loser."

Cornerback Ashley Ambrose said he couldn't keep his eyes off of the volatile Siragusa.

"It definitely inspired me," he said. "He was saying everything I was feeling and it just made me want to go out and do anything in my power to find a way to win."

It didn't take long for Ambrose to have a hand in another Colts comeback.

With New England driving in the third quarter, Ambrose stepped in front of a Drew Bledsoe aerial, giving the Colts the ball at their own 35. Harbaugh took it from there. He completed seven passes in a row for 69 yards. The final one was a 13-yard touchdown toss to Floyd Turner, who did a nice job of catching the ball and then sneaking his toes just inside the sideline in the end zone.

In the fourth quarter, Cary Blanchard had what amounted to a third chance to be the hero. After missing a 44-yard field goal wide left in the first quarter and a 30-yard chip shot wide right in the third, Blanchard had a chance to put the Colts ahead with a 30-yarder with 5:51 remaining in the game. This time, he knocked it down the middle to give the Colts a 10-7 lead they would not relinquish.

This was a game of big plays and big performances.

Lamont Warren, subbing for Faulk for the final three quarters, rushed for a career-high 90 yards and caught six passes for 67 yards.

Harbaugh completed 14 of 19 passes in the second half, including a perfect 10-for-10 in the third. He wound up with 17 touchdown passes on the season, a record for a Colts quarterback since the club moved to Indy in 1984. Jeff George had held the previous record with 16 in his rookie year of 1990.

But none of the big plays was any bigger than those turned in by the defense.

Controlling Their Own Destiny

Ronald Humphrey celebrates as he leaves the field after the Colts' 10-7 victory over New England in the regular-season finale. The victory sent Indianapolis to the playoffs for the first time since 1987. (Photo by Paul Sancya)

With less than three minutes to play in the game, Bledsoe drove the Patriots to the Colts' 15 where they looked to be in position to at least tie the game up and send it into a possible overtime.

But Tony Bennett, who had been double-teamed in pass protection all night, took advantage of a one-on-one matchup against tight end Ben Coates and made the Patriots pay. Bennett came around Bledsoe's blind side and sacked the quarterback for a 17-yard loss and a fumble that was recovered by New England at the Colts' 32. On the next play, Matt Bahr missed a potential game-tying field goal that fell just short with 2:23 to play.

One or two yards, much less 17, turned out to be big for the Patriot kicker.

"You have to make big plays in a big game and I think that's just what we told ourselves in the second half," Bennett said. "We were frustrated at halftime because we just weren't making plays. It could have been anyone but on that play in the fourth quarter I just knew that I had to make something happen.

"You don't get chances in this league very often to make the playoffs and I just think our guys refused to be denied tonight. We didn't want to be remembered as a team that missed the playoffs because we couldn't make the plays."

Another big play was turned in by Jason Belser, who bounced back nicely from a difficult San Diego game the week before. Belser came up with an interception in the final minute that helped seal the victory.

"We were in a quarter-quarter defense and we knew they were going to try and hit the seam with a pass over the middle," Belser said. "I had just missed one on the series before and I didn't want to miss it again. I saw the ball in the air and it looked like a beach ball hanging up in the wind. I knew all I had to do was grab it and pull it in."

The final heroics were saved for Ambrose. The fourth-year cornerback had three interceptions to his credit in four seasons with the Colts coming into the game. That night against the Patriots he had two more. The final one came with 20 seconds to play and allowed the Colts to run out the clock.

Final Score: Indianapolis 10, New England 7.

The Colts were going to the playoffs.

Linebacker Jeff Herrod, who had seen it all in eight seasons with the Colts, summed it up best.

"Eight years of frustration are over," Herrod said. "I'm happy for myself and I'm happy for the other old guys, people like Eugene (Daniel) and Randy (Dixon). We survived 1-15 (in 1991) but all of that is forgotten right now."

With the monkey firmly off his back, Harbaugh smiled for the cameras and just enjoyed the moment.

"We've arrived now. We're going to the big show," he said. "We're one of the 12 best teams in football, right? That's quite an accomplishment considering the schedule we played this year and the adversity we had to overcome.

"I can't imagine feeling too much better than I do right now."

Wait until next week Jim. Wait until next week.

14

The Playoffs: California Here We Come

As the Colts prepared for a date with San Diego in the wildcard playoffs at Jack Murphy Stadium, defensive tackle Tony McCoy said he believed postseason play was a wide-open affair.

"This year, anybody can beat anybody," McCoy said in a story in the *Indianapolis Star*. "And my motto is 'We're anybody'."

The truth is that from the first day of training camp Ted Marchibroda had preached to his troops that first and foremost to set their sights on making the playoffs. Once there, he said, anything would be possible. But if you didn't make it, you would really never know just how good you could have been.

That's the way the Colts were looking at their first-round playoff game. They had made it to the big dance, now the goal was to do some dancing. Everyone in the NFL expected the Colts to be a first-round wallflower, a spectator that was just happy to have received an invitation to the exclusive party. As for actual dancing, people around the league believed it was time for the Colts to clear the floor and let the big boys do their thing.

"There are 12 teams in the playoffs and we are probably 12th in a lot of peoples' minds," Marchibroda said. "But that's fine with me. We wouldn't mind at all being this year's Cinderella story."

It wasn't simply the fact that the Colts were in the playoffs for only the second time since moving to Indianapolis, and the first since the strike-shortened 1987 campaign. Moreover, these Colts were wide-eyed and green behind the ears in other ways as well.

Of the 53 players on the roster, 41 had never participated in a postseason game in the NFL. So with seven days to prepare for this virgin experience, the younger players were counting on the grizzled veterans such as tackle Will Wolford to take them by the hand.

Let 'er Rip

In eight seasons with the Buffalo Bills, Wolford had played in 13 postseason games. He had started in three Super Bowls and thus knew exactly what the formula for success should be.

"Everything just gets turned up a notch," Wolford said. "There's more people interested in you, more media wanting to talk to you and more relatives that you didn't know existed looking for those hard-to-get playoff tickets.

"The important thing is making sure you don't get caught up in everything," he said. "Everyone knows what the stakes are and everyone must prepare themselves in their own way. But when you step on the field for that first playoff game you become aware in a hurry that it's a whole different ballgame."

Teammate Kirk Lowdermilk, who had started seven games in the playoffs while with the Minnesota Vikings, echoed Wolford's sentiments. Lowdermilk said all of a sudden it's like someone turned up the stereo from easy listening to heavy metal.

"It's like the difference between a preseason game and a regular-season game," Lowdermilk explained. "There's that much of a difference. The intensity is higher, there is more on the line and you play like there's no tomorrow. This is what it's all about. Until you've had this experience it's hard to try and pass it on to the next guy. He needs to live it, too.

"If you can win a few playoff games in a row, and get on a roll, you really feel like you've grown up fast as far as what it takes to win in the NFL."

Harbaugh had played in the playoffs but his only experience had been a 1991 first-round loss to Dallas. He said that experience was valuable but it left him wanting more.

"This is what you play the game for, you play it for opportunities such as this one," Harbaugh said. "When people talk about a quarterback's career they're usually going to judge you on how far you were able take your team. I've had a taste of the playoffs but that taste in my mouth is long gone. I want to really be able to get my feet wet this time."

Harbaugh had to be riding a personal high heading into the playoffs. The much-maligned quarterback of the past was the cream of the crop of the present. When the final 1995 quarterback rankings were released following the season, Harbaugh stood alone at the top of the heap.

His rating was 100.7 based on a completion percentage of 63.7, with 2,575 yards, 17 touchdowns and an NFL-low five interceptions. He was only the second Colts player to lead the league in quarterback rating. The other was the legendary Johnny Unitas in 1958 and 1965.

The company Harbaugh shared near the top of the list was impressive. Green Bay's Brett Favre was second at 99.5, followed by Troy Aikman of Dallas at 93.6, Steve Young of San Francisco at 92.3 and Miami's Dan Marino at 90.8.

"I'm not crazy enough to say I belong in that company over the long haul, but for this year anyway I think I may have proved something to some people," Harbaugh said. "This year has been memorable and now I just need to keep finding ways to make it even more memorable."

It had been a memorable season indeed, and one that just seemed to get better at every turn. A good example had been an NFC game Sunday that the Colts normally would not have given a second thought as to which team won.

The Playoffs: California Here We Come

But Atlanta, in rallying for a 28-27 victory over San Francisco, put huge smiles on the faces of Colts management. The victory gave the Falcons a 9-7 record which kicked in a clause in the Jeff George trade to Atlanta that enabled the Colts to get a better draft pick in 1996.

The deal was that if Atlanta won nine games or more, and George started at least 75 percent of those games, the Colts would get a first-round pick in 1996 rather than a second-rounder. Had the 49ers held on to win, the Colts would have been left clutching that second-round pick. Instead, they had a first-rounder and later in the spring would use the pick to draft wide receiver Marvin Harrison out of Syracuse.

"It's about time we caught a few breaks like that," Marchibroda said with a smile.

◆   ◆   ◆

As playoff preparations began, the Colts were well aware of the tall order that was ahead of them.

First up was a red-hot San Diego team that had closed the season with five consecutive victories. If they could survive the hostile environment they were sure to face at Jack Murphy Stadium, the next stop would be Kansas City, where visiting teams rarely make themselves at home and where the Chiefs had the AFC's best 1995 record at 13-3.

If they somehow survived those two games, which would be akin to climbing Mount Everest, the next challenge would likely be a road game against Pittsburgh, or perhaps Buffalo, a team they had already lost to twice this season.

Probably waiting in the Super Bowl would be Dallas, but San Francisco and Green Bay looked like strong possibilities as well.

But none of those other opponents was on the minds of the Colts this week. Instead, the San Diego Chargers possessed more than enough possible trouble areas for the Colts to worry about.

Sure, the Colts had played San Diego just two weeks before, and the game had gone down to the wire before John Carney's 43-yard field goal with three seconds remaining lifted his team to a 27-24 victory.

Sure, the Colts had proven to themselves that they could play on the same field with a very good San Diego team.

Sure, the Colts had begun to gain some respect around the league.

But the Chargers already had it. In fact, many were of the belief that as well as San Diego had been playing of late it wasn't out of the question to think they could make the Super Bowl. And if they did, it would be a repeat performance. The year before, San Diego had knocked off Pittsburgh in the AFC title game at Three Rivers Stadium to advance to the Super Bowl clash in Miami against San Francisco.

The Chargers had a potent running attack but it wasn't '94 Pro Bowl standout Natrone Means who was leading the charge. Means suffered a pulled groin muscle Nov. 5 against Miami and hadn't played since. To that point in the season he had gained 728 yards in eight games and appeared well on his way to a second straight Pro Bowl. But the injury forced him to spend six weeks on the inactive list.

Let 'er Rip

With four games to play in the regular season, and the Chargers in need of a picker-upper, coach Bobby Ross turned to rookie fourth-round draft pick Aaron Hayden to get San Diego moving in the right direction. Hayden had spent the first nine games on the physically unable to perform list as he was still battling back from a broken leg he suffered in the final game of his collegiate career at the University of Tennessee.

But Hayden had not taken long to show he belonged in the NFL. In his four starts, he gained 387 yards (an average of 96.8 yards per game) with three touchdowns and a 3.7 yards-per-carry average. Two weeks prior, in a game against the Colts in the RCA Dome, Hayden had rushed for 96 yards on 22 carries.

Adding double trouble for the Colts was the fact that Means had been cleared to practice the week before the playoffs and Ross had insisted that his veteran back would see some duty against Indianapolis. Add to those two players the names of Ronnie Harmon as well as former Colts draft pick Rodney Culver and the Chargers would likely be ready to run.

But San Diego was more than just a single-faceted team. As the Colts saw in the first meeting, Stan Humphries was a capable quarterback and Tony Martin was more than just a capable receiver.

Defense on the other hand, was likely San Diego's strongest suit. With linebacker Junior Seau, one of the best in the game, patrolling the middle of the field or blitzing at a moment's notice, you never knew just what might happen. As for stopping the run, the Chargers had limited Marshall Faulk to 48 yards on 15 carries when the two teams had played two weeks before.

Put it this way, the Colts went into the San Diego game knowing they would be in for the fight of their lives. It just came down to how much fight these dogs with horseshoes on their helmets would be able to muster.

Many believed the key going into the game for the Colts would be Marshall Faulk.

If the second player selected in the 1994 draft could put together one of his money performances on national television the Colts should at least be able to hang around and have a chance to win the game late. But if Faulk continued to struggle with the nagging bruised knee injury that kept him out of most of the New England game the week before, the Colts could find their backs against the wall.

Faulk did his best to downplay all the talk about his returning to San Diego where he played collegiately at San Diego State. He also didn't want to admit just how much his knee was really still hurting. In both cases, he was very successful.

"I'm looking at it as just another game that we have to win," Faulk said in an interview with members of the Indianapolis media a few days before the game. "I don't want to take it as any special case or anything like that. You win, you're in. You lose, you go home. That's basically it."

Faulk still had fresh memories about the Chargers based on his playing time against them two weeks before. He said he was impressed with their abilities.

"They're pretty tough," Faulk said. "They're real aggressive. They flow fast at times, too fast at times. They blitzed us a lot. I looked at the film and I missed a lot of pickups. Jimmy (Harbaugh) had a couple of bad reads. We made a couple of bad checks. But we were still in the game.

"Minimize our mistakes and we have a better game."

There's no doubt Faulk was hoping that he could at least have a better game. His '95 numbers had been decent but they didn't stack up well against his '94 performance. In '95, he had rushed for 1,078 yards. As a rookie, the number had been 1,282 yards.

One number in particular really stood out like a flashing neon sign in Faulk's running statistics — his gains of 2 yards or less on a carry. Out of 289 possible carries, 138 had been for 2 yards or less.

"Nothing has been easy for me this year but I'm still the same runner," Faulk said. "As a player, as a competitor, I don't go out thinking anyone is better than me at any point."

Faulk had the same confidence in his team.

"I don't think there's a team out there that we can't compete with."

◆　　　◆　　　◆

As much fun as it was making the playoffs, things were bittersweet for Colts general manager Jim Irsay.

With his father, Robert Irsay, still in the hospital after suffering a November stroke, it wasn't as easy to enjoy the Colts' stretch run.

In an interview with Mike Chappell of the *Indianapolis Star*, Irsay talked about how much he wished his father could share in the Colts' triumph of making the playoffs.

"It has been a very difficult time — it's hard to believe it's been a month-plus (since the stroke) — and I wish dad was able to enjoy it more than he has," said Jim Irsay. "What makes it worse is knowing how tough things have been over the last 25 years or so. As you know, he has taken a lot of flak over the years.

"People don't realize that there are very few enjoyments of being an owner," Irsay said. "I remember seeing (San Diego owner) Alex Spanos at the Super Bowl last year and how much he enjoyed the entire situation. You could see it was a special time for him. I know dad would have liked to have been able to share this special time with his family and friends."

Jim Irsay said the playoffs had offered his family a lift.

"In a way (the playoffs) have been a lift for everyone," he said. "It means so much to my dad, myself and the rest of the family to be here after working so hard for such a long time. It has kept the spirits up through a very tough time.

"Dad can't be here for this, but he is the owner of this team and he is the reason it is where it is," he added. "This is a great tribute to him."

As it turned out, the elder Irsay's condition would not improve for some time. As of spring 1996, Irsay was still confined to a hospital bed but his family was growing

Let 'er Rip

more encouraged that he may be back at his Carmel estate by early summer of '96. The trip home actually would come on May 5. After spending 3½ months in intensive care at St. Vincent's Hospital and another three months in a Westside rehabilitation facility, the elder Irsay returned to his residence in Carmel, Ind.

"It's going to take time...Anyone who has had a stroke will tell you that," said Irsay's wife, Nancy, in an article in the *Indianapolis Star*. "There are still big battles ahead. And Bob has his periods where he tires and maybe gets a little discouraged.

"But there's a definite improvement and that is so encouraging," she added. "Bob is working hard. His main goal is to get well. Some of his doctors are surprised at how far he has come, but I'm not. I've been there from the beginning and I know...he's a fighter."

As positive as things were looking in the spring, things weren't nearly as cheery as the Colts began their playoff run.

It was interesting and sad in a way that the man who had spent so much of his life trying to build the Colts into a winner, was not going to be able to fully enjoy the club's brightest moments since moving to Indianapolis in 1984.

When Roosevelt Potts went down with a knee injury in the regular-season game against San Diego Dec. 17, rookie running back Zack Crockett knew his shot at playing time in the National Football League had arrived.

In the week leading up to the season finale against New England, Crockett worked extra hard at preparing himself for that first real shot at NFL work.

But when game time rolled around, it was Lamont Warren who was getting the call the majority of the time on running plays. Crockett was used as a lead blocker but that was it.

His line that day — no carries, no receptions, no yards.

His line for the regular season — one carry, no yards; two receptions, 35 yards.

And so it wouldn't be surprising to learn that Crockett had very few expectations as he awoke the morning of December 31, 1995, to prepare to play the San Diego Chargers in an AFC wildcard matchup later that day.

"I figured the game plan was going to be to get Marshall the ball as many times as possible and then maybe spread a few carries around to me and Lamont (Warren). I really had no other expectations for what might take place."

Things changed after Faulk handled the ball for the first time in the game. He took a handoff, broke to the outside and gained 16 yards. It was a vintage Faulk run, made in front of many former fans of his at San Diego State, and it appeared to be just what the running back needed to launch him into a big day in the Southern California sun.

But Faulk came up clutching his knee. He got up on his own, but limped to the sideline. No one knew it at the time but that would be Faulk's final run of the 1995 season.

The Playoffs: California Here We Come

Suddenly, Crockett found himself in the spotlight again. And with the Chargers poised to stop Warren, Crockett had no idea how many times his number was about to be called.

"I still really didn't expect anything to change," Crockett said. "I figured with such a good backup at tailback in Lamont Warren that he would pick up the load and get all of Marshall's carries. I thought I might be used in some blocking situations but I was the fullback so I didn't think Marshall going down would have much of an effect on me.

"Some of the older guys told me I had to step it up and play the best ball I've ever played," Crockett said. "But they told me to have fun, too. And that's what I tried to do."

His Colts teammates and fans of the horseshoes watching coast-to-coast on national television shared in Crockett's fun. The rookie running back from Florida State didn't know it then, but by the same time the following day he would be a household name at every breakfast table in America.

Headlines everywhere called his performance the "Zack Attack."

The conversations likely always went something like, "How about that rookie running back for the Colts yesterday? Man, did he ever steal the show. He's got a great future ahead of him. What's his name again?"

The name was Crockett and his performance against the Chargers was truly magical.

He carried the ball 13 times for 147 yards and two touchdowns. The touchdown runs were a pair of back-breakers, the first going for 33 yards and the second for 66. The 147 yards and the 66-yard run were both postseason franchise records.

And that's from a club that has had the likes of Alan Ameche, Lydell Mitchell, Tom Matte and Eric Dickerson in its backfield.

"I'm shocked," were the only words Crockett could say at first after flashing a smile that rivaled that of Magic Johnson. "To have come in like I did and step it up and make the big plays, well all I can say is that God really blessed me today."

It was as if someone upstairs had finally taken all of that *Lord Help Our Colts* stuff seriously.

At one point during the day, Faulk walked up to Crockett on the sidelines to offer some encouragement. Both players had Nike shoe contracts, and earlier in the week Faulk had given Crockett a new pair of shoes to try. It was those shoes that Crockett wore on his record-breaking day.

"Marshall walked up to me in the third quarter and told me 'It's got to be the shoes'," Crockett said. "I did like the way they felt. They were light and they felt good. I don't know if it was the shoes or not but something was going right.

"Marshall really helped me a lot in the game because he was giving me constant encouragement," he said. "When you know a guy like that is in your corner you feel like you can do anything."

With the Colts trailing 10-7 with less than two minutes to play in the first half, Crockett made his first memorable rumble through the line. The Colts had moved to the San Diego 33, where they were hoping at the very least to give Cary Blanchard a few extra yards of distance before a potential game-tying field-goal attempt.

Zack Crockett picked the perfect time to have his best game as a pro. Against San Diego, the rookie fullback from Florida State rushed 13 times for 147 yards and had touchdown runs of 33 and 66 yards. (Photo by Paul Sancya)

On second-and-10, Harbaugh saw something he didn't like, audibled at the line, and handed the ball to Crockett. With the defense perhaps on its heels after Harbaugh had burned them for four consecutive completions on the drive, Crockett hit left tackle, bounced to the outside and went 33 yards untouched for the score. Safety Shaun Gayle should have been able to come over and push Crockett out of the bounds in the final 10 yards, but fell down on the play.

Running backs coach Gene Huey, who was singing Crockett's praises throughout the day, said the offensive line deserved a great deal of credit for Crockett's success as well. On the 33-yarder, he said, the hole was big enough that anyone could have found it.

"Sunday (the offensive line) really accepted the challenge," Huey said in a second-day story in the *Indianapolis Star*. "On Zack's 33-yard run, you could have driven a semi sideways through the hole. Kirk Lowdermilk, Joe Staysniak and Jason

Mathews walled off the back side. Will Wolford and Randy Dixon did an outstanding job sustaining blocks on the front side."

Crockett said he was in the right place at the right time.

"I took the handoff to the left and all of a sudden there's this incredible hole for me to run through," he said. "It was like the parting of the Red Sea. Once I got through it I was able to use my speed to outrun the defensive backs and get to the end zone.

"Once I got to the end zone, it was like a dream come true," he said. "I hadn't been in the end zone since preseason so it was a very special moment for me."

He would have another moment like it in the second half that would prove to be even bigger than the first one.

The second run was also a thing of beauty with the entire team leveling some big-time blocks. San Diego's John Carney had just knocked down a 30-yard field goal to bring the Chargers to within one at 21-20 with 11:53 remaining in the game.

But on the first play following the ensuing kickoff, Crockett put the exclamation point on his day's performance. The play was a sprint draw, the same play that Faulk had gained so much yardage on in the St. Louis game early in the season. Crockett took the handoff deep in the backfield between his own 25- and 30-yard lines, bounced off left tackle and began his long gallop toward pay dirt.

Wolford made a big block at the point of attack and Warren made a couple of big blocks on the play. The first came at the line of scrimmage and the final one was way down field.

"I had some great downfield blocking on that one," Crockett said following the game. "I got the blocks and just followed them to the Promised Land. It was just one of those runs when you tried to follow your blockers. I followed Lamont and a few other guys down the field and they just paved the way for me."

When he got to the end zone, he had picked up 66 yards, the Colts were ahead 28-20 and the crowd of 61,182 was eerily quiet with 11:28 showing on the clock in the fourth quarter.

But for Colts fans it would get even better.

Three plays after Crockett's TD run, the Colts got the ball back on a Jason Belser interception and 32-yard return to the San Diego 23. On a drive that would take six plays and run three minutes and 31 seconds off the clock, the Colts would score again on a 3-yard run by Harbaugh.

Suddenly, the score was 35-20 and the Chargers were making off-season travel plans.

The final score was the same: Indianapolis 35, San Diego 20.

As Belser came off the field and headed into the tunnel, he screamed "Show some respect for those horseshoes, baby!"

Tony Siragusa was his usual animated self.

"Nobody wants us to be here but that's just tough," he said. "We're here and we're planning on sticking around awhile."

Let 'er Rip

♦ ♦ ♦

The victory over the Chargers was rich in story lines with Crockett's burst into the limelight leading the way.

But the defensive secondary was also basking in postgame notoriety. The same secondary that had been burned beyond recognition when the two teams had played two weeks before, had shined when it counted the most in the playoffs.

In the first 15 games, the Colts secondary had just 10 interceptions. In the victory over New England and now San Diego in the playoffs, the Colts had tallied seven more including four against the Chargers.

"It was like we were a different team two weeks ago in terms of the way we're playing," said cornerback Ray Buchanan. "We knew we had to tighten things up and play more man-to-man and (defensive coordinator) Vince Tobin believed in us. He told us to play tighter and be more aggressive and that has been the difference."

Ashley Ambrose said the better play had to do with focus.

"I think it has been a matter of concentrating on the ball more," said Ambrose, who tipped a pair of balls in the first half that resulted in interceptions. "Right now, we're not even thinking about the run. We know our front seven is good enough that we can concentrate solely on coverage and taking care of business.

"That hasn't always been our first thought," he added. "I just think we feel right now, if we can stop the pass, we're going to win the game."

In the first meeting between the two teams, the Colts got killed on the post routes. This time, the cornerbacks were more conscious of the safeties and more focused on preventing the big play.

"What I don't think we realized the first time we played was that San Diego wins by making big plays in the passing game and having a solid running attack," said safety David Tate. "Today, we took away the big plays. When they had to rely totally on the short stuff, it took them out of their rhythm."

In the first meeting Martin had 10 catches for 168 yards, including touchdown catches of 51 and 38 yards. This time, he was limited to three catches for 39 yards.

"Their safeties played real well," said quarterback Stan Humphries. "They weren't going to give up the big plays. We had to be patient and take everything underneath and that's what we tried to do. But a couple of balls bounced off of hands and were intercepted.

"I picked a bad day to have a bad day," he said. "I didn't play very well today and when I don't play very well bad things are going to happen."

Humphries completed 23 of 47 passes for 292 yards with two touchdowns but four costly interceptions.

In the first meeting, Jason Belser had assumed the responsibility as the goat after getting burned on a pair of touchdown passes. This time, he made all the plays including a pair of interceptions that he returned for 68 yards. He now had three interceptions in the last two weeks.

The Playoffs: California Here We Come

Stephen Grant returns an intercepted pass 13 yards. It was one of four passes intercepted by Colts defenders in a 35-20 playoff victory in San Diego. (Photo by Paul Sancya)

"We're just playing opportunistic defense," Belser said. "We know we can't sit back, we have to make the plays. We feel like no one really respects us and because of that it's kind of fun being the underdog."

Linebacker Trev Alberts said it's amazing how different a team can look by simply making a few more big plays in a game.

"That was the difference for us," Alberts said when he looked back on the season a few months later. "Players quit being tentative and just decided they were going to go for it. Instead of worrying about what might happen if I don't get this interception or if I underthrow this pass, they were taking all the chances.

"And as everyone was beginning to see, we were on a roll, and all of the chances were working out just the way we had planned them."

Let 'er Rip

Duke Tumatoe's weekly take on the game went this way:

The Colts made the playoffs
For the first time in years
Went out to San Diego
and the Colts kicked the Bolts' rears.
Lord help our Colts. Lord help our Colts.
Oh I'm out of control
They're going to the Super Bowl (well, maybe)
But at least .... We're going to Kansas City, Kansas City here we come.
We're going to Kansas City, Kansas City here we come.
They beat the spit out of San Diego
Wow, are they having fun.
Zack Crockett took the ball
Oh what a surprise
He's awful speedy
For a man that is that size.
They're going to Kansas City, Kansas City here they come.

15

The Playoffs:
We're Going to Kansas City

The bookmakers in Las Vegas poured the ingredients into the pot when their opening line for the AFC's second-round matchup favored Kansas City by as many as nine points over the Colts. By game time, the number would be up to 10.

The Chiefs stirred the pot early in the week when they hinted in print that the Colts might not truly be a formidable foe.

But Jason Whitlock should be the man credited with turning the heat up on the stove and causing the contents to come to a boil.

The columnist from the *Kansas City Star*, who claimed to have Indiana roots, did about as good of a rip job on an opposing team that could possibly be done.

And not surprisingly, the Colts got hold of a copy in Indianapolis. And before too long, everyone in the locker room had his own personal copy.

The first column, which characterized the Colts as a bunch of losers who had no business being in the AFC playoffs, was bad enough. But the one that the players picked up and read the day of the game in the Sunday, Jan. 7, edition of the *Kansas City Star* was even more of a gem.

Wrote Whitlock: "Last week I told you why you shouldn't take the Indianapolis Colts seriously.

"I explained to you that for more than a decade the Colts were the most ineptly managed sports organization in America. I relayed to you that Jim Irsay, the owner's son and the Colts' general manager, has no right handling the joystick of a Nintendo football game let alone handling the checkbook of a pro sports franchise. I discussed with you the many failed coaching and quarterback "eras" (often called "errors" in Naptown) in the Colts' Indianapolis history.

"Those examples should have helped you understand why I, a native Hoosier, am unable to respect the Colts as a legitimate playoff team.

Let 'er Rip

"They're also the reason current Hoosiers refuse to take the Colts seriously. (The Colts, in the middle of a playoff drive, were unable to sell out the 60,000-seat RCA Dome for their final two home games).

"Well, today I'm going to leave the Colts' sorry history alone. Today I'm going to tell you why beginning at 3 this afternoon the Chiefs, the No. 1 seed in the AFC playoffs, should whip the snot out of the 1995-96 Colts.

"If the Chiefs play with typical Marty Schottenheimer intensity, the final score should be around 28-6 in favor of the homeboys."

The story went on to tell how there was no way a team without Marshall Faulk, and with Jim Harbaugh, could possibly score against the stingiest defense in the NFL in terms of fewest points allowed.

Defensively, Whitlock did say that he liked the Colts' linebackers, but proceeded to trash the defensive linemen.

"The problem is the Colts don't have much talent along their defensive line. Tony Bennett and Bernard Whittington, natural outside linebackers, play as ends. Tackles Tony Siragusa and Tony McCoy are effort guys, not playmakers."

If he had thought about it 24 hours later, Ted Marchibroda really should have sent Whitlock a game ball. He deserved it.

◆   ◆   ◆

Defensive tackle Tony McCoy picked up the paper fairly early that morning after a bout with the flu that had him up vomiting most of the night before the game.

On very little sleep, McCoy was already in a foul mood. Peering through bloodshot eyes, McCoy slowly let Whitlock's words sink in. It was as if someone had thrown a bucket of cold water in his face.

"It was that respect thing all over again," McCoy said. "I know it's something you've got to earn but we had just beat a pretty good San Diego team the week before. We had also beaten San Francisco and Miami in the regular season.

"But every time you'd pick up a paper from out of town, it was the same old story," he said. "These are just the same old Colts and they won't be around very long. I know as I read that I just hoped that somehow that's what Kansas City was believing, too. Because if they were, they were in for a rude awakening."

Maybe it was the change in climate going from frigid Indianapolis to sunny San Diego and back, or maybe it was simply flu season, but the bug hit the Colts hard the week before the game with the Chiefs.

But no one single area was hit any harder than the defensive line. Tony Siragusa was in bed hooked up to an IV solution to attempt to keep him from getting dehydrated. Rookie Ellis Johnson was also sick, and McCoy was doing everything in his power to ward off the flu.

But he was losing the battle.

Before he went to bed Saturday night, he asked trainer Hunter Smith for some cough medicine to help him sleep. He said later he didn't remember what dosage Smith had told him to ingest. But when the syrup didn't seem to work right off the bat, McCoy kept taking swigs of the medicine. In a two-hour period, he drank the entire bottle.

"I thought I heard him say take some every so-and-so hours, but I ended up taking the whole bottle in one night which I will never ever do again," McCoy said.

McCoy said after being up most of the night, the effects of all the medicine really hit him around 4 a.m. It was so bad he called Smith and told him he was "throwing up all over the place" and wanted to know if there was anything the trainer could do. Smith arrived immediately and called for the team doctor to come and check McCoy out.

"I told the doctor I felt light-headed and dizzy, and he said that was all the cough syrup that I had drank," McCoy said. "Both the doctor and Hunter just kept looking at me with disbelief that I had really drank the whole thing. But I paid for it. I was sick all morning, into the early afternoon, on the bus to the game and in the locker room as we were getting ready to take the field.

"I can never remember feeling that badly and still finding a way to play."

But to McCoy's way of thinking he really didn't have any choice. Siragusa, who the night before had assured McCoy he would be in the lineup the next day, did not even make the trip from the hotel to the stadium. He was too sick to even get out of bed.

Johnson was also feeling lousy, but the two former University of Florida Gators knew it was going to be their responsibility to somehow slow down what many considered one of the best offensive lines in the National Football League.

A deeply religious man, McCoy said it was only after a personal prayer session inside the shower area of the visiting locker room at Arrowhead Stadium about an hour before the game, that he somehow found the will and energy to play against the Chiefs.

"I just prayed and asked God to help us go out and play a real strong game, and to help me overcome the way I was feeling," McCoy said. "And people tell me I shouldn't bring religion into the game, but for me that's the only way I know.

"And when I got up from praying it was like a peace upon me," he said. "I remember stretching out on the cold field and Dave Walston, one of our trainers, came up to me and said that with all the guys who were sick today, 'We really need you to take the battle'. And I looked him in the eye and I said with a firm believing voice and with a peace about me, 'Hey Dave, we're going to win this game. Period.'

"You have a lot of games where you think you have a good shot at winning, but I can honestly say that the Kansas City game was the first game I have ever played that I knew no matter what we did we were going to find a way to win the game," he said. "I believe that God came into my heart and just told me that everything was going to be all right."

Trev Alberts said the knowledge that many of their big guys in the middle were sick just made the Colts dig a little deeper as a team.

"When you have adversity like that, guys just pull together," Alberts said. "I think the closeness of our team really grew in those last three games. We knew we needed those guys, but we also knew if they weren't able to go that someone was going to step up and make the plays.

"It's just the way our team had come to believe in each other."

Let 'er Rip

Indianapolis Colts defenders Tony McCoy (61) and Bernard Whittington (95) wrap up Kansas City running back Marcus Allen during 1995 playoff action. The Colts defeated the Chiefs, the team with the best record in the NFL, 10-7. (Photo by Paul Sancya)

The Playoffs: We're Going to Kansas City

♦ ♦ ♦

If there was one lesson the Colts learned in the 1995 season, it was that they had the talent to play with anyone in the NFL.

On paper, there would be those that would dispute that claim as the Colts took their show on the road against Kansas City, a team with the best record in the AFC at 13-3.

The cornerstone of Kansas City's success was the "Sudden Death" defense. The Chiefs allowed just 284.3 yards per game in total offense, an NFL-low 4.3 yards per play, and another NFL-low 15.1 points per game. Against the run, the Chiefs had been tough allowing just 82.9 rushing yards per game. Individually, no player had rushed for more than 100 yards against Kansas City in 16 games.

In the final four games of the season, all played in December, Chiefs opponents had rushed for an average of 50 yards per game and 2.6 yards per attempt.

Defensive tackle Joe Phillips said it was all about pressure.

"The focus is on us, the guys up front, using our talents and just being physical," Phillips said in an article in the *Indianapolis Star*. "You try to penetrate, go through the offensive linemen's shoulders and create a new line of scrimmage a yard or two deeper than the original one."

Phillips and the other starting tackle Dan Saleaumua had combined for 172 quarterback pressures and 11.5 sacks. Neil Smith, at left end, led the Chiefs with 12 sacks. Pro Bowl linebacker Derrick Thomas had another big season, recording eight sacks, and Tracy Simien had a big year at the middle linebacker position, leading the team with 106 tackles.

On offense, Kansas City had all the punch necessary to go deep into the playoffs. The running game, spearheaded by Marcus Allen, averaged 138.9 yards per game, and quarterback Steve Bono had done a solid job as the replacement for the retired Joe Montana.

As for the intangibles, Kansas City had plenty of playoff experience and ranked as the only NFL team to reach the playoffs the past six seasons. And playing at home, in one of the league's loudest outdoor venues, the Chiefs had been nearly unbeatable. Over a four-year span, Kansas City had won 27 of 32 games at home. This season they were 8-0 in the friendly confines of Arrowhead Stadium.

But the bottom line for the Colts was after you took away all the fluffy statistics and the numerous reasons why the Chiefs should advance to meet Pittsburgh for the right to attend Super Bowl XXX, one simple fact remained — the game still had to be played.

McCoy, for one, felt deep in his heart that the Chiefs were not taking that fact into consideration. In his mind, he believed Kansas City was not expecting much of a fight out of its dome-stadium opponent venturing into a city with a game-time temperature of 19 degrees and a wind chill of minus 9 degrees.

"I remember standing on the sidelines and just getting the feeling that Kansas City was not ready for a fight," McCoy said. "They wanted a quickie. They wanted to come in and put the game out of reach early and start thinking about how to beat

Pittsburgh next week. They didn't expect us to fight. They figured we would be happy to have made it there but that none of us would really believe we could win the game.

"And that's where they were wrong," he added. "Dead wrong."

Linebacker Jeff Herrod said he felt it was a total lack of respect. And he felt the media had to shoulder a great deal of the blame.

"The media had Kansas City believing that these were the same old Colts, that we couldn't play in the cold and that we didn't have much of a chance because we were going up against the team with the best record in the AFC and a great run-stopping defense," Herrod said. "Then they had a lot of success on that first series of the game and they really started to believe all those things.

"But the second series was a different ballgame and from that point on I think they started changing their opinions of us," Herrod added. "At first they thought it was going to be a cake walk. But I remember the second series looking over into their huddle and you could just tell that they were thinking, 'These guys are crazy. We're in for a dogfight'.

"What people have to realize is that the game isn't won in the media, the game is won on the field," he said. "And that's where we won it was right there in the middle of the field."

Alberts was another one who believed the Chiefs may have gotten a little too caught up in what people were saying about them.

"There's some of this mystique I think when you play teams like the 49ers, the Cowboys and even the Kansas City Chiefs," Alberts said. "The national television exposure just builds them up to be almost super human. It's like this offensive line is just so big and so strong, you'll never be able to stop their running game.

"I remember coming off the field after the first series in some of those games against the Chargers, the Chiefs and even the Steelers. Their line was supposed to be these big guys and they all had beards and they were supposed to be real tough guys. And we'd come off the field and look at each other and say, 'Hey, these guys aren't any different than anyone else we play.' They're good players, but half the battle is just believing that they aren't any better than we are.

"I think as we started beating some of those big teams, guys started realizing, 'Hey, we can play with anybody.' And we should beat anybody. That confidence lets you play less tentatively and that's a big key in the playoffs."

"Don't Forget To Fight," had been a season-long slogan of the Indianapolis Colts. And never before had it been any more apparent than in front of 77,594 die-hard Chiefs fans at Arrowhead Stadium.

Forget that the Colts didn't have Marshall Faulk at running back. Forget that Roosevelt Potts was back home in Indianapolis watching this on television. Forget that Tony Siragusa was back in his hotel room, trying to prop himself up enough to view the game on TV. Forget that starting guard Randy Dixon also was injured to the point where he couldn't play.

"This win symbolizes what our team is about," Marchibroda said. "We were without four starters but we had reserves make key contributions. Lamont Warren and Zack Crockett performed well in the absence of Faulk and Potts. Ellis Johnson played for Tony Siragusa, and Kipp Vickers started for Randy Dixon at left guard.

"All season long we have had guys who were ready when their time came and the effort at Kansas City was no different."

Adversity had been like a long-lost friend to this club before in 1995, and the Colts almost seemed to embrace their underdog role in the second-round playoff matchup.

When Kansas City took a 7-0 lead with 29 seconds remaining in the first quarter on a 20-yard pass from Steve Bono to Lake Dawson, who could have possibly known that the Chiefs would not score another point over the final 45 minutes of the game?

This one was a defensive gem with just enough offense thrown in to get the Colts over the top.

Jim Harbaugh didn't look like the NFL's top-rated passer as he struggled to a 12 of 27 performance for 112 yards. But on an 18-play, 77-yard drive that consumed 8 minutes and 40 seconds of the second-quarter clock, Harbaugh was masterful. He converted five third-down situations and eventually hit Floyd Turner for a 5-yard touchdown pass to tie the score at 7-7 with 6:49 remaining in the half.

Cary Blanchard's 30-yard field goal with 2:48 to play in the third quarter would prove to be the difference in a 10-7 Colts victory.

For the majority of the season, Faulk was the main man in the Colts' backfield.

Against San Diego the week before, rookie Zack Crockett had stolen the show with his 147-yard performance against the Chargers.

Against Kansas City, the flavor of the week was Lamont Warren. Originally a sixth-round pick of the Colts in 1994, a player many felt was the steal of the draft, finally got his big chance and he didn't disappoint.

All Warren did was rush for 76 yards against a team that allowed just 82.9 yards per game on the season to the best running backs the NFL had to offer. The Colts would end up almost doubling that total with a 147-yard effort against the Chiefs.

And he made his share of big plays. On the game-tying touchdown drive in the second quarter, the Colts had a fourth-and-1 at the Chiefs' 38. The give went to Warren who gained 4 yards to keep the drive alive.

But this one belonged to the defense. They did a nice job bouncing from a 4-3 to a 3-4 defensive set, changed coverages often, and allowed only one completion of more than 20 yards in the game. The Colts held Kansas City to 281 yards in total offense and Steve Bono was as flustered as a quarterback could be. He completed 11 of 25 passes for 122 yards but threw three second-half interceptions. He was eventually replaced by backup Rich Gannon for one final drive in the fourth quarter.

Tony Bennett said the way things were going he was happy to see Bono with the ball.

"I knew if we put the ball in Bono's hands, we'd have a pretty good chance of beating them," Bennett said.

Ray Buchanan said Bono was simply out of rhythm.

"We knew something wasn't right with him," Buchanan said. "We took away a little of his music. It was like we turned on a little rap music and he couldn't dance to it."

Another one having difficulty in the rhythm department was kicker Lin Elliott. Elliott had missed just six field goals all season. Against the Colts, he was zero-for-three from 35, 39 and 42 yards.

The last one was the toughest to take for Chiefs fans. Gannon moved the Chiefs to the Indianapolis 25 with less than a minute to play, where Elliott was left with a 42-yard attempt. But from the moment the ball left his foot it was headed wide left and the Colts were on their way to Pittsburgh.

Zero-for-two prior to that potential game-tying kick, Elliott was greeted at the line of scrimmage by a great deal of taunting and heckling by all 11 members of the Colts' defense.

"I was yelling at him and telling him he was a sorry kicker and that it was too bad they were going to have to cut him after the game," said Buchanan. "But I wasn't the only one talking. It started with me but then all of a sudden there were 11 of us screaming. But you've got to remember that was our future right there. This guy who was kicking the ball was about to determine our future.

"So we were trying to rattle him, the weather was bad and the pressure was on him," Buchanan said. "But he had to have the heaviest leg in the NFL at that point and time and we knew that.

"When he ended up missing that field goal, I think everyone's vertical jump went up to 41 or 42 inches."

Tony Siragusa, watching the game on television back in his hotel room, said he deserved some of the credit for Elliott's misfortunes. He said every time Elliott would attempt a field goal he would punch the remote control and change to another channel. When he returned on the first two attempts, he found that the score hadn't changed.

On the final one late in the fourth quarter, Siragusa said when he switched back the ball was just leaving Elliott's foot.

"But it was going left, way left right from the start," Siragusa said. "Like I told the guys later, whatever I can do to help the team I want to do."

While several Kansas City players tried to insist that the Chiefs had lost the game more than the Colts had won it, Marchibroda made it perfectly clear that his club had fought through the adversity and conquered their foe.

"This is no fluke," Marchibroda said. "Nobody picks us but that's fine with us. We're the dead-end kids."

Looking back, Harbaugh passed it off to total belief in the organization as a team.

"We were just a bunch of ragamuffins in the eyes of the national media," Harbaugh said. "Nobody expected us to be there, very few wanted us to be there, but the fact remained — we were there."

Duke Tumatoe sang his weekly song like this:

An incredible, inspiring, exceptional victory
The Colts stood tall.
But it was so cold
Cary Blanchard must have felt like he was kicking a bowling ball.
Lord help our Colts (But think about the Chiefs' kicker)
Lord help our Colts (A great career in used cars coming up for him)
The Colts defense was on the money.
They made Steve look just like Sonny (Bono that is).
Lord help our Colts.
The Colts keep on winning
They will not be denied.
But I can't understand
How the point spread can be so wide.
Lord help our Colts. Lord help our Colts.
Hey, let's change the name of our home
To the RCA Underdog Dome.
Lord help our Colts. Lord help our Colts.
We're playing for the AFC championship
Go Colts, Let 'er rip.
Lord help our Colts.

◆   ◆   ◆

Eight thousand people who wanted the Colts there went against the advice of the National Weather Service and took to the roads heading toward the Indianapolis International Airport shortly after the game had ended.

When the Pacers had reached the NBA's Eastern Conference finals in back-to-back years in 1994 and 1995, the fans had made a ritual of meeting the team at the airport.

With the Colts due there a few hours later, fans began congregating at the westside air terminal.

That night on the WIBC postgame radio show, which had been extended three hours over its normal two-hour length, the word first came through during a traffic report. Despite the fact that the city was under a snow emergency, the traffic reporter said the fans were refusing to stay away.

"The traffic is backed up over a mile trying to get off at the Airport Expressway off I-465," said the traffic reporter. "Just be careful out there and don't be in a big rush to get anywhere. The Colts are still more than an hour away."

When WIBC went back on, host Jim Barbar reiterated the plea. "No one is going to tell you not to go out there, but please be extra cautious if you do."

Cary Blanchard (14) and Chris Gardocki (17) celebrate after Blanchard's go-ahead field goal in the playoff game against Kansas City. (Photo by Paul Sancya)

WIBC's Kevin Lee ventured to the airport to get some live postgame show guests from the Colts that were departing the plane. Those who were interviewed talked about how special it was to feel like the city of Indianapolis was behind the Colts.

"This is great," Harbaugh said in a television interview. "We've been hoping to earn the fans' respect here for a long time and hopefully this is a good first step toward doing that."

Buchanan said the fans' presence at the airport sent a distinct message to the team.

"It made us feel like not only had we come a long way, but our fans had come a long way, too," he said. "It felt so good to know that the fans in our city were behind us now. It was really a great feeling just looking at all of those people as you came through there."

McCoy offered the Christian perspective:

"The Bible says charity begins at home, so if you don't have respect at home then you really can't get respect anywhere else," McCoy said. "For me, I felt like this proved that we had finally captured the respect of our fans. That they believed in us, they believed that we could do it and they really were supporting us.

"To be out in that type of weather and that late at night, that was quite an accomplishment," he said. "As a player and for us as a team it made us believe we had finally gained a measure of respect from our fans."

16

The Playoffs: One Step From the Super Bowl

There was a sign hanging inside the Colts' locker room at their West 56th Street complex that Ted Marchibroda had put up shortly after they returned from training camp in late August.

It spoke of an expectation to improve on the .500 finish of the 1994 season. The sign read:

"Work Hard ... and then some.

Mentally Prepared ... and then some.

8-8 ... and then some."

Just prior to the first playoff game with San Diego, Marchibroda added one line to the bottom of the sign. It read:

"The playoffs ... and then some."

As the Colts prepared for the AFC title game matchup with the Pittsburgh Steelers, suddenly "and then some" was more than just a phrase written on a placard. All of a sudden, "and then some" was just 60 hard-fought minutes of football from becoming a reality.

True to form, the Indianapolis playoff run had served as reinforcement for Colts players that they were a better team than people around the NFL believed. Still, the opening line in Las Vegas following the 10-7 victory over Kansas City was double digits in favor of Pittsburgh. The line opened at 10½ and was as high as 11½ during the week.

"I hope it goes to 20," said cornerback Ray Buchanan. "We have never paid any attention to what some gamblers in Las Vegas think. Sure, it's a slap in the face but if people have been taking their advice all season, I'd say some people out there have lost a whole lot of money."

Ted Marchibroda was another one who was miffed by the odds posted for the AFC title game.

"I just don't understand the logic," Marchibroda said. "We beat a team on the road that was in the Super Bowl last year, then we beat a team on the road that had the best record in the NFL this year.

"It just doesn't make a lot of sense to me."

As the Colts attempted to go about their business as usual at their practice facility during the week, some subtle changes were occurring in Indianapolis.

First, a flood of media had arrived to camp out at Colts headquarters and catch up on all the Colts stories they hadn't written over the last few weeks. For the most part, the media blitz had been light as the majority of national media members kept expecting the Colts to go away. When they still had a pulse with only four teams left in the NFL, writers and broadcasters from across the country began descending upon Indianapolis, many with the same single question in mind.

"Who are these guys?"

Director of public relations Craig Kelley and his staff did their best to keep the visiting media satisfied, and Colts players had been expecting a little extra attention ever since they knocked off San Diego at Jack Murphy Stadium in the first wildcard round.

Marchibroda had also taken steps to make sure his young team didn't use the opportunity of a national soapbox to provide locker room fodder for the Pittsburgh Steelers or the week before, against the Chiefs.

Marchibroda spoke to his team the Monday before the Kansas City game and gave them a subtle warning: Be smart, don't say anything controversial, don't guarantee a victory and don't bad-mouth your opponent.

The Colts simply hadn't had many chances to bask in the national spotlight in 1995. Bill Tobin had been very outspoken on the subject before the season began, believing the Colts deserved a much better television slate following an 8-8 record the year before.

But the NFL wasn't listening. Out of the 59 preseason and regular-season matchups carried by the various networks in 1995, the Colts were on national television just once — a season-ending home game carried by ESPN against New England.

But Marchibroda didn't expect all the attention to become a distraction.

"I think it will be a minor part of the week," Marchibroda said. "Our players are extremely focused right now and they don't need someone reminding them to concentrate on the task at hand. These guys want nothing better than to keep proving their doubters wrong."

Another nuance in the week before the AFC title game was a run on Colts merchandise around the city, as it seemed everyone wanted a Colts sweatshirt to wear to parties that would be taking place around the city come Sunday afternoon. Several local sporting goods outlets sold shirts with the words "Let 'er Rip" on the front, capitalizing on Marchibroda's infamous words to Jim Harbaugh.

By the end of the week, "Let 'er Rip" shirts were no where to be found, Jim Harbaugh and Marshall Faulk jerseys were all but gone in stores around the city, and pretty much anything with blue or a horseshoe on it had been scooped by loyal fans wanting to get behind their team the best way they knew how.

"It was a fun week," Buchanan said, looking back. "We had all seen it with the Pacers so we knew it was possible. But now they were dressing up for us. We wanted more than anything else to give those people a few extra weeks to want to wear their Colts clothes and we did everything in our power to make that wish come true."

At a Pacers-Bucks game at Market Square Arena the Thursday night before the AFC title game, the public address announcer made mention of the fact that Jeff Herrod was in the house. When he was spotted, an 87-second standing ovation followed.

Asked if it was the longest standing ovation of his career, Herrod just smiled.

"It was my first standing ovation," he said.

◆   ◆   ◆

Respect was not easy to come by for the 1995 Indianapolis Colts.

Prior to the 19th game of the season, the matchup against Pittsburgh, T.J. Simers, a sportswriter for the *Los Angeles Times* laid the Colts low.

Forget that this was a team that had beaten Miami twice and San Francisco once during the regular season. Forget that they had cruised into San Diego in the wildcard round and knocked off the defending AFC champions. Forget that they went into the less than friendly confines of Arrowhead Stadium and stunned the Kansas City Chiefs, the team with the best record in the NFL.

Forget it all because Simers, like the majority of his colleagues in the national media, had his blinders on when it came to the Colts. All that mattered to Simers' way of thinking was that the Colts didn't have a snowball's chance in hell against the Pittsburgh Steelers.

His column, under the heading "Analysis" on game day, told the whole story.

"Will the Colts win? Come on, will the Colts score?

"Only three teams have failed to score a point in the history of AFC championship games, and today the Colts are a promising candidate to become the first team in NFL history to be shut out twice in an AFC championship game.

"The Baltimore Colts, playing without top running backs Norm Bulaich and Tom Matte, still had Johnny Unitas at quarterback on Jan. 2, 1972, and yet were humbled, 21-0, in Miami.

"The Indianapolis Colts will be without running back Marshall Faulk (knee) against the Pittsburgh Steelers' defense, ranked third in the NFL, and will be scrambling to find the end zone with Jim Harbaugh at quarterback.

"The Colts, with a lineup one might expect to see in the second half of an exhibition game, will run the ball with Lamont Warren and Zack Crockett and throw it to Sean Dawkins, Floyd Turner and Ken Dilger."

And on and on it went.

Joe Rutter, a sportswriter for the *Pittsburgh Tribune*, saw it this way:

"On paper, it appears to be a bigger mismatch than the Harlem Globetrotters and Washington Generals.

"On one side of the line of scrimmage in today's American Football Conference championship game will be a Steelers defensive unit which was second in the National Football League at stopping the run, establishing a club record for fewest rushing yards allowed.

"On the other side, trying to cut through toothpick-sized gaps in that defensive front, will be a couple of guys named Zack and Lamont. Two running backs who weren't even starters for the Indianapolis Colts until two weeks ago."

Another writer from the *Pittsburgh Tribune*, Jerry DiPaola, wrote:

"Who are these Indianapolis Colts and what are they doing in Pittsburgh today, amidst all the snow and ice and Super Bowl hype?

"Take a stroll outside Three Rivers Stadium — where kickoff for the American Football Conference championship game between the Steelers and Colts is set for 12:30 p.m. — and ask any fan to name five Colts starters.

"You would have better luck setting up an iceball stand at Gate A."

It wasn't that the club didn't simply have any respect but rather it ran deeper than that. A good majority of the national media in particular, believed the Colts were a joke.

Pittsburgh coach Bill Cowher didn't help the Colts' identity crisis any at the beginning of the week before the game when he was asked about Indianapolis. His reply: "I couldn't even give you their starting lineup. I know Jim Harbaugh is the starting quarterback and Ashley Ambrose is a pretty good cornerback. Beyond that I couldn't tell you much."

From the national media to opposing coaches to the oddsmakers in Las Vegas, the Colts spent the season begging for a little respect.

But everywhere they turned it was the same story. Jokes were still being made, doors were still being slammed in their faces, and to a man the Colts were a club that wondered aloud what they needed to do to make people believe they were for real.

"It's hard for people to respect us," said Tony Siragusa. "After we got in (the playoffs), people told us it was going to get crazy with all the media around here. We were waiting but they didn't come. Then we beat San Diego in the wildcard game and we were waiting but they didn't come. Then we beat the Chiefs and we were waiting but they didn't come.

"We know if we can beat Pittsburgh that they'll come but that's because those guys won't have anyplace else to go."

Jeff Herrod said respect is something that must be earned.

"Things are so much different than they were when we were really a bad team, a bad organization," Herrod said. "I know, I was here. I was part of all the bickering in the late 1980's. I was part of the 1-15 season in 1991. I have been as low as you can get to where you really wonder if you want to play football anymore.

"But those days are behind us. The last couple of years have been totally different. The coaching staff has us believing in ourselves and we have made big strides toward becoming a respectable team. But you still have to earn people's respect.

The Playoffs: One Step From the Super Bowl

"I honestly believe we did that this year," he said. "I think this season will prove to be the cornerstone, the building block from which our football team will benefit for years to come."

As the Colts buses pulled out of the practice facility and made the 10-minute ride to Indianapolis International Airport on Friday afternoon for their flight to Pittsburgh, a large yard sign was waiting for them at the end of the drive leading on to 56th Street.

The professionally lettered metal sign sounded the alarm one more time about the lack of respect the Colts were receiving from around the NFL. The sign read:

"LATEST ODDS: Pittsburgh — minus 11. LET 'ER RIP."

There also was a sign up in Three Rivers Stadium, but this one had nothing to do with the Colts. It had to do with some unfinished business for the home team that was ingrained in their memories since the AFC championship game from the season before.

The banner in the north end zone was simplistic in its message:

"Three more yards."

Three yards. That's all that stood between the Pittsburgh Steelers and a date with San Francisco in Super Bowl XXIX at Miami's Joe Robbie Stadium. The Steelers were on San Diego's 3-yard line with just over one minute to play and trailed 17-13. On fourth down, Neil O'Donnell's pass into the end zone was deflected by linebacker Dennis Gibson.

"When that game ended, Three Rivers Stadium became the world's biggest funeral parlor," Steelers defensive end Brentson Buckner said in an article in the *Indianapolis Star*. "The guys in our locker room don't ever want to experience that feeling again."

"We learned a big lesson last year," O'Donnell said. "We don't want to have to re-learn that lesson again."

Against the Chargers in '94, Pittsburgh didn't have a good enough running game to adequately stack up against the San Diego defense. The result was the Steelers threw the ball 54 times, despite the fact they didn't trail until less than six minutes remained in the game.

In '95, the Steelers had become more diversified. The running game with Bam Morris was still utilized, but it wasn't the primary focus. Instead, Ron Erhardt's offense often employed five-receiver sets and would spread the field. The Steelers had a diversified passing attack, with the luxury of having a solid running game to mix things up. The combination allowed Pittsburgh to lead the AFC in points scored with 406, rank sixth in the NFL in total offense and eighth overall in passing offense.

And then there was the always-tough defense with guys like Kevin Greene and Greg Lloyd and Carnell Lake leading the way.

"We developed a running game and we play tough defense, and I think they are associated with the Pittsburgh Steelers," Cowher said. "We won't ever lose that. I think being able to run the football creates a mentality and a makeup that has a degree of toughness about it.

"But I believe we've opened up some things on offense," he said. "I believe there is a confidence now that we can play games in the 30s and win them. I'm not sure that existed before this year. But that emphasis typifies this city. I don't think they'd take to the run-and-shoot."

◆　　　　　◆　　　　　◆

As the Colts stepped out into the sea of Terrible Towels in Pittsburgh on Sunday January 14, they knew they had arrived. With the past becoming a distant memory, Herrod said he was living a dream.

"I was in a daze for a while," Herrod said. "That first series we went out there, and after the starting lineups and all of that I didn't know where I was. After all the bad experiences I had here, I never dreamed I would ever be in an AFC championship game. It was overwhelming.

"Then it was early in the first quarter and I came up with an interception and all of a sudden I snapped out of it," he said. "Not only was I in the AFC title game but I was also holding on to the ball. It got me really fired up for the rest of the game."

Buchanan agreed with the characterization of the early going feeling like a dream sequence.

"It was almost like somebody had to snap us out of this bubble," he said. "When we walked out there on the field and looked up into the stands, looking at all the media and seeing how much attention the Colts were getting, it just made you feel good.

"I believe everybody had butterflies but it wasn't a bad butterfly," he said. "It was an anxious, get ready type of feeling. We knew what we had to do and all of us believed we could pull it off. We felt the world wasn't ready for the Indianapolis Colts to be in a Super Bowl, but we couldn't worry about that.

"We felt like everything was working our way and we were going to go out there and find a way to pull it off again."

What they didn't have going for them, though, was the ability to sneak up on their opponent.

San Diego may have been looking past the Colts to a matchup with Kansas City, and the Chiefs may have also taken the boys in blue a bit lightly. But the Pittsburgh Steelers were having none of that.

In fact, Pittsburgh coach Bill Cowher nipped all references to the Cinderella Colts in the bud the first opportunity he had.

"I don't think anybody is a Cinderella team at this time of the year," Cowher said in a teleconference midweek. "All four teams that are left have to be good football teams or they wouldn't be there."

He also scoffed at the suggestion that the Colts might be in awe of the AFC title game, or the Terrible Towels that would be waving in Three Rivers Stadium. Following wins on the road against San Diego and Kansas City, Cowher didn't think a trip to Pittsburgh would be a problem.

"I don't think they'll be intimidated by anything right now," Cowher said.

As the game unfolded the Colts looked anything but intimidated. They traded punches with the Steelers for the majority of the game's first 30 minutes and led 6-3 with less than a minute to play on a pair of Cary Blanchard field goals.

But just when everything seemed to be going right, they suddenly went all wrong.

One missed official's call — one big-time miss — resulted in a Pittsburgh touchdown with 13 seconds remaining in the half and a 10-6 Steelers lead at intermission.

On third-and-goal from the Colts' 5-yard line, Neil O'Donnell dropped back to pass. He looked, he looked and he looked some more and finally found Kordell Stewart in the back of the end zone for a touchdown that made it 10-6.

The only problem was that Stewart had stepped out of bounds on the back line and came back in to make the TD grab. The problem was that no official saw it take place.

"Nobody obviously saw him step out of the end line," said referee Bernie Kukar. "If they did, it would have been a penalty.

"It appears as if it happened so close to one of our officials that he probably didn't look down at his feet. He was looking to see if there was any contact. Unfortunately, he only has two eyes."

And unfortunately for the officials in question — field judge John Robison and back judge Tim Millis — NBC had plenty of cameras on the play and several got a definitive look at Stewart stepping out of bounds.

"When I sensed him coming I looked down but by then he had already apparently stepped out," Robison said. "From the time I looked until he caught the ball I didn't seem him step out."

Not surprisingly, the play sparked renewed interest from people across the country to bring back instant replay. The play, according to NFL officials, would have been a reviewable call under the old instant replay rule. Later, the league agreed to bring back replay on an experimental basis for 10 games during the 1996 preseason.

Had the play been reviewed, and reversed, the Steelers would have been penalized with a loss of down and Pittsburgh would have been forced to attempt a game-tying field goal.

Ted Marchibroda, who had never been a big proponent of instant replay, was one who had changed his mind with one play.

"I think it should return," was all Marchibroda would say about the play.

As controversial as that play turned out to be, the Colts would have probably half a dozen other plays to look back on in this game that could have turned the tide.

As tackle Will Wolford said it was a game of 'what ifs'.

"You can probably look at 15 or 20 plays in that game and say 'What if?' What if this happened? What if that happened?," he said. "There were so many woulda, coulda and shoulda's. It just leaves you kind of numb."

One of the biggest for Colts fans came with just under four minutes to play in the game and the Colts clinging to a 16-13 lead and in possession of the football. After taking the 16-13 lead on a 47-yard touchdown pass from Jim Harbaugh to Floyd

Let 'er Rip

Indianapolis receiver Floyd Turner races past a Pittsburgh defender on his way to the end zone for a touchdown that put the Colts ahead of the Steelers in the fourth quarter of the AFC championship game. (Photo by Don Larson)

Turner, the Colts were faced with a third-and-1 situation at their own 31. The give went to Lamont Warren, who appeared to have all kinds of room on a sweep around the left side.

But out of nowhere came cornerback Willie Williams on the blitz. He dove at Warren's feet and was able to trip the running back up from behind for no gain. To make matters worse for the Colts, Williams wasn't even supposed to be blitzing on the play but decided to take a chance when he realized strong safety Myron Bell did not hear the blitz call.

"He made a great play," Warren said in an article in the *Indianapolis Star*. "He was the only guy not accounted for. All I could see was daylight in front of me. He got me by the shoelace. You have to give their defensive coordinator credit for a great call."

Instead of being able to run some valuable time off the clock and/or force Pittsburgh to burn its remaining timeouts, the Colts were forced to summon Chris Gardocki to punt the ball away.

Taking the ball at their own 33, the Steelers went 67 yards in eight plays with Bam Morris scoring on a 1-yard run to make it 20-16 Pittsburgh with 1:34 to play in the game.

The Steelers' scoring drive also had its share of incredibly close moments.

With 2:25 remaining in the game, Pittsburgh was faced with a fourth-and-three at the Colts' 47. The Colts came with a blitz but the rush didn't get there in time. Instead, O'Donnell was able to fire a 9-yard completion to Andre Hastings to keep the drive alive.

"That play was unbelievable," O'Donnell said. "I fired the ball as hard as I could and said, 'if he wasn't going to catch it, it would go through him to another guy'."

O'Donnell was looking for Yancey Thigpen on the play, instead he settled for Hastings as the ball went through three defenders to reach its target.

A couple of plays before, Quentin Coryatt had just missed an interception on a ball that appeared to carom off his hands at the Colts' 40.

"It's something that's going to hurt me for a long time, but I have to live with it," Coryatt said. "The receiver ran a slant pattern. I broke on the ball and I didn't expect (Pittsburgh receiver Ernie Mills) to be behind me. I think we kind of collided when I had the ball. The bump knocked the ball loose."

Following the big fourth-down catch by Hastings, Mills made the catch of the game when he came down with a 37-yard grab from O'Donnell to take the ball to the Colts' 1. He beat Ashley Ambrose, who slipped coming out of his backpedal on the play with 1:51 remaining in the game.

The play was called "87-Move-Go" which drawn up on the chalkboard has Thigpen and Mills running exactly the same route but on different sides of the field.

"I took a quick peak left and then I went back over to Ernie's side," O'Donnell said. "Ernie made a great move on his guy and I gave him a chance to go get it. I told him in the huddle that I was going to give one of those guys a chance to go get it."

Mills came up with the diving catch, just getting his second foot in bounds at the 1. Two plays later, Morris scored the go-ahead touchdown.

♦   ♦   ♦

But one minute and 34 seconds seemed like an eternity to Captain Comeback.

Harbaugh had brought the Colts back so many times before that if he failed to drive his club back down the field toward the Steelers' end zone, it would have seemed totally inappropriate.

"The great thing was that nobody panicked," said Wolford. "We had been there before and we expected to find a way to do it again."

In retrospect, Harbaugh would credit his team with having a tremendous amount of heart. Everyone that was in the huddle on the final drive completely believed the Colts would find a way to win.

"I give our guys all the credit," Harbaugh said. "Their hearts are as big as (Three Rivers) Stadium. I love them for that. You can't come any closer than we did to making the Super Bowl."

The final drive began for the Colts at their own 15. Eighty-five long yards stood between Indianapolis and a trip to Tempe, Ariz.

Floyd Turner (88) enjoys the moment after scoring a touchdown in the fourth quarter that put the Colts ahead of Pittsburgh. (Photo by Don Larson)

Captain Comeback wasted no time. Harbaugh, who completed 21 of 33 passes for 267 yards, began by hitting Lamont Warren on an 8-yard completion, and followed it up with an 18-yarder to Brian Stablein. Later on fourth-and-two just inside midfield, Harbaugh found Sean Dawkins for 13 yards.

On first down at the Steelers' 38, Harbaugh scrambled for nine yards, then killed the clock with 5 seconds remaining.

All of which set up the season's final play, the Hail Mary to Aaron Bailey that wasn't answered.

"God doesn't care about football," said Harbaugh in the postgame locker room. "But he does give us blessings, like this entire season."

The locker room was quiet for a long time when the game was over, with several players sitting in front of their lockers sobbing openly. It was some consolation to come so close, but at the same time it had offered no chance to begin facing the reality that a loss in a conference title game can bring.

"It's tough to come that close and not continue on to play another day," Trev Alberts said. "And it really hurts when you look back on all the plays that we had an opportunity to make but didn't. That was what really hurt. We had been making those plays for three or four weeks but when we really needed them, we couldn't quite make them.

"It's a big-time cliche, but we left there with our heads held high," he added. "We had nothing to be ashamed of. No one ever thought we'd get that far and we almost wound up playing Dallas in the Super Bowl."

Colts general manager Jim Irsay remembers the scene as he found it upon arriving in the locker room.

"I just walked in and it was dead silence," Irsay recalls. "Craig Erickson came up to me and said 'Jim, you might want to go in the trainer's room. Jim (Harbaugh) is hurt and you might want to just check in on him.' "

When Irsay got to him, Harbaugh looked like the typical bruised and battered warrior. There was blood on his uniform from a dislocated finger he had suffered on the final drive. And Kevin Greene and Greg Lloyd and company had issued him a pretty good pounding throughout the afternoon.

"I went and I saw Jim Harbaugh first and he just looked at me and he said, 'You know you can't get any closer than that. It was a hell of a run.'

"And that just summed it up," Irsay said. "It really was a hell of a run and like Harbaugh says, God doesn't control those scores. It was a great memory. Like I've said before, the Cowboys may have won the Super Bowl, but I think we had way more fun."

◆   ◆   ◆

Respect finally came in various ways within minutes after the Colts fell to the Steelers.

Network analysts praised the Colts for a valiant effort. On ESPN's *SportsCenter*, the Colts were lauded for a job well done. Everywhere you turned, someone had something nice to say about an organization that for so long had wallowed in bad reviews.

The national pro football media contingent that had gathered in Pittsburgh also gave the Colts their due. For one shining moment, unfortunately in a loss, the Colts had earned the respect of the professional football community.

The stories all said pretty much the same thing: the Colts showed heart, pride and determination. Had a call gone this way or that, they might have made it to the big dance. Many said the Colts had been one of the NFL's brightest stars in postseason play.

Chicago Tribune columnist Bob Verdi did a particularly nice job of capturing the moment in a column the next day written about Harbaugh.

The story read:

"Jim Harbaugh, who has choreographed so many miracles this winter, could have said he'd simply run out of time. But a winner doesn't make excuses, even if he's lost his biggest game.

"So Harbaugh, as usual, took the high road. His white uniform pants were speckled with blood from a sliced right index finger, and the middle digit on the same hand was wrapped after being dislocated on that last drive, too.

" 'Maybe now I'll be able to throw spirals,' Harbaugh rasped, smiling faintly. 'And maybe we can build on this. We showed courage, but the scoreboard is what counts.'

"That's where Harbaugh looked Sunday for a verdict. The desperation play was dubbed 'Rocket'. Three guys deep and hope. His pass from the 29-yard line had plenty of hang time, enough for almost half the warriors in Three Rivers Stadium to congregate, including Aaron Bailey, who'd done two years at the College of DuPage.

" 'It was such a crowd, I couldn't see what happened,' Harbaugh went on. 'I thought he'd caught it. Then I just stared up at the replay. Once, twice. Then I knew. But it's been a beautiful year. Just beautiful.'

"The Indianapolis Colts, good to the last drop, lost this gritty AFC championship to the Pittsburgh Steelers 20-16. Bailey almost caught the ball that would have sent Athletes Anonymous to Super Bowl XXX. The scruffy wild cards almost won three road games in three time zones, almost became the first dome team to go to the prom, almost ...

" 'But it was beautiful,' Harbaugh said. 'Chemistry, love, togetherness. Those things don't show up on paper. If people thought Peter McNeeley was coming out of the locker room today, they got Mike Tyson instead.' "

The well-deserved accolades were finally being passed out. The callers to WIBC's postgame show that night kept the switchboard lit for more than five hours. While some called to complain about the officiating, not one was calling to be critical of the Colts.

In the eyes of the people of Indianapolis, the Colts had arrived.

The scene at Indianapolis International Airport that night was one that will not easily be forgotten by the estimated crowd of more than 13,000 Colts fans that jammed the Continental Airlines concourse.

The mood was uplifting and spirited. By the time the plane touched down in Indianapolis at 7:15 p.m. local time, fans had worked themselves into a fevered pitch. Factions of the crowd kept things lively with a series of chants.

As players got off the plane and began the 600-foot walk back to the baggage claim area, the crowd broke into one long thundering ovation.

All of the local television stations were on hand and most were providing live interviews back to their viewers. WIBC was also on hand with live accounts, capturing the mood at the airport for the final hour before the players arrived and coming through with one interview after another after the plane had touched down.

The Playoffs: One Step From the Super Bowl

In one of many big plays for the Colts, Lamont Warren is pulled down from behind by Pittsburgh's Willie Williams on a crucial third-and-1 play as quarterback Jim Harbaugh (4) watches. Indianapolis was forced to punt after failing to pick up the first down. (Photo by Don Larson)

Offensive guard Joe Staysniak said it really meant a lot to the team to walk off the plane and see the reception that was waiting.

"It had been a relatively quiet flight home and people were pretty down about the game," he said. "But when we walked out and saw the bright lights, and then the huge mass of people, it just made you feel like what we had accomplished hadn't gone unnoticed."

Other players had similar reactions. Buchanan said the moment almost moved him to tears. Harbaugh said it gave him a warm feeling in his stomach. McCoy said it was unforgettable.

"It's something I'll never forget for as long as I live," said McCoy. "I just felt like we had finally gotten some of the respect we deserved, and it was the fans that were really letting us know how they felt.

"Respect is a funny thing that way," he said. "If you have the respect of your mother and your father then you feel like you can live your life in a positive way. It's the same in football, when you have the respect of your peers and your fans, you feel like you've taken a huge step.

"I think we took that step and our fans took it with us."

17

Unfinished Business

To Lindy Infante's way of thinking, when the National Football League season comes to an official end with the Super Bowl each January there are 29 teams in the league with one definite thing in common.

They all have unfinished business.

"There's really only one team in the NFL that feels good when the season is over and that's the team that wins the Super Bowl," Infante said.

"Because if you have a bad year and you're not in the playoffs you feel bad. If you go right to the wire and just miss the playoffs you feel bad. If you lose in the first round of the playoffs you feel bad. If you lose in the second round of the playoffs you feel bad. If you get to the conference title game and you lose you feel bad. If you make it to the Super Bowl and you lose you feel bad.

"So the only team that truly walks away at the end of the year feeling they finished the job they started is the one team out of 30 that wins it all," he said. "It may sound crazy, but that's the way most people in this league look at things."

Given that thought process, Infante has yet to be truly satisfied in a 12-year run in the NFL that has included stints with the New York Giants, Cincinnati, Cleveland, Green Bay and now Indianapolis.

But he's been close. Oh so close.

In 1981, he was the offensive coordinator at Cincinnati when the Bengals won the AFC championship before losing to San Francisco 26-21 in Super Bowl XVI in Pontiac, Mich.

In both 1986 and 1987, Infante was the offensive coordinator when the Browns made it to the AFC title game both years, losing to Denver each time. And then in 1995, he came oh so close again with the Colts before dropping the 20-16 decision to Pittsburgh in the AFC championship game.

"I remember driving home from Pontiac after we lost the Super Bowl and feeling pretty down because we hadn't totally finished what we started," he said. "That was a pretty good team, too, but because we lost that one game that's what people will always remember. If you're satisfied to be second best, you'll never have what it takes to strive to be number one."

At the same time, Infante also doesn't believe that you can spend too much time thinking about what might have been.

Like with the '95 Colts. Sure, people will talk about what could have happened if Lamont Warren doesn't get tripped up in the backfield, or if Quentin Coryatt comes up with a timely interception, or if the official sees Kordell Stewart step out of bounds before making a touchdown catch, or on and on and on.

The same was true in Cleveland. In the first AFC title game loss to the Broncos, the Browns were eliminated following John Elway's 98-yard drive for a touchdown. The following season, it was the Browns that marched down the field for the potential go-ahead score, but were the victims of a fumble inside the Denver 5-yard line.

"You want so badly to watch the Super Bowl and say, 'Damn that could be us out there', but it doesn't do you any good," Infante said. "You have to keep things in perspective in this business or you'll go nuts."

But as Infante points out, the rehashing only serves as therapy for so long. After a while, it's simply a reminder of past failings and at that point you have to let it go.

"If you really want to, you can play that 'If' game in every game you play during a season and come up with 15 or more plays that could have swung the game a different way," he said. "But what does it accomplish? Nothing. If you spend so much time worrying about the past, you'll just go crazy.

"You've got to make yourself look back and say, 'Hey, it was a pretty damn good year.' That's what you've got to dwell on. You can't dwell on the bad things because they'll eat you alive."

As the Colts headed for the 1996 season, the general feeling on the team was that 1995 was a good first step. But that's all it was, a step. A building block by which you just wanted to work harder to get back and have a shot at going to the big dance once again.

Trev Alberts believes the major thing the success of 1995 will do is raise the level of expectation.

"The level of expectation is just so much higher this year," Alberts said. "You talk to people in the community and the first thing they say is, 'Super Bowl this year, right?' If it were only that easy. People have to realize there's a lot of luck that goes along with getting that far but the big thing is you have to give yourself the opportunity.

"Number one, you've got to make the playoffs and hopefully find a way to get a home game," he said. "I think everyone in our locker room understands that this isn't something that can be a once every 10 years type of thing. This has to become a habit for our club. When it does, I just know we'll be back knocking on the door of the Super Bowl once again."

Alberts believes the level of expectation also has to rise among his teammates.

"This has got to be something we expect out of ourselves and that's half the battle, expecting you should be there," he said. "Toward the end of last year I know we began to have that expectation. The great teams expect themselves to win. If we want to be a great team that's what our number one goal has got to be."

Some off-season changes, particularly in the offensive line, carried with them some big question marks heading into the 1996 season. Tackle Will Wolford had signed a free agent contract with Pittsburgh, cornerback Ashley Ambrose had gone the free agency route to Cincinnati, and it appeared as if the Colts were not going to bring back Kirk Lowdermilk, Joe Staysniak or Randy Dixon.

Still, Alberts remained optimistic.

"We had enough changes that it might have shaken things up a bit but I think we have enough of the core people that were here last year," he said. "We have enough people that went through the whole ride that there is still that sense of unfinished business. We can use all the cliches we want but the bottom line is that we realize we're in an excellent position to do something real special for this team and this community.

"And you've got to hold on to these times and never let go," he added. "That's why you see us hold a two-week voluntary camp after minicamp and everybody is here. Absolutely everybody. Because everybody wants to be a part of that. Everybody wants to be a part of a winner and the kind of thing we went through last year. Success breeds success and I think that's what we're all here for."

Another linebacker, a nine-year veteran out of Mississippi, said 1995 simply gave him and his teammates a taste of the good life.

"We had some success but we still have a lot to prove," Herrod said. "We have to go to training camp and still have that fire burning inside us that we had in the playoffs last season. We need to start strong in September, something that we really haven't done since I've been here. We always start slow and finish strong. If we could start strong and finish strong, we could finally play that home playoff game we all talk about.

"I think we all dream about what it would be like to play in a playoff game in the RCA Dome with all of our fans going crazy," Herrod said. "It would be great. Maybe it will happen this year."

Herrod said he was happy to finally taste the playoffs, but said it just made him want for more.

"I had always heard guys throughout the years say 'Hey man, you just don't know what the playoffs are like. It's everything you can imagine and a whole lot more. It's one of those things you've just got to experience.'

"I'm thankful I had that taste but what it did for me was make me feel all young again, and it makes me want to work even harder to try and reach that goal again."

For the first time in many years, Herrod said he entered the off-season not carrying the excess baggage of all the negatives the organization had endured over the years.

"Finally, all of those bad times seem to be a long ways away, and that feels really good," Herrod said. "I really don't think of those times anymore. I just think of all the

Indianapolis Colts defenders swarm around a Buffalo ball carrier during action in 1995. It was plays like this that give the Colts reason to believe that 1996 will be even better. (Photo by Paul Sancya)

successes and the positive things that have happened and it gets me excited about what could happen this season."

Buchanan said the success of 1995 served as an off-season motivator. All of a sudden, there was a push to work harder than ever before.

"I really think every player on this team will tell you they think they deserved to be in the Super Bowl last year," Buchanan said. "But we came up just a little bit short. And that means this year in the off-season we just had to work harder than ever before to continue to get better. Status quo doesn't cut it when you have 16 teams on your schedule that are going to be taking you seriously.

"The days where teams go against the Colts and figure it's going to be an easy win are over," he said. "Now teams are coming in here expecting a dogfight. And we've got to give it to them."

Buchanan believes the combination of hard work and good front office moves will be the keys to success.

"We have to work as hard as we can to get better and Bill Tobin is going to have to do his job to bring in the right athletes to make sure we take the right steps," Buchanan said. "Maybe we're going to have some difficult times early on with the offensive line, and then at the same time maybe they'll come through right away. But the one thing we don't want to do is disappoint each other and let each other down. As long as we work as hard as we can in the off-season that shouldn't be a problem."

Buchanan, one of the flashier and higher profile Colts players, says he's playing this game simply to add some jewelry to his wardrobe. Above all, Buchanan yearns for a Super Bowl ring.

"I think that every athlete here more than anything else would like that ring," Buchanan said. "Once you get that close where you almost feel like you had it on your finger, you never know when the opportunity is going to present itself again. It's our jobs to find a way to chase that ring once more."

◆ ◆ ◆

Zack Crockett's successes at Florida State taught him one valuable lesson.
Never be satisfied.

And because of that, despite the fact his team made it to the AFC title game his rookie season, Crockett has a difficult time accepting third or fourth best.

"I think as a team we learned a lesson in the Pittsburgh game and that's that the taste we got was a good one but it made us want for even more. For two games it was a sweet taste, but the Pittsburgh game left us feeling bitter. We have a bad taste in our mouths.

"I think we know now that we can't settle for less," he said. "You have to find a way to go back and do even better. Until you win the big one, you can never be completely satisfied. I learned that at Florida State and so I am never satisfied unless I'm a part of the team that's the last one standing."

Crockett was a member of the Seminoles' national championship team in 1993. In his four seasons there, Florida State was never ranked lower than No. 5 overall in the final polls.

"At Florida State we always expected to win, no matter who we were playing and that is something we have to get to around here," he said. "It was just my rookie season but I really think we were beginning to feel invincible down the stretch here last season and that's the way you've got to feel."

The 1996 schedule promised to give the Colts plenty of opportunities to be successful once again.

In the all important month of September, the Colts were to open the regular season with a home game against new head coach Vince Tobin and the Arizona Cardinals. The second game was a road trip to the Meadowlands to play the New York Jets.

Ken Dilger stretches for yardage after making a catch against the New York Jets at the RCA Dome. (Photo by Paul Sancya)

"We've got to have early success," Infante said. "If you have that early success you don't put yourself behind the eight-ball too quickly. If you struggle, sometimes it can take you a while to get out of that rut."

Another big reason the Colts need to perform well in those first two games is that game three is a trip to Dallas to play the World Champion Cowboys. It will only be the second time in 13 seasons in Indianapolis that the Colts have traveled to Dallas to play the Cowboys. The other time was 1984.

Following the Cowboys game, the Colts will play Miami at home, have an open date, travel to play Buffalo, and then come home to host Ted Marchibroda's Baltimore Ravens followed by Bill Parcells' New England Patriots.

In the second half of the season the Colts will play Washington, Miami, New England, Cincinnati and Kansas City on the road, while games with San Diego, New York, Buffalo and Philadelphia will be played in the RCA Dome.

The games with San Diego at home and Kansas City at Arrowhead Stadium should be particularly interesting especially given the outcomes of the 1995 playoff matchups against those teams.

"If we can take care of business I think we have a schedule that gives us opportunities to be successful," Buchanan said. "And that's all we can ask for is a chance to be successful. I think this group of players has come a long way and now believe very much in each other.

"I think all of us are just excited to get out on the field and see if we can take that next step."

◆   ◆   ◆

Think about unfinished business and the replay of the final play of the 1995 season once again plays in the mind.

Harbaugh rolling out, putting the ball in the air, and Bailey coming within inches of making one of the greatest catches in NFL history.

But not surprisingly, it's Bailey that heads into the 1996 season looking to put fate to the test. He knows he'll never get a chance in the same way, but he would at least like to see his Colts teammates have a shot at getting into the Super Bowl.

"I think we've got the nucleus to get back there again, but we just have to stick together and not let anything distract us from that goal," Bailey said. "We feel like we were the better team against Pittsburgh, but we didn't prove that on the field. Now we've got to find a way to get back to that game so that we can prove we belong in the Super Bowl."

Bailey knows what the chances are of the Colts making that return trip through the playoffs and into the AFC title game, but for now anyway, it's the only chance he's got.

"I know I have to stay within myself and stay within my own personal limits but at the same time I hope to get a shot to really contribute this season," he said. "The more opportunities I get, the more I will forget about that final play of last season.

"Part of me never wants to forget it, and another part of me knows I have to get past it," he said. "But when I think of 1996, all I can think of is that as a team and as an individual there's a whole lot of unfinished business waiting for the Indianapolis Colts."

A whole lot of unfinished business.

Let 'er Rip

Music by Duke Tumatoe
Lyrics by Duke Tumatoe and Tom Griswold

On the sidelines stands coach Ted.
I overheard what he said.
Mr. Harbaugh let's begin.
We came here today to win.
Let 'er rip. Let 'er rip.

Marshall and Crockett are breaking loose.
On the 'D' we've got the Goose.
Rosey and Sean and old Eugene
all part of this blue machine.
Let 'er rip. Let 'er rip.

Blanchard makes those uprights split.
Trev and Tony always make the hit.
Floyd and Aaron and Big Play Ray.
The men in blue are gonna win today.
Let 'er rip. Let 'er rip.
Let 'er rip. Let 'er rip.

The Indy Colts they make us proud.
Getting crazy and getting loud.
We're in the playoffs and I suspect.
We're finally getting some respect.
Let 'er rip. Let 'er rip. Let 'er rip.

About the Author

Terry Hutchens is a sportswriter for the *Indianapolis Star* and *News* and has been covering the Indianapolis Colts since 1989. Married and the father of two sons, Hutchens has won two national awards from the Professional Football Writers Association of America, including a first place in the game stories category in 1995.

A native of Portland, Ore., he grew up in Southern California, where he worked for newspapers in Fullerton and Orange County before coming to Indiana. He graduated with honors from Indiana University in 1989 and now teaches a sportswriting class at Indiana University-Purdue University in Indianapolis.

Build your Sports Library with Masters Press!

Masters Press has a complete line of sports books to help coaches and participants alike "master their game." All of our books are available at better bookstores or by calling Masters Press at 1-800-9-SPORTS. Catalogs available by request.

Boom Baby!
The Sudden, Surprising Rise of the Indiana Pacers

Conrad Brunner

The most extensive account of the history of the NBA's Indiana Pacers ever written. Charts the 1993-94 season, when the team climbed to within a few seconds of its first-ever berth in the NBA finals.
$14.95, ISBN 1-57028-036-3

Holding Court:
Reflections on the Game I Love

Dick Vitale

with Dick Weiss

Former NBA and college head coach, and legendary ESPN and ABC Sports college basketball analyst Dick Vitale candidly shares his insights and opinions on significant issues facing basketball as well as other sports-related topics.
$22.95 (hardcover), ISBN 1-57028-037-1

Vintage NBA:
The Pioneer Era (1946-1956)

Neil D. Isaacs

(Foreword by Bill Bradley)

Players, coaches and officials give personal accounts of the Pioneer Era of the National Basketball Association, and how the league overcame point-shaving scandals, other gambling problems and off-court escapades.
$16.95, ISBN 1-57028-069-X

The NBA Finals:
A 50-year Celebration

Roland Lazenby

Relive the excitement that has grown with each NBA championship series over the last 50 years, from the days when the Finals wasn't a big deal to the 1996 event won by the Chicago Bulls, who many believe to be the best NBA team ever. (This is not an official NBA publication.)
1-57028-103-3, $19.95

Ted Williams' Hit List

*Ted Williams
with Jim Prime*

Ted Williams, one of baseball's most revered players, ranks his 25 best hitters of all time, naming the almost-made-its and should-have-beens, as well. Williams provides insight into not only the actual facts of each player's career, but their discpline and devotion to the game.
1-57028-078-9, $19.95

Airballs:
Notes From the NBA's Far Side

Roland Lazenby

This veteran pro hoops writer gets behind the scenes of pro basketball's staged events for a look at the real people. This book captures the best and worst of the NBA, all in one rollicking ride.
$14.95, ISBN 1-57028-070-3

A Buckeye Season
The Inside Story of the Glory and Heartbreak of Ohio State's 1995 Season
Jeff Snook

A riveting, behind-the-scenes look at the 1995 Ohio State football season. Author Jeff Snook takes the reader through an entire season with coach John Cooper's players.
1-57028-071-1, $14.95

Brave Dreams
A Season in the Atlanta Braves' Farm Sytem
Bill Ballew

In Brave Dreams, author Bill Ballew recounts a season in the minor-league system of the Atlanta Braves, a system he calls one of the best in professional baseball. Ballew not only looks at each team's struggle to finish on top but also at individual players, some who realize their dreams of playing big-league ball, but many others whose dreams are shattered by the competetion as well as they politics and other harsh realities that are a part of playing for pay.
1-57028-081-9, $14.95

Super Bowl Chronicles
A Sportswriter Reflects on the First 30 Years of America's Game
Jerry Green

Author Jerry Green, a sportswriter for the *Detroit News* and one of a handful of journalists to cover every Super Bowl, provides behind-the-scenes looks at the players, the parties, the locker rooms and the press conferences.
1-57028-050-9, $14.95